The Gang

THE Gang

A STUDY OF 1,313 GANGS
IN CHICAGO

Frederic M. Thrasher

ABRIDGED AND
WITH A NEW INTRODUCTION BY

James F. Short, Jr.

PHOENIX BOOKS

 Chicago & London

THE UNIVERSITY OF CHICAGO PRESS

Library of Congress Catalog Number: 63-20899

The University of Chicago Press, Chicago & London
The University of Toronto Press, Toronto 5, Canada

TO MY MOTHER
EVA LACY THRASHER
AND MY FATHER
MILTON B. THRASHER
THIS BOOK IS
GRATEFULLY AND AFFECTIONATELY
DEDICATED

Editor's Preface

The title of this book does not quite describe it. It is a study of the gang, to be sure, but it is at the same time a study of "gangland"; that is to say, a study of the gang and its habitat, and in this case the habitat is a city slum.

Gangs are not confined to cities, nor to the slums of cities. Every village has at least its boy gang, and in the village, as in the city, it is composed of those same foot-loose, prowling, and predacious adolescents who herd and hang together, after the manner of the undomesticated male everywhere. Gangs flourish on the frontier, and the predatory bands that infest the fringes of civilization exhibit, on the whole, the same characteristic traits displayed by the groups studied in this volume. The thirteen hundred gangs investigated in Chicago are typical of gangs elsewhere. Gangs are gangs, wherever they are found. They represent a specific type or variety of society, and one thing that is particularly interesting about them is the fact that they are, in respect to their organization, so elementary, and in respect to their origin, so spontaneous.

Formal society is always more or less conscious of the end for which it exists, and the organization through which this end is achieved is always more or less a product of design. But gangs grow like weeds, without consciousness of their aims, and without administrative machinery to achieve them. They are, in fact, so spontaneous in their origin, and so little conscious of the purposes for which they exist, that one is tempted to think of them as predetermined, foreordained, and "instinctive," and so, quite independent of the environment in which they ordinarily are found.

Indeed, social life is so necessary and so fundamental to the existence of human nature that society has sometimes been conceived to be an innate trait of the individual man. This is so far true that human beings have at any rate shown themselves capable of creating a society out of the most umpromising materials. Children, abandoned to their own resources, find companionship in dolls, make friends with dogs and cats, and, if necessary, create imaginary personalities, with whom they are able to live on the very best of terms. Solitary persons, on the other hand, establish intimate and personal relationships with their physical environment and find "sermons in stones, books in running brooks."

It is therefore to a certain extent true that the society in which we live is predetermined and innate. We spin our social relations, somewhat as the spider spins its web, out of our own bodies.

On the other hand, the specific character of our society, the type, is always more or less determined by the sort of world, physical and social, in which we happen to live.

And so gangs, like most other forms of human association, need to be studied in their peculiar habitat. They spring up spontaneously, but only under favoring conditions and in a definite milieu. The instincts and tendencies that find expression in any specific form of association are no doubt fundamentally human, but it is only under specific conditions that they assume the forms and exhibit the traits that are characteristic of any existing type. And this is true of gangs. It is this that makes them worth studying; it is this that assures us that they are not incorrigible and that they can be controlled.

It is not only true that the habitat makes gangs, but what is of more practical importance, it is the habitat which determines whether or not their activities shall assume those perverse forms in which they become a menace to the community. Village gangs, because they are less hemmed about by physical structures and social inhibitions of an urban environment, ordinarily do not become a social problem, certainly not a problem of the dimensions and significance of those which constitute so obvious and so obdurate a feature of city life.

The gangs here studied are not a product of the city merely, but they are at the same time the product of a clearly defined and well-recognized area of the city, particularly of the modern American city. It is the slum, the city wilderness, as it has been called, which provides the city gang its natural habitat. The slum is a wide region, which includes various other characteristic areas, each inhabited by its own specific type. The slum is not simply the habitat of gangs, but it is the rendezvous of the hobo, and Hobohemia, already described by Nels Anderson, in an earlier volume of this series, is a minor division of the city slum.

The slum includes also the areas of first settlement to which the immigrants inevitably gravitate before they have found their places in the larger urban environment. The racial "ghettos," which now shelter and set apart from the rest of the community Negroes and Chinese as they once sheltered and segregated Jews, are invariably located in the slum. The Jewish ghetto still exists, but the slum, as far as the Jew is concerned, is at present only an area of first settlement. Negroes and Chinese, on the other hand, still find it difficult to live beyond the pale.

ROBERT E. PARK, *Editor*
University of Chicago Sociological Series

November 1926

Author's Preface

This volume is designed to present the sociology of the gang as a type of human group as it has been revealed in a study of 1,313 gangs in Chicago. It will probably have considerable interest for the general reader in that it deals with the relation of the gang to the problems of juvenile demoralization, crime, and politics in a great city. It may be used also as a supplementary textbook in courses of study dealing with the city, collective behavior, juvenile delinquency, and social pathology.

Such formulations as are presented, however, must be regarded as tentative hypotheses rather than as scientific generalizations. Certain of the suggestions made here may prove fruitful in dealing with the practical problems which the gang foments, but the investigation has probably raised more questions than it has answered. Too great precision, furthermore, must not be claimed for the materials collected, although every effort has been made to render them accurate. The study is primarily an exploratory survey designed to reveal behavior-trends and to present a general picture of life in an area little understood by the average citizen. It is hoped that the book will encourage additional study in this field and indicate some interesting lines for further research.

The task of collecting and preparing the data presented, which occupied a period of about seven years, was only brought to a successful culmination through co-operation from a great variety of sources. Limitations of space do not permit definite acknowledgments to all the social agencies and individuals who have rendered assistance. The author is deeply indebted to the Chicago boys' work agencies, both public and private, for their friendly interest in the investigation and their frequent co-operation in some special phase of the study. He is also under obligation for assistance in making the study and in preparing the manuscript for publication to the Local Community Research Committee of the University of Chicago.

Particular thanks are due the following persons, all of whom co-operated in some special way: William L. Bodine, O. J. Milliken, I. D. Stehr, J. C. Parrett, Wallace W. Kirkland, G. B. Stephenson, O. Wander, Joseph L. Moss, Benjamin Blinstrub, Ed. Borcea, G. M. Martin, Mrs. W. L. McMaster, Jessie Binford, Mary McDowell, Harriett Vittum, Donald F. Bond, Judith Strohm, Joel D. Hunter, Winifred Raushenbush, Robert D. Klees, John H. Witter, Francis D. Hanna, Charles F. Smith, H. B. Chamberlin, Jack Robbins, C. H. English, Roy E. Dickerson, Herbert Asbury, Clifford R. Shaw, Albert E. Webster, Claudia Wannamaker, Edwin A. Olson, Ruth Shonle, Ferdinand Kramer, Leon F. Whitney, Nels Anderson, Paul B. Bremicker, George B. Masslich, V. K. Brown, Theodore J. Szmergalski, and Allen E. Carpenter. More specific acknowledgments are made in the text where possible.

The following agencies (of Chicago, if not otherwise indicated) have co-operated with the author: Better Government Association of Chicago and Cook County, Boys' Brotherhood Republic, Boys' Club, Boys' Court, Boy

Scouts of America, Central Council of Social Agencies, Chicago–Cook County School for Boys, Parental School, Public Schools, Crime Commission of the Association of Commerce, Department of Compulsory Education, Department of Public Welfare, Federation of Settlements, Juvenile Court of Cook County, Juvenile Detention Home of Cook County, Juvenile Protective Association, Municipal Court, Park and Playground Systems, Police Department, Railroad Detective Departments (Private Police), Social Settlements, Union League Boys' Club, United Charities, United Jewish Charities, University of Chicago, and Young Men's Christian Association.

The author is under especial obligation to Robert E. Park, editor of this series, who read the manuscript and the proofs and who has made many suggestions of great value with reference to the interpretation of the materials and the preparation of the manuscript. He wishes also to express his deep gratitude to Ernest W. Burgess for his unfailing interest in the study and for many valuable suggestions, and to William I. Thomas and Ellsworth Faris for valuable suggestions and standpoint.

FREDERIC M. THRASHER

CHICAGO, ILLINOIS
November 1, 1926

Introduction to the Abridged Edition

The task of abridging[1] and "introducing" a modern classic is both challenging and frustrating—challenging because elmination of material poses problems of remaining faithful to the essential point of view and basic conclusions of the original, while placing it in historical perspective and assessing its current relevance; frustrating because so little still is known concerning many of the basic questions.

No one conversant in the social sciences would challenge the designation of Thrasher's work as a "modern classic." It is so for a variety of reasons. It stands, first of all, after more than three and a half decades as the

[1] I am indebted to Ray A. Tennyson for helpful suggestions concerning the abridgment. This Introduction has benefited from critical reading by several colleagues, including especially Albert J. Reiss, Jr., Richard W. Boone, David Bordua, Charles Cooper, Donald Garrity, Donald Gibbons, Robert A. Gordon, Solomon Kobrin, Henry McKay, Walter Miller, Fred Strodtbeck, and Stanton Wheeler. The entire project reflects work done under grants from the Behavior Science Study Section of the National Institute of Mental Health, the Ford Foundation, and the President's Committee on Juvenile Delinquency and Youth Crime. Thanks also are due staff members and collaborators for work done under these grants, and the Program for Detached Workers of the Y.M.C.A. of Metropolitan Chicago, without whose co-operation our research would be impossible.

most comprehensive study of the phenomenon of adolescent gangs ever undertaken. So complete was it that, at least in part because of this fact, no other great survey of its type has been undertaken.

The Gang is a great book also because of the social climate of the day in which it was written, and because many of the significant people of that day were associated with it. The list of acknowledgments in the original edition reads almost as an introductory "Who's Who" of the juvenile court and its ancillary services, of city planning and social welfare in its broader sense, encompassing a host of social problems, and of the "Chicago school"— its originators and their students who came on to teach the rest of us. For all of these people the city was a laboratory par excellence, and Thrasher was one of its pioneers. His was one of the first of the great sociological monographs to come from the students of W. I. Thomas, Robert E. Park, and Ernest W. Burgess. Nels Anderson's *The Hobo*[2] was published while Thrasher was making his survey, and the works of Wirth, Cavan, Shaw and McKay, Zorbaugh, Frazier, Landesco, Cressey, Reckless, Hayner[3] and others were soon to come. This

[2] University of Chicago Press, 1923.

[3] Louis Wirth, *The Ghetto* (Chicago: University of Chicago Press, 1928); Ruth Shonle Cavan, *Suicide* (Chicago: University of Chicago Press, 1928); Clifford R. Shaw, *Delinquency Areas* and *The Jack-Roller* (Chicago: University of Chicago Press, 1929, 1930); Clifford R. Shaw and Henry D. McKay, *Social Factors in Juvenile Delinquency, Report on the Causes of Crime for the National Commission on Law Observance and Enforcement*, Vol. II (Washington, D.C.: U.S. Government Printing Office, 1931); and Shaw and McKay, *Juvenile Delinquency and Urban Areas* (Chicago: University of Chicago Press, 1942); Harvey W. Zorbaugh, *The Gold Coast and the Slum* (Chicago: University of Chicago Press, 1929); E. Franklin Frazier, *The Negro Family in Chicago* (Chicago: University of Chicago Press, 1932); John Landesco, "Organized Crime in Chicago," Part III of *Illinois Crime Survey* (Illinois Association for Criminal Justice, 1929), pp. 827–1087; Paul G. Cressey, *The Taxi-Dance Hall* (Chicago: University of Chicago Press, 1932); Walter C. Reckless,

was an age of unprecedented enthusiasm for discovery in American sociology, and Chicago was its center. The old "Green Bible"[4] called upon students to observe and record social life in every conceivable setting, and to generalize its forms and processes. This was the essential spirit of the "Chicago school," and it is the spirit of *The Gang*.

"THE GANG" AS SOCIOLOGY AND AS FACT

The Gang is a product not only of the enthusiasm of the Chicago school but of its methodology and theoretical orientation as well. Assessment of its contemporary relevance requires evaluation in terms of these matters and of the findings of later research.

Leaders of the "Chicago school," said Richard Wright, "were not afraid to urge their students to trust their feelings for a situation or an event, were not afraid to stress the role of insight, and to warn against a slavish devotion to figures, charts, graphs, and sterile scientific techniques."[5] Theirs was more the spirit of the "social survey"—"a study, undertaken by men who believed that social facts well presented would point the way to reform of the conditions and ways of living at or below the poverty line."[6] The emphasis of the "Chicago school" of sociologists was on "how to get facts" and on their

---

Vice in Chicago (Chicago: University of Chicago Press, 1933); Norman Hayner, *Hotel Life* (Chapel Hill: University of North Carolina Press, 1936).

[4] Robert E. Park and Ernest W. Burgess, *Introduction to the Science of Sociology* (Chicago: University of Chicago Press, 1921; 2d ed., 1924).

[5] Richard Wright, Introduction to the first edition of *Black Metropolis: A Study of Negro Life in a Northern City* by St. Clair Drake and Horace R. Cayton (New York: Harcourt, Brace & Co., 1945; reprinted in the revised and enlarged edition, Harper & Row, Publishers, 1962), I, xix.

[6] Everett C. Hughes, Introduction to the Torchbook Edition, *ibid.*, p. xxxvii.

dissection and classification, rather than social reform, but reform was consciously close to the surface for most of its participants, including Thrasher.

Thrasher's entire life attested to his identification with this methodological perspective. He stood, as Dan Dodson notes *in memoriam*, "between education as an art and sociology as a science."[7]

When it was first written, *The Gang* was hailed as "an advancement in the general-survey and case-study method" and as "superior to earlier studies of the gang in that its conclusions grow out of concrete material."[8] No latter-day assessment is likely to alter this judgment. Yet we do not know specifically how Thrasher collected his material. We know that its collection required seven years and that a variety of data collection techniques were employed, including utilization of census and court records, personal observation, and personal documents collected from gang boys and from persons who had observed gangs in many contexts. But we do not know precisely how Thrasher chose his informants, and we have no way of evaluating their reliability or representativeness. In the light of reports of his later research experience, and his critical appraisal of the research of others, confidence in what is reported as fact in the book seems justified.[9]

By comparison with later developments in systematic observation and experimentation with small groups, how-

[7] Dan W. Dodson, "Frederic Milton Thrasher (1892–1962)," *American Sociological Review*, XXVII (August, 1962), 580–81.

[8] Kimball Young, "Frederic M. Thrasher's Study of Gangs," Analysis 37 in Stuart A. Rice (ed.) *Methods in Social Science: A Case Book* (Chicago: University of Chicago Press, 1931), pp. 525–26.

[9] See, for example, Frederic M. Thrasher, "How To Study the Boys' Gang in the Open," *Journal of Educational Sociology*, I (January, 1928), 244–54; and "A Community Study," *Religious Education*, XXV (May, 1930), 398–400.

JUNIOR VICE KINGS

A group of Junior Vice Kings "making it" down Roosevelt Road. Gang boys gain status not only by breaking the law but by more conventional ways as well.

ever, Thrasher's material is unsystematic and incomplete in essential details. He did not have as much information on any one gang as did Whyte, for example.[10] His personal documents and his observations lack sufficient detail concerning particular behavior episodes to permit group process analysis.[11] The study's greatest strength, its comprehensiveness, suffers from lack of analytical sophistication in "holding constant" variables which might have further elucidated the nature of many aspects of gang variety. These criticisms are tempered by the fact that modern methods of small group observations had not yet developed, and by the failure, with few exceptions, of more recent social scientists to apply these methods in the natural settings of groups.[12] Furthermore, because of technological innovations in social science methodology we are in danger of losing much of the strength of Thrasher's observational methods. In many studies today, "Observation is reduced to the minimum considered necessary to developing a questionnaire yield-

[10] William Foote Whyte, *Street Corner Society: The Social Structure of an Italian Slum* (Chicago: University of Chicago Press, 1943; 2d ed., 1955).

[11] Cf. James F. Short, Jr., and Fred L. Strodtbeck, "The Response of Gang Leaders to Status Threats: An Observation on Group Process and Delinquent Behavior," *American Journal of Sociology*, LXVIII (March, 1963), 571–79.

[12] Cf. Whyte, *op. cit.;* also Leon Jansyn "Solidarity and Delinquency in a Street Corner Group," unpublished M.A. thesis, University of Chicago, 1960; Muzafer Sherif, O. J. Harvey, B. Jack White, William R. Hood, and Carolyn W. Sherif, *Intergroup Conflict and Cooperation: The Robbers Cave Experiment*, a publication of the Institute of Group Relations (Norman: University of Oklahoma, 1961). The recent work of Walter B. Miller in Boston and of the Youth Studies Program at the University of Chicago are the most intensive investigations of gangs undertaken since the days of Thrasher and, immediately thereafter, of Shaw and his associates. See Walter B. Miller, *City Gangs* (New York: John Wiley & Sons, forthcoming), and James F. Short, Jr., and Fred L. Strodtbeck, *Group Process and Gang Delinquency* (forthcoming).

ing answers which can be 'coded' or 'programmed' for processing by machines. Fewer skilled observers and more standardized interviewers are used."[13] It should be noted, of course, that there are countertrends and that the issue is not observation *or* interviews, experimentation *or* paper-and-pencil tests, but rather the development of more systematic methods of observation and data reduction and the combination of methodologies for optimal results.[14]

Perhaps the greatest weakness of most of the studies conducted by the "Chicago school" was, as Shils has pointed out, that they "did not set out to demonstrate any explicitly formulated sociological hypothesis."[15] Thrasher, too, was heir to this weakness. Like many others he chose to "illustrate with direct, first-hand reports some process or interrelationship which appeared to Park to be of crucial significance in the modern world or in human behaviour in general."[16]

Thrasher's data were neither collected nor analyzed in terms of hypothesis testing. He described his work as "an exploratory survey" and the "formulations" of the book as "tentative hypotheses rather than as scientific generalizations," but he does not really concern himself either with building hypotheses or with relating them in systematic fashion. As a consequence, the data are not suitable for hypothesis testing. Often they seem, in fact, confusing, even contradictory, to the student who would

[13] Hughes, Introduction to the Torchbook Edition, *Black Metropolis*, p. xxxvii.

[14] See, for example, Howard Becker, Blanche Greer, Everett C. Hughes, and Anselm Straus, *Boys in White* (Chicago: University of Chicago Press, 1961).

[15] Edward Shils, *The Present State of American Sociology* (Glencoe: Free Press, 1948), p. 10.

[16] *Ibid.*

attempt to state or test hypotheses. We are told, for example, that gangs are characterized by loyalties and codes which bind more strongly than any other human tie, and by tendencies to instability and disintegration; profanity is "the common language" of the gang world, yet some of them also are "righteous" gangs whose code requires punishment for swearing. The gang is a "primitive democracy," but racial and ethnic identities form the basis for much gang conflict. Clearly, Thrasher recognized many variations, but he made almost no attempt to conceptualize such differences in a way which would account for them or relate them systematically to other (variable) characteristics of gangs or gang boys. Thus, for example, the very wide age differences which Thrasher notes in his gangs seem clearly to be relevant to many of the topics discussed, yet they receive scant treatment in the book. He recognizes age differences and refers to them briefly in the early part of the book and again in discussing "Sex and the Gang" and "The Gang and Organized Crime," but no attempt is made to relate age in any systematic way to the varied behaviors described. Similarly, Thrasher does not conceptualize the difference between conflict which is carried out as one of the focal activities of the gang and conflict which is functional to other purposes. The chapter on "Gang Warfare" treats as though they were cut of the same cloth the fights of adolescent gangs, the warfare of adult organized criminal gangs, and family feuds.

The failure to conceptualize such differences gives some of Thrasher's material the appearance of naïveté, an appearance which is enhanced in part by social changes which have occurred since the days of the "Roaring Twenties" out of which Thrasher's work grew, changes such as the repeal of Prohibition, greater freedom of sexual behavior and discussion, automation, the exten-

sion of governmental welfare services on a vast scale, and
the development of a "buy now, pay later" economy
with attendant financial exploitation of economically
marginal populations, including adolescents. Some would
add the "vanishing" of adolescence as a socially struc-
tured period during which young people are permitted
exploration and experimentation in "growing up" prior
to their entry into adulthood.[17]

Students of gangs today are likely also to feel that
Thrasher, and Park in his preface, fail to recognize systematic variations in the structure and behavior of gangs.
It is probable that they recognized the likelihood of vari-
ation, but felt that its exploration was less important at
the time than was documentation of the gang as "a
specific type or variety of society."

Today there is much emphasis on varieties of delinquent subcultures and on types of gangs which are the
carriers of different subcultural forms. Dodson has said
that Thrasher "was perhaps a forerunner of Whyte, Cole-
man, Cohen and others who are presently concerned with
youth subcultures. . . ."[18] Thrasher, in fact, includes
much material which is relevant to current theories.
Recent enthusiasm for abstract conceptualization, particularly of varieties of delinquent subcultures, has outstripped the data at hand, and we are badly in need of
new empirical studies, several of which fortunately are
under way. In any case, it is well to recognize that
variety occurs against a background of ganging as a general form of human association. Recent data suggest that
variations in delinquent subcultures develop at least in
part in the course of interaction within and between

[17] Cf. Edgar Z. Friedenberg, *The Vanishing Adolescent* (New York:
Dell Publishing Co., Inc., 1962), and Erik H. Erikson, *Childhood and
Society* (New York: W. W. Norton & Co., 1950).

[18] Dodson, *op. cit.*

gangs, and that they cannot be accounted for solely in terms of social structural considerations such as have dominated most recent theories.[19]

"THE GANG"—A CONTEMPORARY VIEW

Much has been written on the subject since the first publication of *The Gang*. Many social changes have occurred which are important in understanding just how this book "fits" today. The temptation is great to sift through the book, with comments here and there concerning changes and similarities, later evidence which confirms, modifies, or disconfirms. We choose, instead, to organize our discussion around three major issues: (1) gangland, including considerations of race and nationality; (2) patterns of gang behavior and etiological considerations; and (3) problems of delinquency control.

The ecological distribution of gangs today probably is very similar to that described by Thrasher. I say "probably," because no later survey as comprehensive as Thrasher's has been made and some doubt exists concerning the classification scheme by which Thrasher was able to "count" his 1,313 gangs. There is no doubt that the delinquent gangs which occupy the attention of the police remain concentrated in "inner-city" areas. The difference is that these areas have changed somewhat in physical appearance, they have expanded greatly, and their ethnic composition has changed. The "prairies" of yesterday have been filled in, by and large, and their place taken by dingy alleys in the midst of overcrowded slums. A few of the latter have fallen before the bulldozers of urban redevelopment. Public housing, and in some in-

---

[19] See, for example, the work of Walter Miller, *op. cit.*, and Short and Strodtbeck, "The Response of Gang Leaders to Status Threats." See, also, Robert A. Gordon and James F. Short, Jr., "Social Level, Social Disability and Gang Interaction," unpublished manuscript, 1962.

A LAWNDALE ALLEY

In the heart of the West Side gangland, an area plagued by gang conflict over the past few years. This is now an area of rapid population transition similar to those in which Thrasher found gang concentration.

stances higher income private housing, have risen in their stead.

As Negroes have increased their numbers and proportion in Chicago's population, the "Black Belt" has expanded greatly and Negro gangs have come to be the major gang problem in the city. (Compare document 116.) In 1960 Negroes constituted 22.9 per cent of the population of the city, and 24.2 per cent of the "Total Boy Population from 20 to 24 Years of Age Inclusive," to use Thrasher's phrasing. (The latter figure compares with 3.7 per cent in 1920.)

The old ethnic identities within the white community are less important today. As the flow of immigration has slowed to a trickle compared to an earlier period, "culture conflict" between immigrant generations and their children has become less important as a general process in gangland. Some of the former ethnic identities are preserved, however, in the argot of the gang world, e.g., the "Jewtown Egyptian Cobras," a large Negro gang located in the old Maxwell Street open-market area. Among white boys, ethnic identity has lost much of its importance in the gang, though distinctions often are made among the newer white immigrants—the Mexican and Puerto Rican. Certainly it is no longer true that "The majority of gangs in Chicago are of Polish stock," though Polish ethnicity still is important in certain areas of the city, notably in the South Chicago steel mill district and the "near northwest side."

Douglas Park still is the scene of gang warfare, but now instead of Polish and Jewish boys doing battle (see document 110), Negro gangs engage in the internecine conflict which has become famous through the mass media. Lawndale was an area of very rapid shift from white to Negro in the 1950's. During this period and into the sixties it was the primary locus of gang conflict in Chicago.

The primary gang conflict areas in recent Chicago history can be divided into two basic types:

(1) Areas which have undergone very rapid transition from white to Negro, such as the West Side along Roosevelt Road and the Congress Street expressway. Here was found the fullest development of the conflict subculture, with Negro gangs fighting other Negro gangs. Here were (and are) the West Side Egyptian Cobras, the Vice Lord Nation, the Chaplains, Imperial Chaplains, Braves, Cherokees, Racketeers, and many others.

(2) Areas on the fringes of expansion of the "Black Belt." These were primarily in the South, though other areas of the city were not immune. In such areas conflict most often occurred between white gangs, sometimes organized specifically for the purpose of "keeping the Niggers out," and Negro boys who were the vanguard of the Negro invasion. The latter were in most cases not organized as gangs, though in some cases they became so.

In both types of area conflict was carried out among adolescent boys, though in the latter case there was much evidence of widespread support from the white adult community, both institutionally and as individuals. During the summer of 1960, for example, it was noted in the Grand Crossing Park area that Negro teen-agers were frequently chased out of the Park, while adults were not molested. White adults frequently gave tacit approval to the white teen-agers and at times such support became overt and aggressive. A few boys whose families had moved out of the area romanticized a role for themselves as "defenders of the community" and for a time returned to the area to maintain personal contacts and to keep up the struggle with those who remained. Most of the boys regarded the conflict with Negro boys as a sort of game, adopting the attitude that "Next year they'll be chasing us out of the Park." This did not materialize, however, because the white boys simply ceased to use the park once Negro supremacy in the "game" had been established.

We have referred to two types of gang conflict areas. The question arises whether the forces giving rise to and perpetuating gang conflict differ between the two. Certainly the precipitating forces would appear to be different. Racial antagonisms are involved in the "border disputes" of the first type, while in the second type the combatants are all of one race. Before jumping to the conclusion that the *conflict orientation* of white gangs opposing Negro invasion is caused by racial antagonism, it should be noted that the white gangs in question have a history of prior conflict among themselves, on the basis of other ethnic or neighborhood identities. Still, these gangs lack stability, and there is no evidence even in the past that their conflict orientation was of the same variety as the Negro gangs on the West Side. When, between the summers of 1959 and 1962 the Youth Studies Program of the University of Chicago sought to locate white conflict gangs of this variety, there were none to be found. And the Negro gangs studied were not equally conflict-oriented—some not at all. An adequate theory must account for such differences.

Among the more important empirical discoveries which have occurred since Thrasher, and which are of significance to delinquency theory, are those having to do with lower class culture, and especially with Negro lower class culture. Whyte, and others after him, told us a great deal about *organization* in the slums, in contrast to the earlier (including Thrasher) emphasis on *disorganization*.[20] Slum areas which were identified as

[20] Whyte, *op. cit*. See, also, W. Lloyd Warner and Paul S. Lunt, *The Social Life of a Modern Community* (New Haven: Yale University Press, 1941); and August B. Hollingshead, *Elmtown's Youth* (New York: John Wiley & Sons, Inc., 1949).

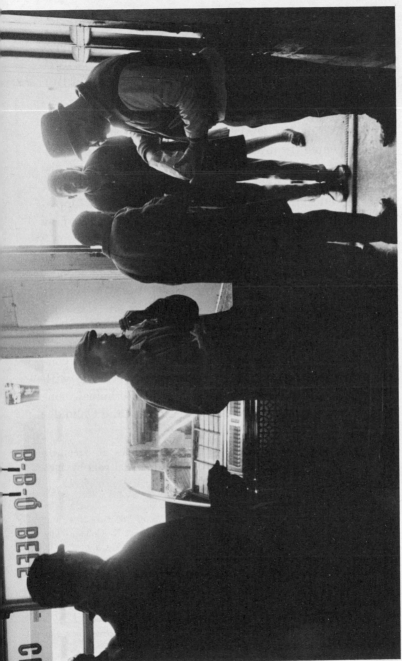

A DETACHED WORKER

A detached worker meets members of the Junior Vandals and Midget Navahoes
in a restaurant hangout on the Near North Side.

"interstitial" were found in many cases to stabilize around lower class cultural forms. Much still is to be learned concerning the nature of lower class "institutions" such as "quarter parties," storefront churches, and "policy," and how these fit into the larger social structure. Whyte, and Drake and Cayton for Negro culture,[21] documented the interdependence of such "deviant" phenomena and conventional institutions. With these discoveries, social disorganization lost some of its appeal as a theoretical frame of reference, and it came to be supplemented by considerations of social structure[22] and by more intense study of lower class social systems.[23] Among the more recent developments in this process has been a revitalization of interest in juvenile delinquency, and particularly in "delinquent subcultures" which are hypothesized to characterize some adolescent gangs.

Several "delinquent subcultures" have been described since Thrasher wrote *The Gang.* Most of these were anticipated in Thrasher's book, but they have been conceptualized differently. The classification scheme with perhaps the broadest currency describes criminal, conflict, and retreatist subcultures.[24] Cloward and Ohlin describe these subcultures as follows:

> One is based principally upon criminal values; its members are organized primarily for the pursuit of material gain by such

[21] St. Clair Drake and Horace R. Cayton, *Black Metropolis* (New York: Harcourt, Brace & Co., 1945).

[22] Robert K. Merton, *Social Theory and Social Structure* (rev. and enl. ed.; Glencoe: Free Press, 1957). See, also, Albert K. Cohen, "The Study of Social Disorganization and Deviant Behavior," Chapter 21 in Robert K. Merton, Leonard Brown, and Leonard S. Cottrell, Jr. (eds.), *Sociology Today* (New York: Basic Books, Inc., 1959).

[23] See, for example, Oscar Lewis, *Five Families* (New York: Basic Books, Inc., 1959). The most thorough study of lower class culture specifically in relation to gangs is reported in Walter B. Miller, *op. cit.*

[24] See Richard A. Cloward and Lloyd E. Ohlin, *Delinquency and Opportunity* (Glencoe: Free Press, 1960), p. 20.

illegal means as extortion, fraud, and theft. In the second, violence is the keynote; its members pursue status ("rep") through the manipulation of force or threat of force. These are the "warrior" groups that attract so much attention in the press. Finally, there are subcultures which emphasize the consumption of drugs. The participants in these drug subcultures have become alienated from conventional roles, such as those required in the family or the occupational world. They have withdrawn into a restricted world in which the ultimate value consists in the "kick."

Thrasher did not talk about delinquent subcultures, but his material is relevant to their delineation. He distinguished between "diffuse" and "solidified" gangs, "conventionalized" and "criminal" types. He sketches diagrammatically alternative possibilities concerning the forms of collectivity which the gang may take as well as natural history "stages in the development of the gang." (See chapter iv.) The attempt is one of generating "possible relations to other types of collective behavior," however, rather than logical combinations or generalized models of cause and effect. It is taxonomic rather than hypothetical-deductive or explanatory, but the case materials are relevant to current theories which attempt to explain and predict. Chapter viii, "Junking and the Railroads," contains excellent material relative to "opportunity structures" for illegitimate enterprise in the form of fences and other customers who purchase stolen goods, parents who condone and encourage theft, and whole neighborhoods which support such illegitimate activities. Thrasher was aware also of the importance of "political" connections in the case of a gang which enjoyed "practical immunity from prosecution."[25]

Thrasher conceptualized gang conflict very little beyond observations of its function in promoting group

[25] Cf. Solomon Kobrin, "Sociological Aspects of the Development of a Street Corner Group: An Exploratory Study," *American Journal of Orthopsychiatry*, XXXI (October, 1961), 685–702.

consciousness and morale (see chapters ii and iii). Chapter ix, on "Gang Warfare," however, presents material descriptive of adolescent gang warfare, on the one hand (documents 92, 94, 100, 104, and 105), and the warfare of adult criminal gangs on the other (documents 95, 96, 102, and chapter xviii, "The Gang and Organized Crime").

Observations concerning the use of alcohol among gang boys are dated to a greater extent than is most of the book. He wrote in the middle of the prohibition era. Liquor, while reasonably available to adults who took the trouble to inquire, was much less accessible to young people. Today, use of alcohol is probably the most common "delinquent" activity engaged in by gang boys, being reported for nearly 90 per cent of approximately 600 boys studied in a recent Chicago project.[26] Apparently, also, drug use was not a serious problem among Thrasher's gangs, whereas 40 per cent of the gang boys recently studied had smoked "pot" (marijuana) and 10 per cent had used "hard" narcotics such as heroin. Thus, Thrasher did not describe or differentiate gangs of drug users, at least in part because there were none to describe.

But, why did he not differentiate conflict and criminal gangs? There is, first of all, no certainty that the types which have been described existed at the time Thrasher was writing—or now for that matter. There is considerable evidence of "overlapping" in conflict, criminal, and retreatist patterns of behavior within gangs, in Thrasher's data and in more recent empirical investigations.[27] It may be, too, that the specialized adaptations delineat-

[26] See James F. Short, Jr., Ray A. Tennyson, and Kenneth I. Howard, "Behavior Dimensions of Gang Delinquency," *American Sociological Review*, XXVIII, 415.

[27] *Ibid*. See also Herbert A. Bloch and Arthur Niederhoffer, *The Gang* (New York: Philosophical Library, 1958), Part IV.

ed by Cloward and Ohlin should be regarded as "ideal types" isolated for theoretical and heuristic purposes, rather than as descriptions of reality. Or, the extreme patterns may exist, but they may be very rare as compared with more versatile, amorphous, and general delinquent subcultures, as proposed by Cohen.[28] It has been suggested that varieties of delinquent subcultures develop from such "parent" subcultures in response to conditions in the external environment—such as criminal opportunities and the culture of the local neighborhood—and to processes internal to the group—such as skills represented in the membership, clique differentiation, leadership ability, and stability.[29]

The state of organized crime was changing rapidly at the time of Thrasher's study. Thrasher was aware of many variations and changes, and chapter xviii presents their documentation and conceptualization. The chapter does not present a theory concerning the relation between adolescent gangs and the different forms of organized crime. Kobrin, Cloward and Ohlin, Spergel, Miller, and others have attempted to fill this gap in Thrasher's material.[30] The fact that it has taken so long to get around to the matter, and that these efforts are today debated with such vigor, testifies to the complexity of the task and perhaps to Thrasher's acumen rather than his oversight.

The very scope of Thrasher's investigation, his methods, and his primary purpose also stood in the way of the-

[28] Albert K. Cohen, *Delinquent Boys* (Glencoe: Free Press, 1955).

[29] See Albert K. Cohen and James F. Short, Jr., "Research in Delinquent Subcultures," *Journal of Social Issues*, XIV, No. 3 (1958), 20–37; also, Short and Strodtbeck, "The Response of Gang Leaders to Status Threats."

[30] Solomon Kobrin, "The Conflict of Values in Delinquency Areas," *American Sociological Review*, XVI (October, 1951) 653–62; Irving Spergel, "An Exploratory Research in Delinquent Subcultures," *Social Service Review*, XXXV (March, 1961), 33–47; Miller, *op. cit.*

oretical development. The task of statistical manipulation of more than 1,300 cases on which very little data in
common were collected was an impossible barrier to conceptualization beyond relatively crude classification.
Early in the book, however, we are given probably the
most important clues to the nature of the entire enterprise. Park writes in his Preface, "Gangs are gangs,
wherever they are found," and Thrasher enjoins, "the
gang is a protean manifestation . . . . each has to be
considered on its own merits." Thus, the effort was directed toward documentation of the gang as "a specific
type or variety of society" and toward documentation of
features common to the gang as a form of association
admist the almost infinite variety represented by individual gangs.

Moving beyond Thrasher's classification scheme to
more recent efforts to understand patterns of gang behavior, it is necessary to distinguish between *subcultures*
and gangs, or other organizational forms of individuals
who are the *carriers* of a particular subculture or subcultures. Not all delinquency which is subcultural in
nature takes place within gangs.[31] A subculture is a
"way of life" which has become traditional among members of a particular category or subgroup of individuals
within a larger society which shares a common culture,
e.g., occupational (M.D.'s, farmers, bankers, truck drivers), regional (southerners, "down easters," midwestern-
ers), and age (children, adolescents, young adults, middle
aged, and aged).[32] Any individual—including gang boys
—inevitably belongs to several of these subcultures,
though they are not of equal importance to him personal-

[31] For an instructive example, see the analysis by Albert J. Reiss,
Jr., of "The Social Integration of Queers and Peers," *Social Problems*,
IX (Fall, 1961), 102–20.

[32] See Albert Cohen's discussion of subcultures in *Delinquent Boys*.

HANGING

A worker and some of his boys. Detached workers spend much of their time in such informal situations.

ly or to an understanding of his behavior. A member of the Egyptian Cobras, for example, is a lower class Negro adolescent male, as well as an Egyptian Cobra. Each of these "membership" categories has subcultural implications for the boy. If he is employed, this too may have an important bearing on his subcultural orientations, as will the type of job he has. So, too, if he is married, from the South, in school or out, and a host of other background and associational patterns which characterize him as an individual. Amidst this welter of sometimes conflicting identities it is important to note that subcultures "are acquired only by interaction with those who already share and embody, in their belief and action, the culture pattern."[33] If a boy does not interact with fellow schoolmates at all or in such a manner that he becomes immersed in their activities and identified with the school program, this particular subculture may influence him very little, except perhaps in a negative way. Similarly, without continuous interaction with other carriers of a particular subculture, its hold on an individual is likely to weaken. Even frequent interaction with other participants in a subculture may not carry over into behavioral settings in which participants of the subculture are not involved. Witness, for example, the office girl who becomes a "Beat" in the Village at night; or the gang boy who holds a job during the day and spends his evenings on the corner.

The latter case provides an opportunity to discuss what appears to be one of the characteristics of lower class gang boys which provides an important clue to their behavior. Its etiological implications can be illustrated by the experience of gang boys in the world of work. Experiments which have sought to secure jobs for gang boys have been reasonably successful in job location and

[33] *Ibid.*, p. 13.

placement, but they have been notably unsuccessful in keeping the boys on jobs. A part of this job instability doubtless is due to purposive exploration by the boys in search of greater vocational opportunities and aptitudes. A large part, however, is due to job failure because of excessive absence or tardiness, arrest, or misbehavior on the job. These types of failure are related to the boy's participation in gang life in obvious ways, and in ways which are more subtle. As Bordua has pointed out, Thrasher was sensitive to the fact that "long-term involvement in the 'free undisciplined' street life with money at hand from petty theft and with the days devoted to play was not exactly ideal preparation for the humdrum life of the job."[34] Once on the job, long hours on the street with a gang at night with or without consumption of alcohol, are not conducive to punctuality in the morning. Involvement in delinquent episodes with other gang members is another clear case of the gang "causing" job failure. What is not so obvious is that many gang boys do not possess the knowledge and the social skills which are required to function outside their circumscribed lower class and gang worlds. It appears that they recognize the moral validity and the legitimacy of "middle class" values, but they are ill equipped to perform adequately in middle class institutional contexts, and their gang associations further hamper such efforts as they are able to muster in this direction.[35] They

[34] David J. Bordua, "Delinquent Subcultures: Sociological Interpretations of Gang Delinquency," *Annals of the American Academy of Political and Social Science*, CCCXXXVIII (November, 1961), 134.

[35] See James F. Short, Jr., Fred L. Strodtbeck, and Desmond S. Cartwright, "A Strategy for Utilizing Research Dilemmas: A Case from the Study of Parenthood in a Street Corner Gang," *Sociological Inquiry*, XXXII (Spring, 1962), 185–202; also, Robert A. Gordon, James F. Short, Jr., Desmond S. Cartwright, and Fred L. Strodtbeck, "Values and Gang Delinquency," *American Journal of Sociology* (forthcoming).

xxxviii   INTRODUCTION TO THE ABRIDGED EDITION

do not, for example, know how to go about an employment interview, how to dress and comport themselves. These are skills which can quickly and reasonably effectively be imparted to the boys by special counseling. More basically, however, and more difficult to change, the boys tend to lack skills associated with ordinary interpersonal relationships—in simply "getting along with" people. Further, many characteristics of gang life on the streets—the highly aggressive means of establishing a "pecking order," the exploitation of each momentary situation for whatever immediate pleasure can be derived, the flouting of conventional middle class values and authority—are hardly calculated to inculcate or to encourage the development of these skills.

Observation suggests that the ability to get along with people is one of the basic skills associated with gang leadership. It seems likely that the boys recognize the catalytic function of the few who possess these abilities and they reward them with leadership positions.[36] Similarly, and not unexpectedly, observation suggests that gang boys who possess these qualities have better job records than do those who lack them.[37]

Among the social skills which facilitate social interaction, particularly in modern urban society, is the ability to change roles with ease, to move from one subculture

[36] This, quite in contrast to the view advanced by Yablonsky that gang leaders are the most seriously emotionally disturbed boys. Our data suggest that the latter more often are fringe members who often attempt to achieve leadership by aggressive means or by involving the group in conflict with other gangs in order to create leadership opportunities. Cf. Lewis Yablonsky, "The Delinquent Gang as a Near Group," *Social Problems*, VII (Fall, 1959), 108-17.

[37] These observations are unsystematic. A research program designed to follow up work experiences with employers as well as gang boys is under way with support from the President's Committee on Juvenile Delinquency and Youth Crime, under my direction. Ernest Lilienstein is chiefly responsible for this phase of the research.

to another. This skill is instilled in their children at an early age by middle class parents. They are taught, for example, that "company" involves a different set of expectations at the dinner table than does "family," that Sunday School requires "dressing up" in manners as well as customary garb. Teachers are defined for their children as a special category of persons, to be respected and obeyed, the schoolroom and the playground are differentiated in terms of behavioral expectations. By admonition and by parental example, the middle class child is prepared to "role play" in appropriate ways.

The lower class child is likely to be poorly prepared in those respects, and there is evidence as well of a higher incidence of conditions which block nurturant and in other ways gratifying personal relationships within lower class, as compared with middle class, families.[38] Further, within the lower class, non-gang boys are found to have more successful adjustments in school and to come from more stable families.[39]

These and other findings suggest that the gang represents for the boys a social system which in many ways is *alternative* to and competitive with more conventional systems rather than simply supplementary to them. Cohen has hypothesized that gang boys become especially dependent on the gang as they become alienated from other groups. Recent evidence suggests, in addition, that the gang is not as stable or as rewarding a social system

[38] The literature on this point is extensive, from early social surveys to more recent studies. See, especially, Sheldon and Eleanor Glueck, *Unravelling Juvenile Delinquency* (New York: Commonwealth Fund, 1950); and Albert Bandura and Richard H. Walters, *Adolescent Aggression* (New York: Ronald Press Co., 1959).

[39] See Jonathan Freedman and Ramon Rivera, "Education, Social Class, and Patterns of Delinquency," paper read at the annual meeting of the American Sociological Association, 1962; Ramon Rivera, "Occupational Goals: A Comparative Analysis," unpublished M.A. thesis, University of Chicago, 1963.

as it has been assumed to be, largely on the basis of early case histories from Thrasher and others.[40] Even in these there is evidence of great instability in gang membership, structure, and length of life. It does not take an uncomfortably large inferential step, furthermore, to interpret Thrasher's cases in terms a good deal less carefree and happy-go-lucky than Thrasher himself was wont to do. His descriptions of the wanderings of gang boys away from home and school sound a decidedly romantic note, but it may be questioned whether such an unstable existence provided the nurturance and security needed by the boys perhaps even more than the gratifications inherent in "new experience." Thrasher was impressed with the *independence* of gang boys (chapter xvii). A more modern psychological perspective suggests that such an unstable existence is likely to lack many of the rewards of close interpersonal relations.

Thrasher was sensitive to the boys' perspectives concerning their experiences and the world around them. He urged keeping channels of communication open between adults and adolescents. The closing paragraph in chapter vi, "The Rôle of the Romantic," is especially relevant:

> *To understand the gang boy one must enter into his world with a comprehension, on the one hand, of this seriousness behind his mask of flippancy or bravado, and on the other, of the rôle of the romantic in his activities and in his interpretation of the larger world of reality.*

The "social disability" thesis holds that a significant part of the "seriousness behind this mask of flippancy or bravado" stems from the lack of social skills possessed by many gang boys and the deprivation of interpersonal grati-

[40] Cf. Edward Rothstein, "Attributes Related to High Social Status: A Comparison of the Perceptions of Delinquent and Non-Delinquent Boys," *Social Problems*, X (Summer, 1962), 75–83; Lewis Yablonsky, *The Violent Gang* (New York: MacMillan Co., 1962); and Bandura and Walters, *op. cit.*

BLONDE AND KING

The girl asked the photographer to take a picture of her chewing on this "cat's" ear. The level of sexual sophistication of gang youngsters appears to be higher than it was forty years ago.

fications consequent to this lack. Thrasher felt that the "pull" of the gang lay primarily in its *play* motif and in the spirit of adventure to which it catered. Bordua has protested that, by contrast, according to more recent theories, "it does not seem like much fun any more to be a gang delinquent," that "Cohen's boys and Cloward and Ohlin's boys are driven by grim economic and psychic necessity into rebellion."[41]

The point, however, is not that the gang is not a rewarding experience for the boys. If this were the case, gangs would likely cease to exist except as ephemeral groupings of momentary duration. Many groups have long histories, and there is evidence of considerable clique stability even within gangs whose shifting membership and "attendance" on the corner suggest fluidity and instability. The point, rather, is that even within the gang, upon which the boy comes to be dependent for a large share of interpersonal gratification, interaction in many respects is not rewarding and lacks characteristics essential to the fulfilment of these needs. It has been suggested that some of the delinquent activities of gang boys, as well as symbols which are adopted for gang identification, such as names, styles of dress and hair-do, etc., represent the adoption or contrivance of "tasks which justify dependence between members and call for co-operation in a common enterprise," thus enhancing the potentials of gang participation for such gratifications.[42] Delinquent

[41] Bordua, *op. cit.*, p. 136. See, also, David J. Bordua, "Sociological Theories and Their Implications for Juvenile Delinquency," Children's Bureau, *Juvenile Delinquency: Facts and Facets*, No. 2 (Washington, D.C.: Government Printing Office, 1960); and "Some Comments on Theories of Group Delinquency," *Sociological Inquiry*, XXXII (Spring, 1962), 245–60.

[42] Robert A. Gordon and James F. Short, Jr., *op. cit.* There is evidence, too, that gang delinquents are *less intelligent* than non-gang boys from the same neighborhoods, and that delinquents are less intelligent

activities become shared and demanding problems which call for co-operation. Jansyn's finding, that delinquent episodes occur frequently in response to low gang solidarity, is consistent with such a view[43]—similarly, Thrasher's point that "A stable unity does not develop in the diffuse type of gang . . . until it becomes solidified through conflict" (chapter xviii).

While they do not depend on one another, the "social disability" hypothesis is consistent with theories which stress the *status* problems of gang boys as of primary etiological significance for both the formation of delinquent subcultures and the precipitation of delinquent episodes.[44] The status argument may be summarized briefly: It is held first of all, that lower class boys tend to be ill prepared by family background and cultural heritage to achieve in the context of middle class institutions such as the school, the church, and the job. There are many ways to overcome the barriers to status which are thus created, such as by being a star athlete or possessing some other skill which compensates for poor preparation and enables the child to "catch up." To the extent that the child is poorly prepared and without compensatory resources, he is likely to be downgraded in the status hierarchies, both child and adult, of relevant institutions. Among the alternatives open to him is the creation of an

---

than non-delinquents when social class is held constant. See Albert J. Reiss, Jr. and Albert Lewis Rhodes, "Delinquency and Social Class Structure," *American Sociological Review*, XXVI (October, 1961), 720–32; and Kenneth I. Howard, Alan E. Hendrickson, and Desmond S. Cartwright, "Psychological Assessment of Street Corner Youth: Intelligence," unpublished paper from the Youth Studies Program, University of Chicago, 1962 (mimeographed).

[43] Jansyn, *op. cit.*

[44] Cf. Cohen, *Delinquent Boys;* Cohen and Short, *op. cit.;* and Short and Strodtbeck, *op. cit.*

alternative status universe in terms of which he can achieve. This requires others who are similarly disposed at least to the extent that they, too, are willing candidates for such a status universe. Since many lower class boys are "in the same boat," there is no shortage of supporters for such a solution to common status problems. Cohen has suggested that in the process giving rise to the delinquent subculture, the criteria of status come to be defined in terms of *opposition* to criteria by which participants previously have been found wanting.[45] Whether or not such a "reaction formation" occurs, it is clear that the criteria of status defined by the new subculture must be responsive to the needs of the participants. Such "focal concerns" of lower class culture as toughness, excitement, and smartness (in the sense of ability to "con" and live by one's wits, rather than academic achievement) are readily available to provide guidelines for such criteria.[46]

Once the gang has become an important vehicle for status achievment, the elaboration of symbols and activities enhances status possibilities within the gang. Thrasher saw the process of conflict in many forms as a necessary element in developing group consciousness within the gang. There can be little doubt that conflict serves this purpose. Beyond this, conflict between gangs may enlarge the status universe of gang boys very appreciably. Networks of gang "nations" comprised of Senior, Junior, Midget (sometimes even down to Pee Wee!), roughly age-graded segments of a gang, and the "alliance" of gangs with the same name, and sometimes with different names, in different areas of the city serve this purpose

[45] Cohen, *Delinquent Boys.*

[46] For elaboration of the focal concerns of lower class culture, see Walter B. Miller, "Lower Class Culture as a Generating Milieu of Gang Delinquency," *Journal of Social Issues*, XXIV (No. 3, 1958), pp. 5-19.

"PILL POPPERS"

"Pill poppers" making the scene. One of the most common forms of narcotics usage by adolescents is the consumption of pills intended for medicinal purposes. Marijuana and heroin also are used by some groups.

well.[47] One's "rep" is determined not only by his status within the gang, but in relation to the "rep" of his gang in the world of conflict gangs.

The relation between gangs and subcultures is not the same for all "delinquency orientations." Subcultures orientated around drug use, for example, are less closely tied to membership in particular gangs than are conflict subcultures. Participation in drug use legitimizes an individual to a considerable degree throughout the subculture. Status here is judged in terms of one's "kick," and his "hustle," rather than gang identification.[48] A drug user makes connections relatively easily even in different cities, once he is known and accepted as an insider to the subculture. A participant in a conflict subculture, by contrast, is likely to feel extremely ill at ease when in strange territory, particularly if he is not with his own gang. Though we have little firm knowledge, adolescent criminal subcultures seem to be characterized less by gang rivalry than by rationally directed theft activities and, in contrast especially to conflict gang boys, a desire to remain inconspicuous in order to avoid detection, jeopardizing protective arrangements, outlets for stolen goods, etc. Such subcultures may be organized around a variety of "rackets," and the skills demanded by these will determine status among participants. This is most fully developed among adult criminal subcultures, many of which are the models of adolescent varieties.[49]

[47] See New York City Youth Board, *Reaching the Fighting Gang*, Donald J. Merwin (editor), 1960; Cohen and Short, *op. cit.*, Cloward and Ohlin, *op. cit.*; and James F. Short, Jr., "Street Corner Groups and Patterns of Delinquency: A Progress Report," *American Catholic Sociological Review*, XXIV (Spring, 1963), pp. 13–32.

[48] See Harold Finestone, "Cats, Kicks and Color," *Social Problems*, V (July, 1957), pp. 3–13.

[49] See Edwin H. Sutherland, *The Professional Thief* (Chicago: University of Chicago Press, 1937).

The argument of subcultural theorists is that delinquent behavior occurs because it is sanctioned by the subculture. Indeed, say Cloward and Ohlin, "the criminal subculture *prescribes* disciplined and utilitarian forms of theft; the conflict subculture *prescribes* the instrumental use of violence; the retreatist subculture *prescribes* participation in illicit consummatory experiences, such as drug use."[50] Though there is disagreement among competing theories on *reasons for the existence* of these norms, in each case behavior is seen as motivated in terms of *status requirements* of the boy's gang, or world of gangs, characterized by the norms of the particular delinquent subculture.

Cloward and Ohlin suggest that delinquents are *selective* in their withdrawal of support from conventional norms and that delinquent subcultures represent the patterning of selective processes in relevant areas, e.g., property rights, the use of violence, and drug use. Even given such selective processes, however, we must account for the manner in which norms so generated become translated into *behavior*. We know that the bulk of even the most delinquent boy's waking hours are spent in non-delinquent activity. What precipitates delinquent episodes, and who is involved?

A beginning is made toward answering these questions in Thrasher's case materials. "Enemies" are chased from the gang's territory and, if caught, beaten. Forays are organized in response to real or imagined challenges from other gangs. Boys who are hungry steal food, and the search for excitement leads to a variety of episodes. There is evidence that such episodes cannot be understood simply as a response to basic needs such as were posited by Thrasher, however, or to group norms. Presumably the norms are reasonably constant for a gang,

[50] Cloward and Ohlin, *op. cit.*, p. 14.

xlviii INTRODUCTION TO THE ABRIDGED EDITION

at least over short periods of time. Yet delinquency is episodic, and it rarely involves all members acting together. It is a focal activity, but not the most common activity of gang boys, individually or collectively.

Status considerations of gang boys help to answer these questions. It is found, for example, that when leaders of gangs perceive their status to be threatened, they seek to reaffirm or re-establish their leadership. Among conflict-oriented gangs and others in which toughness is a valued characteristic, this reaction often takes the form of aggression directed outside the group.[51] A group of retreatists which were studied did not react aggressively when challenged. Instead they chose to engage in the one activity which set them apart from their challengers, namely, drug use. Thus, group process and subcultural considerations operate together in the explanation of delinquent episodes.

Some evidence exists that "status threats" to which gang boys may respond in a delinquent manner are not limited to challenges to leadership. The threat may be to his masculinity or his status as an (aspiring) adult or as a member of a particular gang quite aside from his position in the gang.[52] If the "social disability" thesis is correct, the range of situations which is perceived as threatening may be greater, and their ability to respond to such threats in other than an aggressive or retreatist manner more limited for gang boys than for their non-gang peers. Such reactions may be experienced individually or collectively, but for the gang boy the response is likely to

[51] Short and Strodtbeck, "The Response of Gang Leaders to Status Threats," argue that this is the case because gang leaders have limited resources for internal control of the group.

[52] See James F. Short, Jr., "Anomie and Gang Delinquency," in Marshall B. Clinard (ed.), *Deviant Behavior and Anomie* (New York: Free Press of Glencoe, forthcoming).

occur within the gang context and so to implicate other members of the gang.

Most of this section is in the nature of hypothesis, rather than demonstrated fact. In nearly forty years we have gone little beyond Thrasher except in terms of conceptualization and research methodology. Advances in these two areas have not as yet joined forces sufficiently to bring answers to the sorts of questions which have been posed. The "necessary job of sociographic description of slum life" is far from complete.[53]

Although Thrasher did not believe the gang "caused" delinquency and crime (see chapter xvii), it was clear to him, as it is clear today, that gangs are a major influence on their members. Gangs provide the social setting for much delinquency and crime and are extremely important to the control of these phenomena.

Thrasher's studies convinced him that juvenile delinquency was extremely difficult to control, and that the control of ganging and the redirection of gangs was of primary importance to the problem. His chastisement of conventional institutions for their failure to provide socializing experiences consistent with the needs of gang boys sounds a familiar, almost contemporary, note, as does his highlighting of the social gap between adolescents and adults. Thrasher was not naïve enough to believe that "wholesome recreation" was the solution to the problem, for such programs would have to *"compete with the vigorous freedom of exciting gang life"* (chapter xvii).[54]

[53] Bordua, "Some Comments on Theories of Group Delinquency," *Sociological Inquiry*, XXXII, 260.

[54] A detached worker's poignant observation concerning an apartment where some members of his gang spent their time while the mother of one of the boys was working is appropriate: "Up there they got booze, women,

Perhaps the most revealing commentary on Thrasher's views in this area lies in the fact that we still must echo most of his six points for crime prevention programs. Certainly the call for programs "based upon social research rather than the superficial type of survey often employed by social agencies" is well taken. Recent efforts in this direction are not the first ever to be undertaken, but they promise to be among the most thorough.[55] The Federal Delinquency Program which was initiated in 1961 calls, as did Thrasher, for co-ordination of community-wide efforts to control delinquency, and for program innovations and experimentation when existing facilities are inadequate.[56] Grants are being made to many cities, counties, universities, and local agencies, for planning and demonstration programs, training and curriculum development projects, all aimed at controlling juvenile delinquency. If Thrasher could observe this flurry of activity he might well remark, "It's about time!"

THE ABRIDGMENT

Readers familiar with the work will note that two chapters in the original edition have been eliminated in

and freedom from adult control. Now, what program can compete with that!" (From the files of the Youth Studies Program at the University of Chicago.)

[55] The Chicago Area Project, initiated by Clifford Shaw following his own research conclusions, was perhaps the earliest and most significant such program. See Solomon Kobrin, "The Chicago Area Project—A 25-Year Assessment," *Annals of the American Academy of Political and Social Science*, CCCXXII (March, 1959), 19–29.

[56] See "The Federal Delinquency Program Objectives and Operation under the President's Committee on Juvenile Delinquency and Youth Crime, and the Juvenile Delinquency and Youth Offenses Control Act of 1961" (Public Law 87–274) (Washington, D.C.: Department of Justice, Department of Health, Education, and Welfare, Department of Labor, November, 1962).

the abridgment: chapter vi, "The Movies and the Dime Novel," and chapter x, "Wanderlust." The technology of mass communications has changed so greatly in forty years that this chapter is of little current interest. Television has been added, and movies are quite different today. Gang boys seem less "addicted" to movies than in Thrasher's day, now that the novelty of the media has worn off. The dime novel has given way to comic books and the "slick" magazines as purveyors of sex and violence. Still little is known concerning the influence of any of these media on the behavior of gang boys, or of children generally. There has been much speculation, but little evidence, as Thrasher noted many times.[57] "His studies of movies convinced him that the meanings they conveyed were not the same for the child as for the adult. He believed that they did not contribute to social disorganization."[58]

"Wanderlust" depicted gang boys' "roaming, roving, and exploring activities" as a "quest for new experience," following W. I. Thomas. The main thesis, that "the great outside world is a place of mystery and mythical wonders," is of interest because it may help us to understand the fear of going outside their "area" which is found among many gang boys. We know very little of the extent and nature of "bumming" today, or of its significance to adolescent adjustment. Thrasher's impression, and our own, was that "Usually the gang becomes fairly well attached to a definite locality and wanders only occasionally beyond its frontiers." (p. 166 in the original edition). "Bumming" seems not to be a major problem

[57] See Frederic M. Thrasher, "Education Versus Censorship," *Journal of Educational Sociology*, XIII (January, 1940), 285–306, and "The Comics and Delinquency: Cause or Scapegoat," *Journal of Educational Sociology*, XXIII (December, 1949), 195–205.

[58] Dan W. Dodson, *op. cit.*

among gang boys today. For Negro gang boys it is difficult because of their high social visibility. Perhaps those
among gang boys who might have been inclined to take
to the road have been siphoned off into Beatnik adjustments. In any case, it was decided not to include the
chapter in this edition because its speculations seemed to
add little to the present state of knowledge concerning
gangs.

A few of Thrasher's original "documents" have been
eliminated, some because they seemed of questionable
relevance and some because of doubts concerning their
reliability. Original document numbers have been retained to facilitate reference to the unabridged edition.
The entire Bibliography, which Thrasher added to the
1936 impression, and many footnotes have been removed. Bibliographical items added in 1936 are largely
superseded by later works and contribute very little to
an understanding of Thrasher's work. Footnotes eliminated represent research or theories upon which Thrasher
based his views or which supplemented his work, and are
chiefly or historical interest. Readers primarily interested in history should by all means consult the original
work.

More was eliminated from Part IV ("The Gang Problem") than from any other section primarily because
much of the material seemed badly dated in the sense
that it referred to problems or ongoing programs which
were relatively specific to the period of Thrasher's concern. Thus, description and casual evaluation of delinquency control efforts by a variety of social agencies
during the 1920's and early 1930's was not included, nor
was Thrasher's "Brief outline of a crime-prevention program for a local council of social agencies" (pp. 539–41
in the 1936 impression). Though in the latter Thrasher's
stress on research as the basis of action is well taken, bet-

ter advice concerning both research and agency co-ordination can be obtained from more recent sources. In any case, the experience of several cities in this regard suggests that the matter is far too complex to be reduced to such a simplified sketch.

No text has been added, but sentences have been italicized in a number of instances in order to draw attention to especially significant themes in the book. Hopefully, these will serve as guidelines to the reader, and they are a convenient reference.

CONCLUSION

For sheer scope of the inquiry Thrasher stands alone, and it is doubtful that such an investigation will be attempted again. This is the basic work concerning the gang as a form of social organization. The nature of gangs in terms of etiology and typology, ongoing process, and behavioral consequences still is unfinished business, but in Thrasher a significant beginning was made. If today some of the cases and interpretive sections seem overly romanticized and unsophisticated, it may be due in part to statistical and theoretical sophistication which has outstripped the quality and scope of our data. We are forever indebted to Thrasher for his diligence and perseverance in the monumental task he set himself. It is a tribute to him that the heritage of knowledge and insight which was his legacy to the future is matched in significance by the challenge of questions raised by his work but unanswered more than forty years after he began his research.

JAMES F. SHORT, JR.

WASHINGTON STATE UNIVERSITY
July 1, 1963

Contents

Illustrations

PART I

The Natural History
of the Gang

Introduction

The characteristic habitat of Chicago's numerous gangs is that broad twilight zone of railroads and factories, of deteriorating neighborhoods and shifting populations, which borders the city's central business district on the north, on the west, and on the south. The gangs dwell among the shadows of the slum. Yet, dreary and repellent as their external environment must seem to the casual observer, their life is to the initiated at once vivid and fascinating. They live in a world distinctly their own —far removed from the humdrum existence of the average citizen.

It is in such regions as the gang inhabits that we find much of the romance and mystery of a great city. Here are comedy and tragedy. Here is melodrama which excels the recurrent "thrillers" at the downtown theaters. Here are unvarnished emotions. Here also is a primitive democracy that cuts through all the conventional social and racial discriminations. The gang, in short, is *life*, often rough and untamed, yet rich in elemental social processes significant to the student of society and human nature.

The gang touches in a vital way almost every problem in the life of the community. Delinquencies among its members all the way from truancy to serious crimes, disturbances of the peace from street brawls to race riots, and close alliance with beer running, labor slugging, and corrupt politics—all are attributed to the gang, whose treatment presents a puzzle to almost every public or private agency in the city, which deals with boys and young men.

Gangs, like most other social groups, originate under conditions that are typical for all groups of the same species; they develop in definite and predictable ways, in accordance with a form or entelechy that is predetermined by characteristic internal processes and mechanisms, and have, in short, a nature and natural history.[1]

---

[1] This paragraph is a paraphrase of a statement explaining the origin and growth of the sect; it applies equally to the development of the gang. Robert E. Park and E. W. Burgess, *Introduction to the Science of Sociology*, p. 873.

CHAPTER I

Gangland

No less than 1,313 gangs have been discovered in Chicago and its environs! A conservative estimate of 25,000 members—boys and young men—is probably an understatement, for the census taken in connection with this study is not exhaustive.

It must be remembered in reading the following description of gangland that the writer is presenting only one phase of the life of these communities. There are churches, schools, clubs, banks, and the usual list of wholesome institutions in these areas as well as gangs. The gangs and the type of life described here may not even be apparent to the average citizen of the district, who is chiefly occupied in his own pursuits.

The reader should also bear in mind that the gang is a protean manifestation: no two gangs are just alike; some are good; some are bad; and each has to be considered on its own merits. Many of the gangs mentioned by name in the following account are delinquent groups, for they are usually of the picturesque sort, attracting more attention and receiving names more readily than other types.

THE EMPIRE OF GANGLAND

The broad expanse of gangland with its intricate tribal and intertribal relationships is medieval and feudal in its organization rather than modern and urban.

The feudal warfare of youthful gangs is carried on more or less continuously. Their disorder and violence, escaping the ordinary controls of the police and other social agencies of the community, are so pronounced as to give the impression that they are almost beyond the pale of civil society. In some respects these regions of conflict are like a frontier; in others, like a "no man's land," lawless, godless, wild.

In Chicago the empire of the gang divides into three great domains, each of which in turn breaks up into smaller kingdoms. They are natural areas, differentiated in the processes of human interaction, and having their own characteristic place in the mosaic of the city's life.

The first of these we may call the "North Side jungles"; the second, the "West Side wilderness"; and the third, the "South Side badlands"—names which well characterize the regions so far as gang life is concerned. Gangland stretches in a broad semicircular zone about the central business district (the Loop) and in general forms a sort of *interstitial* barrier between the Loop and the better residential areas.[1]

THE NORTH SIDE JUNGLES

The North Side jungles of gangland lie north of the Loop and the Chicago River, and east of the north branch of that stream, constituting a portion of the unique area known as the "Grand Canyon of Chicago" because of the great diversity of its "social scenery." Here is a "mosaic of little worlds which touch but do not interpenetrate."[2] Along the lake front northward is the "Gold Coast," representing the extreme of wealth and fashion, while in the southern portion we find "Bohemia," the

[1] Not all the statements presented in this study must be understood as applying to Chicago at the time of publication. Conditions change rapidly. The purpose is to present a picture which is more or less typical of a generic situation.

[2] Robert E. Park, *et al.*, *The City*, p. 40.

North Side artists' colony. West of these two areas is a cosmopolitan and rooming-house district which includes the haunts of a gang of dope-peddlers serving North Side addicts; the north stem of "Hobohemia";[3] and "Bughouse Square," a center for hobo intellectuals. This region serves also as a base for such notorious bootlegging groups as the Clark and Erie gangs. Formerly it was the bailiwick of Chicago's most notorious gangster, the leader of the powerful ZZZ gang of "hijackers" and rum-runners, who was assassinated by unknown enemies.[4]

The gangs are most numerous, however, between this region and the north branch of the river, in "Little Sicily," a community of southern Italians. Certain immigrant customs color the gang life of the region. The vendetta is often carried into the quarrels of juvenile gangs, while the Mafia of southern Italy takes the form among criminal groups of secret gangs of the Black Hand, such as the "Gloriannas" and "Little Italy" gang. So notorious are these gang conditions that the southern portion of the colony has sometimes been called "Little Hell." In this area is "Death Corner," the scene of frequent murders. Recently many negro families have invaded "Little Hell," and a colored church now stands two blocks from "Death Corner."

North and westward of "Little Sicily" gangland fringes the industrial properties along the river. Here is a Polish colony called by the gang boy "Pojay Town," in contradistinction to "Dago Town" described above. All the gangs of this region together are known as the "North Siders," and they wage continual warfare across the river bridges with their enemies the "West Siders."

[3] Nels Anderson, *The Hobo*, p. 8.

[4] Names of gangs are omitted and disguises used whenever such procedure seems advisable. Major criminal gangs are designated throughout the study by triple letters.

THE WEST SIDE WILDERNESS

Most extensive of gangland domains is the West Side wilderness which lies south and west of the north branch of the Chicago River, west of the Loop, and north and west of the south branch of the river.

Across these turbid, sewage-laden waters lie the crowded river wards. In the drab hideousness of the slum, despite a continuous exodus to more desirable districts, people are swarming more than 50,000 to the square mile. Life is enmeshed in a network of tracks, canals, and docks, factories and breweries, warehouses, and lumber-yards. There is nothing fresh or clean to greet the eye; everywhere are unpainted, ramshackle buildings, blackened and besmirched with the smoke of industry. In this sort of habitat the gang seems to flourish best.

The gangs of the northern portion of the West Side wilderness center in "Bucktown," a Polish colony adjoining the north branch of the Chicago River, and the home of the widely known "Blackspots," long a community terror.

1. Bucktown has long been known as one of the toughest neighborhoods on the northwest side. A few years ago you couldn't pass through there without taking a trimming. There are plenty of fights still, but it is quieter now. Most of the boys what used to cause the trouble are older and have learned better. Some of them are married, but the younger fellows, 17 and 18! They haven't learned nothing yet![5]

The gangs of this area have formed a general alliance, the "West Siders" against their rivals in "Pojay Town" across the river.

South from Bucktown, the Polish colony continues

[5] From an interview with a gang boy. Many documents of this sort are presented in part or in toto in the text. For ease of reference, they are numbered consecutively. Some documents have been eliminated from the abridgment, but original numbers have been retained to facilitate reference to earlier editions.

along Milwaukee Avenue, the great Polish business street. Here there is a gang in almost every block. The majority of gangs in Chicago are of Polish stock, but this may be due to the fact that there are in the city more than 150,000 more persons of Polish extraction than of any other nationality except the German. [6]

South of this Polish settlement is "Little Italy," with gangs of all ages. With the exception of a few, like the "Spark-Plugs," the "Beaners," or the hard-boiled "Buckets-of-Blood," they are either anonymous or adopt the names of the streets where they "hang out."

Below the Chicago and North Western railroad tracks, the southern boundary of Little Italy, lies a region with relatively few gangs. Immediately back of the Loop the continuity of gangland is broken by a central industrial district, and farther south and west by a rooming-house area, where two-thirds of the residents are said to be transients. Once the abode of Chicago's "Four Hundred," the fashionable dwellings have become the headquarters of labor unions or tenements which house a shifting population of all nationalities. Here, too, are hospitals, clinics, and adjuncts of the medical schools, and also the main stem of "Hobohemia" with "Bum Park" and the "slave market,"as the numerous employment bureaus for the migratory workers are called by the men who patronize them. [7] Although the gangs are relatively few in this region, some of them, like the "Night Riders," are composed of anemic rooming-house children, a distinct type bordering on degeneracy.

West of the industrial section of this area is a negro colony whose gangs, known to the boys of the vicinity as the "Coons from Lake Street," are marooned among hos-

[6] U.S. Census, 1920, Vol. II, *Population*, pp. 1006-9. Figures as to mother tongue of foreign white stock have been used as being the most accurate for comparative purposes.

[7] Nels Anderson, *The Hobo*, pp. 4, 5..

tile gangs of whites. Many of these negro groups are crap-shooting gangs, and some of them, such as the "Bicycle Squad," engage in thievery.

South of the colored district and extending westward to Garfield Park is a so-called "American" area, with many gangs in the poorer sections which abut the elevated lines, the railroad tracks, and the business streets. The notorious and daring "Deadshots" and the adventure-loving Irish and Italian boy "Blackhanders" are among the groups which carry on hostilities with the negro gangs from Lake Street and the Jews to the west and south.

South of the cosmopolitan district described above lies a greatly congested immigrant community where gangs are numerous. In popular parlance this area (the old Nineteenth Ward) has been known as "Moonshine Valley" or the "Bloody Nineteenth." When Jane Addams established Hull-House at Polk and Halsted streets in 1889, the residents were largely German and Irish, but these nationalities have gradually moved out before the influx of Italians, Russians, Jews, and Greeks. Here we find both a "Little Italy" and a "Little Greece," and, recently, gypsies, negroes, and Mexicans have come into the community.

In the northwest portion of this area a gang of dope-peddlers ply their trade. Here, too, the notorious "Cardi-nellis" are still said to have their rendezvous, though their leaders and two of their members have been hanged. Although dominantly Italian, these groups often include men and boys of other nationalities. It was in the heart of Little Italy that the powerful Genna gang had its chain of stills from which flowed much of Chicago's illicit liquor. Halsted, the main business street of the West Side, which is a favorite playground for gangs both young and old, is unusually varied and colorful in this particular section.[8]

[8] See document 55.

Photo by Author

Photo by Author

THE MAXWELL STREET MARKET

In the heart of Chicago's Ghetto is the Maxwell Street Market, the most picturesque spot in gangland. Its triple row of booths on either side display every conceivable ware. To the gang it is a source of excitement and a mecca for thieving. Suggestions of lawlessness are to be found here in stands openly displaying materials for stills and the making of illicit liquor. (See document 56.)

West of the Hull-House community and extending south across Roosevelt Road to Fifteenth Place, is the Ghetto. The Jewish gangs, which belong to this region are less numerous than those of other slum areas, due, it is said, to the "more individualistic spirit of the Jews," but more likely to better organized recreation and family life than is found among the poorer classes of other immigrant groups. Those gangs which do thrive in the Ghetto, of which the old "Boundary Gang" was probably the best known, carry on intermittent warfare with the groups of adjacent regions. They are known as the "Jews from Twelfth Street."

In the heart of the Ghetto is the crowded Maxwell Street market, one of the liveliest and most picturesque spots in Chicago. Some of the Jewish gangs, like Itchkie's "Black Hand Society," a pickpocket "outfit" find excellent opportunity for sport and prey along this thronging Rialto; nor is it overlooked by the gangs of other regions.

West of the Ghetto is Lawndale, an area of second settlement for the Jewish immigrant. Lawndale, with its 75,000 Jews, is typically a middle-class community into which the Ghetto in its growing prosperity has poured three-fourths of its population until more Jews live here than in any other local community in America outside of New York City. Most of the boys' groups of this community take the form of basement clubs. Along Roosevelt Road, however, which appears to be an interstitial business street—a tentacle of gangland extending its baleful influence into an orderly residential area—several notorious gangs of criminals, bootleggers, and rum-runners under Jewish leadership hang out in the restaurants, poolrooms, and gambling dens. One of the most dreaded of these, the WWW's, is noted for the pugilistic prowess of its members; another powerful group, the TTT's, is said to have succeeded the Gennas in the control of illicit liquor manufacture on the West Side.

In the southern portion of the Ghetto is an area known as the "Valley"—the cradle of a powerful gang of robbers, bootleggers, and beer-runners[9] and the present territory of the notorious "Forty-Twos," who started as automobile "strippers" and who have prospered as window-smashing burglars under the energetic leadership of one of their members nicknamed "Babe Ruth" (not a ball player). Several blocks in the western portion of the Valley are now occupied by Chicago's new commission produce market which was formerly on South Water Street. South of the Valley, in a Lithuanian colony, are a large number of street gangs.

West of the Lithuanian settlement and north of the river is "Little Pilsen," a Bohemian area from which many of the residents are rapidly moving before an influx of Croatians and Poles. The houses are becoming dilapidated, and the many basement flats are damp and unsanitary. Here are many gangs of the formally organized type, such as athletic and social clubs. Some have a political complexion, and one vicious gang, whose leader is the son of an office-holder, enjoys practical immunity from prosecution.

West of Little Pilsen is an extensive Polish colony and farther on, a second Bohemian settlement. The numerous gangs in these areas form a widespread group known as the "West Siders," who wage war back and forth over the bridges against the "South Siders," or the "Brightoners," across the river to the south.

THE SOUTH SIDE BADLANDS

South of the Loop and southeast of the south branch of the Chicago River lies the third major division of gangland—the South Side badlands.

A number of gangs largely Italian in membership hang out on the streets between the Loop and Roosevelt Road.

[9] See document 231.

Coming from homes above the stores in a quasi-business district on South State Street, most of the boys, like the "So So's," the "Onions," and the "Torpedoes," lead an irregular life in the street, which is their playground.

South of the Loop, beginning about Sixteenth Street, is the "Black Belt," Chicago's most extensive negro area which stretches southward with varying breadth to Sixty-third Street, a distance of about six miles. In this region of contrasting social conditions are high-class colored residential neighborhoods, as well as "black and tan" cabarets, white and colored vice resorts, and the worst type of slum. Gangs are most numerous in the poorer sections and especially in the so-called "crime spots" where gambling, robbery, and murder are prevalent. The gangs of the Black Belt include: those for whom a pool hall serves as a clubroom and center of interest; gangs of mixed membership, like the "Dirty Sheiks and Wailing Shebas"; and at least one group which specializes in dope-peddling. The "Wolves," "Twigglies," and "Royal Eclipse" are well known in the area.

Immediately beyond Wentworth Avenue, which is the general boundary of the Black Belt on the west, are the "Shielders," a group of several gangs who possess a long, narrow stretch of territory extending from the river on the north southward as far as Sixty-third Street. West of the railroad tracks along Stewart Avenue is a corresponding area about four blocks in width held by their arch-enemies the "Dukies." As the Turks called all Westerners "Franks," so their colored rivals to the east call the gangs from both of these regions the "Mickies," for this was originally an Irish district. At present the northern portion is dominantly Italian, but the gangs maintain the traditional names. The southern part of the Dukies' territory, Canaryville, which is still Irish, has been notorious for its many gangs which are so "hard-boiled" that gang-sters who come out of the district are known as graduates from the "Canaryville school of gunmen."

West of the "Dukies" and south of the river is the old settlement of Bridgeport with its "Archy Road" (Archer Avenue). It is now a Polish and German com-munity, hemmed in by industry on all sides but the south. The history of the region is interesting, in the light of gang development, for here the first gang of which we have secured a record had its beginnings.

2. The earliest settlers in Bridgeport were the Irish who re-treated before the influx of Germans. The latter in turn gave way to the Poles who are in the majority today.

In the sixties everybody had cabbage patches, chickens, and even cows about their places. Most of the mischief committed by neighborhood gangs was breaking fences and stealing cabbages, for there was not much else to take. The men of the community worked near Bubbly Creek at the rolling mills which had about 200 employees, or at the stockyards which employed 1,000.

In 1867 there was a gang of about a dozen fellows, 17 to 22 years of age, who hung around at Ashland and Bubbly Creek. They were fond of gambling at cards. They did not work regularly and waited here to rob the men as they came home with their pay. It is said that they disposed of many a victim by throwing him into the creek. Some of them were sent to the Bridewell, but none ever went to the state's prison.

In the eighties there was a gang of Irish and German lads who had their clubroom in the basement of a saloon on Ashland. An-other group about the same time was the Hickory Street gang—about a dozen fellows from 12 to 18 years of age who met in a base-ment. Here they used to read "dime novels," play cards, study, and drink their beer. Sometimes they copped peaches or bought a pie which they would cut with a safety pin from their suspenders. Some of this group have since become contractors, and one an alderman.[10]

The gangs in Bridgeport which followed the period of the eighties were very active and wielded great political

[10] Interview with a very old resident of the district.

power,[11] but with a few exceptions those of the present time, although numerous, are not so well organized.

South and east of the older portion of Bridgeport is a Lithuanian colony in which many of the boys belong to lawless gangs, which break windows, steal, and hold up children and drunken men on the street.

West of the odorous expanse of pens and packing-houses of the Union Stock Yards is an immigrant colony, dominantly Polish, known as "Back-of-the-Yards." In the northern portion of this area is one of the grimiest, most congested slums of the city. Here, besides the numerous street groups, there are a large number of gang clubs which rent rooms in times of prosperity but give them up in summer or when work is slack. Some indulge in gambling, "moonshine," and sex irregularities as well as in athletics. In this general region and south of it, a long-enduring gang, the XXX's, carries on beer-running and other criminal activities, and holds its power by means of bribery, intimidation, and murder.

Southwest of the "Back-of-the-Yards" area proper, the majority of gangs, organized as athletic clubs, center their activities around Cornell Square, a small park and playground. East of this group and south of Forty-seventh Street are numerous gangs of the "hard-boiled" variety—such as the much feared "White Rocks" and the "Murderers."[12] This region is called the "Bush," and its reputation is such that policemen are sometimes put on duty there, it is said, for punishment.

East and southeast of the Bush is an Irish community including a part of the territory of the "Dukies." This is the *aristocracy* of gangland. Gangs of all kinds are numerous in the South Halsted Street vicinity and around Sherman Park. Many of the well-known athletic clubs,

---

[11] See document 255.

[12] See document 18.

such as Ragen's Colts, are influential in this region where
they own or rent clubrooms.

The South Halsted Street district is also the operating
territory of another major gang of notorious criminals and
rum-runners, the YYY's. This group has at times warred
with the XXX's for control over the affairs of the underworld.

BORDERLANDS AND BOUNDARY LINES

In addition to the three major divisions of gangland,
certain boundary lines and borderlands between the non-
gang areas of the city develop gangs. Threads of social
disintegration tend to follow alongside rivers, canals,
railroad tracks, and business streets whose borders are
manifestly undesirable for residential purposes and permit gangs to thrive in the interstices between very good
residence areas.

In Hyde Park, one of the best residential districts in
the city, there are a number of gangs along the business
streets and in the sections adjacent to the Illinois Central
Railroad. On Fifty-fifth Street, where a rather heterogeneous, congested population lives above the stores and
behind the business buildings, we find about a dozen
gangs, including the "Kenwoods," who have been a problem in the community for years. On Lake Park Avenue
the situation is similar; on Forty-seventh Street are the
"Bat-Eyes," while Sixty-third has the "Dirty Dozen."[13]

These interstitial areas formerly comprised a saloon
district with, it is said, a gang in every two blocks. One
of these, meeting on Lake Park Avenue, had a cave with
a subcellar used for keeping stolen goods and disciplining
unruly members. There were benches around the walls
where members sat in solemn conclave, each in his appointed place. About fifty boys were included in this
group.[14]

[13] See document 13.
[14] S. P. Breckinridge, *The Child in the City*, p. 434.

APPENDED GANGLANDS

In the satellite communities near Chicago, areas develop, under certain conditions, not unlike those of the central empire of gangland. Purely residential and well-organized suburbs of the better type such as Oak Park and Evanston, are practically gangless, for the activities of the children are well provided for in family, school, church, and other established institutions. Even in these regions, however, gangs develop in interstitial zones. In Evanston, along Railroad Street and in "Toad Town," are found characteristic interstitial groups such as "Honey's" gang.[15]

In "West-Town," on the contrary, where life is not well organized there are more gangs on the order of the "Hawthorne Toughs" and the "hard-boiled Crawfords." West-Town, with a population of 55,000, while an integral part of Chicago socially, has a separate municipal government, which seems unable or indisposed to cope with lawless elements. When Chicago's criminal gangs first began to find life difficult within the city limits, they ingrafted themselves into West-Town, and made it "wide-open" with saloons, cabarets, gambling houses, and vice resorts.

South and east of Chicago in the industrial suburbs, such as Blue Island, South Chicago, and West Pullman, gangs are numerous in the immigrant colonies. Hammond, Indiana, an industrial satellite of larger size, has twenty-six gangs, among them the "Bloody Broomsticks," the "Night Hawks," the "Pirates," and the "Buckets-of-Blood," who duplicate the activities of Chicago gangs in little kingdoms of their own.[16]

[15] See document 146.

[1] Unpublished study by J. C. Parrett.

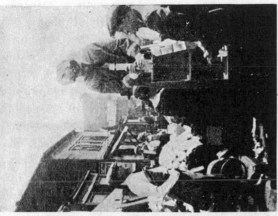

Photo by Author

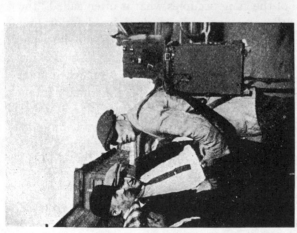

Photo by Author

PICTURESQUE FIGURES IN GANGLAND

The man at the left has on his back two interesting boxes, in one a musical instrument, in the other a green bird. The bird picks out envelopes containing "fortunes" and bearing numbers which entitle the buyer to a cheap but gaudy print.

The fakir at the right is reading the future for a quarter. He places a blank sheet of paper in the mystic tube and after many strange incantations, it comes out with a "fortune" written on it.

GANGLAND IS AN INTERSTITIAL AREA

The most important conclusion suggested by a study of the location and distribution of the 1,313 gangs investigated in Chicago is that *gangland represents a geographically and socially interstitial area in the city*. Probably the most significant concept of the study is the term *interstitial*—that is, pertaining to spaces that intervene between one thing and another. *In nature foreign matter tends to collect and cake in every crack, crevice, and cranny —interstices. There are also fissures and breaks in the structure of social organization. The gang may be regarded as an interstitial element in the framework of society, and gangland as an interstitial region in the layout of the city.*

The gang is almost invariably characteristic of regions that are interstitial to the more settled, more stable, and better organized portions of the city. The central tripartite empire of the gang occupies what is often called "the poverty belt"—a region characterized by deteriorating neighborhoods, shifting populations, and the mobility and disorganization of the slum. Abandoned by those seeking homes in the better residential districts, encroached upon by business and industry, this zone is a distinctly interstitial phase of the city's growth. It is to a large extent isolated from the wider culture of the larger community by the processes of competition and conflict which have resulted in the selection of its population.[17] Gangland is a

[17] The prevalence of gangs in the so-called "poverty belt" or "zone of transition" is further indicated by a survey (made by a private agency) of 173 eighth-grade boys attending schools in one of these areas. It was found that over 82 per cent of these boys (from twelve to fifteen years of age) were not connected in any way with constructive recreational activities. "With the exception of a small number of boys industrially occupied, this 82 per cent passed their leisure time in streets and alleys, shooting craps, playing 'piggy wolf,' and other games, participating in gang activities, or were members of independent unsupervised clubs of their own. While boys would hesitate about acknowledging membership in a 'gang' when it was called by that name, practically all of them did belong to groups that were essentially gangs."

phenomenon of human ecology.[18] As better residential
districts recede before the encroachments of business and
industry, the gang develops as one manifestation of the
economic, moral, and cultural frontier which marks the
interstice.

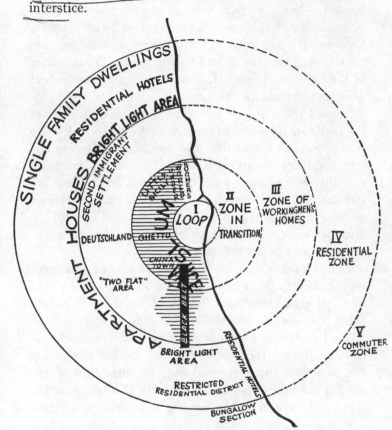

FIG. 1.—THE PLACE OF CHICAGO'S GANGLAND IN THE URBAN ECOLOGY

The shaded portion indicates the approximate location of the central empire of
gangland, which has been superimposed upon E. W. Burgess' chart showing urban areas
in the development of the city. (See E. W. Burgess, "The Growth of the City," Robert E.
Park, et al., The City, p. 55.)

[18] See E. W. Burgess, "The Growth of the City," and R. D. McKen-
zie, "The Ecological Approach to the Study of the Human Community,"
in Robert E. Park, et al., The City. See Figure 1.

This process is seen, too, in the way in which a business street, stream, canal, or railroad track running through a residential area tends to become a "finger" of the slum and an extension of gangland. Borderlands and boundary lines between residential and manufacturing or business areas, between immigrant or racial colonies, between city and country or city and suburb, and between contiguous towns—all tend to assume the character of the intramural frontier. County towns and industrial suburbs which escape the administrative control and protection of the city government and whose conditions of life are disorganized, as in the case of West-Town, develop into appended ganglands. The roadhouses fringing the city, and those occupying positions between its straggling suburbs, represent an escape from society and become important factors in maintaining the power and activities of the gang. The region of 155th Street and South Halsted has been representative of these conditions in the southern part of Cook County.

The city has been only vaguely aware of this great stir of activity in its poorly organized areas. Gang conflict and gang crime occasionally thrust themselves into the public consciousness, but the hidden sources from which they spring have not yet been understood or regulated. Although their importance in the life of the boy has sometimes been pointed out, the literature of the subject has been meager and general. This region of life is in a real sense an *underworld*, through whose exploration the sociologist may learn how the gang begins and how it develops, what it is and what it does, the conditions which produce it and the problems which it creates, and ultimately he may be able to suggest methods for dealing with it in a practical way.

CHAPTER II

Ganging

The beginnings of the gang can best be studied in the slums of the city where an inordinately large number of children are crowded into a limited area. On a warm summer evening children fairly swarm over areaways and sidewalks, vacant lots and rubbish dumps, streets and alleys. The buzzing chatter and constant motion remind one of insects which hover in a swarm, yet ceaselessly dart hither and thither within the animated mass. This endless activity has a tremendous fascination, even for the casual visitor to the district, and it would be a marvel indeed if any healthy boy could hold himself aloof from it.

In this ubiquitous crowd of children, spontaneous play-groups are forming everywhere—gangs in embryo. Such a crowded environment is full of opportunities for conflict with some antagonistic person or group within or without the gang's own social milieu. The conflict arises on the one hand with groups of its own class in disputes over the valued prerogatives of gangland—territory, loot, play spaces, patronage in illicit business, privileges to exploit, and so on; it comes about on the other, through opposition on the part of the conventional social order to the gang's unsupervised activities. Thus, the gang is faced with a real struggle for existence with other gangs and with the antagonistic forces in its wider social environment.

Play-groups easily meet these hostile forces, which give their members a "we" feeling and start the process of ganging so characteristic of the life of these unorganized areas.

3. On a brisk day in May we visited the Hull-House region. Streets and open spaces were alive with boys. With very little direction, there were under way energetic games of all sorts.

At one side of the Goodrich school grounds the "Peorias" were matching skill with a "pick-up" team, the nucleus for some future gang, in a game of playground ball. The "Peoria Strangers," the younger satellites of the group, looked on. In an adjoining portion of the yard, the "Tanners" were playing the "Forquers" for a "pool" of $3.75 which had been put up by the opposing teams. A fight was narrowly averted when the umpire made a "bum" decision and the boys massed about him in a threatening way. At the other end of the lot two more teams were playing.

Small groups here and there were engaged in conversation or side play. Not far away a man was playing "rummie" with four or five young boys with no attempt to conceal the money. A fight in the alley caused a stampede in which the whole "field" rushed precipitately to the fence to see what was the matter.

At the corner of Blue Island and Forquer we found a lively game of ball between the "Reveres" and the "loogins" (second team) of the "Red Oaks." The first team was rooting lustily for its protégés. A gang of little boys had a camp fire in the alley about which they played in Indian fashion. Their fantastic motions gave us an insight into the imaginative world of adventure in which gang boys often live.

Crossing Halsted on Forquer, we met the "Orioles" playing a game of handball against the wall of a building. Although they had developed great skill in dodging, they were greatly handicapped by the interference of vehicles and pedestrians. In the Dore schoolyard the "Guardian Angel Alley Gang" was playing a similar group at ball. Crawling through a hole in the fence, we found the "Arabian Nights," the "Taylors," and the "Comets." At the conclusion of their play, they sang their paeans of victory, like college "pep" songs.

On our return journey, we met the "Black Circles" playing on the corner of Polk and Halsted. Our final stop was at the clubroom of the "Red Oaks," a newly formed social and athletic club which had purchased the charter and equipment of an older organization. The members were sitting quietly about the room playing cards and talking.[1]

THE GANG AND THE PLAY GROUP

There is a definite geographical basis for the play-group and the gang in these areas.

4. In the more crowded sections of the city, the geographical basis of a gang is both sides of the same street for a distance of two blocks. The members are those boys who have played together while their mothers and fathers, as is the custom in those regions, sat in front of their homes and gossiped during the long summer evenings. They know each other as well as brothers or sisters, and as they grow older continue to play together. An investigation showed that groups playing in the schoolyard after school hours are composed of boys living in the vicinity, many of whom do not attend that school during the day. The school is not the basis of this type of gang.

In the less crowded sections where the parks are available, the play-groups which frequent them usually live within a radius of only a few blocks. The whole group has simply transplanted itself to the park. The same thing is true of groups playing on vacant lots: they all come from nearby streets. One may see a group from one section playing against a group from another area, but never parts of two groups from different sections on the same team. From childhood up, members of these play-groups and gangs have been together; they would be in an unnatural atmosphere, were they to play in any other group.[2]

The majority of gangs develop from the spontaneous play-group. As the boys or older fellows of a block or a neighborhood come together in the course of business or pleasure, a crowd, in the sense of a mere gathering of persons, is formed.

5. The new poolroom which came to the neighborhood was a great attraction to the boys. The beginning of the gang came when the group developed an enmity toward two Greeks who owned a

[1] Observations by the author.
[2] Unpublished study by an experienced boys' worker in gangland.

fruit store on the opposite corner. The boys began to steal fruit on a small scale. Finally they attempted to carry off a large quantity of oranges and bananas which were displayed on the sidewalks, but the Greeks gave chase. This was the signal for a general attack, and the fruit was used as ammunition. The gang had a good start from this episode.[3]

On this basis of interests and aptitudes, a play-group emerges whose activities vary from "hide-and-go-seek" to crap-shooting.

6. This was a group of about nine boys, whose ages varied from sixteen to twenty years. There were both Protestants and Catholics, some of whom attended school, while others worked. Their hang-out was in the front room of the home of one of the members, whose mother, known as "Aunt Sarah," allowed the boys the freedom of her house. Two of the number were piano-players. The boys sang, jigged, played cards, or just talked. There was no formal organization, no one was considered as leader, but the word of one or two had more weight than that of others. There was a group-consciousness and most of the wishes of the members were met in the bunch; yet there was no antagonism to outsiders; they never intruded. During the years the bunch lasted no new members were taken in. It disintegrated as members grew up and moved away or married.[4]

Such a play-group may acquire a real organization. Natural leaders emerge, a relative standing is assigned to various members and traditions develop. *It does not become a gang, however, until it begins to excite disapproval and opposition, and thus acquires a more definite group-consciousness.* It discovers a rival or an enemy in the gang in the next block; its baseball or football team is pitted against some other team; parents or neighbors look upon it with suspicion or hostility; "the old man around the corner," the storekeepers, or the "cops" begin to give it "shags" (chase it); or some representative of the com-

[3] Records of the Juvenile Protective Association.

[4] Unpublished manuscript by an experienced boys' worker in gangland.

munity steps in and tries to break it up. This is the real beginning of the gang, for now it starts to draw itself more closely together. It becomes a conflict group.

It would be erroneous, however, to suppose that a gang springs immediately from an ordinary street crowd [5] like Minerva, full-grown from Jove's forehead. The gang has its beginning in acquaintanceship and intimate relations which have already developed on the basis of some common interest. These preliminary bonds may serve to unite pairs or trios among the boys rather than the group as a whole. The so-called "two-boy gang" is often a center to which other boys are attracted and about which they form like a constellation. Thus, the gang may grow by additions of twos and threes as well as of single individuals. The notorious Gloriannas were originally a two-boy gang. [6]

7. Our gang was the outgrowth of a play-group formed by nine boys living in the same block, who became acquainted through the usual outdoor games. Then we began to meet in Tommy's attic. For greater privacy, we built a shack on the alley where we could temporarily isolate ourselves and smoke without the interference of our parents. When my parents were away, we used our basement for a rendezvous, but we were careful to enter by a window so as to escape the attention of the housekeeper.

This desire to escape family supervision marked the beginning of our feeling of solidarity. Our first loyalties were to protect each other against our parents. Sometimes the latter were regarded with great dislike by the gang. The mother of one of the boys, who was very unkind to him, viewed us with equal hatred and once threw a pan of dishwater on us when we were whistling for our pal.

First it was the gang against the members of our households, and then it was the gang against the neighbors. One Saturday morning when we were playing "ditch," Mrs. Apple called the police and told them that we were molesting her property. It

[5] The formation of a gang from a corner crowd is illustrated in document 13.

[6] See document 215.

proved that we had only run across her lawn, and the cop laughed and said that she was too crabby to be living.

Our collective enterprises soon gave us the name "Cornell Crowd," but we preferred to call ourselves the "Cornell Athletic Club" or the "C.A.C." We took in only two new members during our six years' existence, but for them we devised a special initiation. copying some of our stunts from the "Penrod and Sam" stories by Tarkington.

Our solidarity was greatly augmented by our clashes with other gangs, whether in raids or football games. On one occasion when we beat the Harper gang at football. the game ended in a free-for-all fight. We licked them, and after that they were much more friendly, even though we continued to raid each other's hang-outs. We formed an alliance with the Dorchester gang against the "Ken-woods," who called us "sissies" and "rich kids," and when the latter stole the stove out of the Dorchester shanty, we joined forces and invaded Fifty-fifth Street to bring it back.

Danger from other gangs was always sufficient to eliminate internal friction and unite us against the common enemy. On one Hallowe'en, two of our members engaged in a fight, and no argument or pulling could get them apart. Just then another gang came along and hit Tommie with a soot bag, whereupon the combatants immediately forgot their quarrel and helped us chase and beat up the invaders.[7]

THE GANG AND THE FORMAL GROUP

Curiously enough, the gang sometimes develops within a group which is quite different from it in every way. A number of boys, perhaps entire strangers, are brought together by some interested agency and a club is formed. A conventional form of organization is imposed, and activities are directed and supervised. Friendships within the group begin to develop on the basis of common interests and lead to factions and cliques which oppose each other or incur the hostility of the directors. In either case, the clique may serve as the basis for a gang, and its members may begin to meet without supervision at other than the regular times.

[7] Manuscript prepared by a former member of the gang.

Photo by Author

Photo by Author

INNOCENT AND WHOLESOME

Above is a play-group composed of fourteen boys from seven to fourteen years of age living in one block in a residential area. Although without a name, this group has a definite structure with a first and second leader and a definite status assigned to every member and five "fringers." If it were located in a slum, this group would probably be a "gang in embryo."

Below are the Blue Valleys or Young Morgans, a group that has gone beyond the play-group stage and calls itself a "club." Yet it is often from such little "clubs," innocent enough in their beginnings, that the delinquent gang develops.

8. A group of Irish, Jewish, and Italian boys were enrolled in classes for dancing and dramatics at the settlement. As a result of the new friendships and activities which developed, the Italian boys soon formed a gang which, although leaderless, held closely together and carried on many exploits outside the settlement, including civil war with rival gangs. A strong group spirit arose, and the loyalty of the members to each other became marked, manifesting itself especially in times of unemployment. The settlement saw its opportunity and accepted the new group, directing its activities along the lines of hiking and camping.[8]

It often happens that boys expelled either as individuals or as a group from some formal organization are drawn together to form a gang. They have become outlaws, and it is the old story of Robin Hood against the state.

9. A group of eight boys, who had been associated with a club as individuals from two to five years, were suspended because they broke an agreement not to play other baseball teams for money. Twelve sympathizers left the club and joined the outlaws who with their hangers-on now number about one hundred. They met first in a candy store and later rented a cottage. They play baseball for as much as $100 a game. They plan a basket-ball team, equipment for which they will buy from proceeds of a raffle and a dance.

Their problem is to get access to a gymnasium; the playgrounds are full.[9]

10. About twenty Polish boys, "canned" from the settlement, organized a gang that they called the "Corporation." The common object of the group was to do away with the settlement which was notified to this effect. Their hang-out was at a Greek fruit store Only half of them worked at a time. They shared their spending money but not their earnings. They all tended to work at the same place, quitting as a group. They stole balls from the settlement, broke gymnasium windows, and put fake notices on the bulletin boards, but did not cause any serious trouble. Their other activities were robbing fruit stands, cheap holdups, gambling, and baseball. Some of them saw service in the war, which seemed to steady them. Many of them are now drivers of taxicabs and North Side busses, but they still hang together on the street corners.[10]

[8] Study by a settlement worker (manuscript).

[9] Interview with a club director.

[10] Interview with a settlement worker.

In all cases of this type, the function of the common enemy in knitting the gangs together is clearly indicated.

INSTABILITY AND DISINTEGRATION

The ganging process is a continuous flux and flow, and there is little permanence in most of the groups. New nuclei are constantly appearing, and the business of coalescing and recoalescing is going on everywhere in the congested areas. Both conflict and competition threaten the embryonic gangs with disintegration. The attention of the individual is often diverted to some new pal or to some other gang that holds more attractions. When delinquency is detected the police break up the group and at least temporarily interrupt its career. Some new activity of settlement, playground, or club frequently depletes its membership.

11. There were several factors in the break-up of our gang. Two of the members and later others became interested in a boys' club. Dissension then arose because the fellows in the club would not swear and play dice. Mutual dislike came out of this division of interest. Another factor was the building of a Y.M.C.A. on the lot where the gang had its playground.[11]

More often the families of the boys move to other neighborhoods, and unless connections are tenacious the old gang is soon forgotten in alliance with the new. One boy joined an enemy gang when his family moved into hostile territory, because he "did not feel like walking so far."

12. When we lived on Nineteenth and Paulina, I joined the "Nineteenth Streeters," a gang of twelve or thirteen Polish boys. We would gather wood together, go swimming, or rob the Jews on Twelfth Street. When we moved to Twenty-first and Paulina I joined the "Wood Streeters." It was like this. I met a kid and got in a scrap with him. He got two more kids and tried to lick me. A couple of days later on the way to school the same kid came up and said, "Got any snuff?" "Sure!" "Shake a hand!" "Sure!

[11] Gang boy's own story.

You're the kid who hit me." Then we were friends, and I joined the gang. Then we moved to Twenty-third and Wood, then to Hoyne, next to a suburb, and finally back to Twenty-third and Wood. At each of these places I usually went with a different gang.[12]

Sometimes a quarrel splits the gang, and the disgruntled faction secedes.

Marriage   It is interesting to note that marriage is one of the most potent causes for the disintegration of the older groups. The gang is largely an adolescent phenomenon, and where conditions are favorable to its development it occupies a period in the life of the boy between childhood, when he is usually incorporated in a family structure, and marriage, when he is reincorporated into a family and other orderly relations of work, religion, and pleasure. For this reason, the adult gang, unless conventionalized, is comparatively rare and is the result of special selection. From this point of view also, then, the gang appears to be an interstitial group, a manifestation of the period of readjustment between childhood and maturity.

Most gangs are in a condition of unstable equilibrium. Those which endure over a period of years are relatively rare in comparison with the great number of rudimentary forms. It is important to note, however, that the volume of gang life and the sum total of gangs does not change appreciably with changing personnel. With few exceptions, the old gangs are replaced by new ones.

THE ROOTS OF THE GANG

Gangs represent the spontaneous effort of boys to create a society for themselves where none adequate to their needs exists. What boys get out of such association that they do not get otherwise under the conditions that adult society imposes is the thrill and zest of participation in common interests, more especially in corporate action, in

[12] Gang boy's own story.

hunting, capture, conflict, flight, and escape. Conflict with other gangs and the world about them furnishes the occasion for many of their exciting group activities.

The failure of the normally directing and controlling customs and institutions to function efficiently in the boy's experience is indicated by disintegration of family life, inefficiency of schools, formalism and externality of religion, corruption and indifference in local politics, low wages and monotony in occupational activities, unemployment, and lack of opportunity for wholesome recreation. All these factors enter into the picture of the moral and economic frontier, and, coupled with deterioration in housing, sanitation, and other conditions of life in the slum, give the impression of general disorganization and decay.

The gang functions with reference to these conditions in two ways: It offers a substitute for what society fails to give; and it provides a relief from suppression and distasteful behavior. It fills a gap and affords an escape. Here again we may conceive of it as an interstitial group providing interstitial activities for its members. Thus the gang, itself a natural and spontaneous type of organization arising through conflict, is a symptom of disorganization in the larger social framework.

These conclusions, suggested by the present study, seem amply verified by data from other cities in the United States and in other countries.

THE GANG AND THE FRONTIER

That the conception of the gang as a symptom of an economic, moral, and cultural frontier is not merely fanciful and figurative is indicated by the operation of similar groups on other than urban frontiers. The advance of civilization into a wild country is heralded by marauding bands which result both from relaxed social controls and attempts to escape authority. The period before and following the Civil War has been called the "era of banditry," so numerous and so desperate were the outlaw gangs. And what are pirates but "gangs of the seas," which, with some of their lonely or lawless coasts, represent interstitial reaches that fall beyond the scope of organized authority and civil society?[13]

IS THERE A GANG INSTINCT?

The traditional explanation of the gang and one supported by the older type of individual psychology has been to dismiss gang behavior as due to an instinct. ". . . . The gang instinct . . . . is a natural characteristic of our social order, and it would be impossible to uproot it or destroy it. . . . ."[14] "The gang instinct . . . . is recognized in the formation of the small group clubs. . . . ."[15] "Somewhere about the age of ten, the little boy . . . . begins to develop the gang-forming instinct."[16] These are typical statements of the "gang-instinct" explanation. Other writers consider ganging as a special form of the "social instinct"—a difference in phrasing only.[17]

What writers on the gang have attributed to instinct is the result of pervasive social habits arising out of the human struggle for existence and social preferment. It is apparent also that use of the phrases "gang instinct" or "social instinct" in the passages quoted is made without much attempt at a thoroughgoing analysis of the complex

[13] The first known use of the term gang in the English language in the common disparaging sense was with reference to pirates (1623). See Murray's *A New English Dictionary* (Oxford).

[14] Franklin Chase Hoyt, *Quicksands of Youth*, p. 120.

[15] *Annual Report*, Chicago Commons, 1919, p. 19.

[16] J. Adams Puffer, *The Boy and His Gang*, p. 72.

[17] N. E. Richardson and O. E. Loomis, *The Boy Scout Movement Applied by the Church*, pp. 206–7.

conditions underlying the formation and behavior of the gang.

The gang, as has already been indicated, is a function of specific conditions, and it does not tend to appear in the absence of these conditions. Under other circumstances the boy becomes a "solitary type," enters into a relation of palship or intimacy with one or more other boys in separate pairs, or is incorporated into play-groups of a different sort or into more conventional or older groups. What relationships he has with others are determined·by a complex of conditioning factors which direct his interests and his habits. It is not instinct, but experience—the way he is conditioned—that fixes his social relations.

CHAPTER III

What Is a Gang?

What is a gang? What characteristics does it possess which distinguish it from other forms of collective behavior such as a play-group, a crowd, a club, a ring, or a secret society? This is a question which is not answered either by the dictionary or by the scanty literature on gangs. The answer must come from a careful examination of actual cases and a comparison of them with related social groups.

THE INDIVIDUALITY OF GANGS

No two gangs are just alike. The cases investigated present an endless variety of forms, and every one is in some sense unique. In this respect the gang exhibits the principle, universal throughout the natural world, that, although like begets like, the single instance is variable.

Wide divergency in the character of its personnel combined with differences of physical and social environment, of experience and tradition, give to every gang its own peculiar character. It may vary as to membership, type of leaders, mode of organization, interests and activities, and finally as to its status in the community. This fact of individuality must be recognized both by the student who attempts to classify it as a form of collective behavior and by the social worker who deals with it as a practical problem.

A DESCRIPTIVE DEFINITION OF THE GANG

Yet science proposes to discover what is typical rather than what is unique and does so, first of all, by making classifications. Interest centers, therefore, not so much in the individual gang for itself as in the characteristics which set it off from other types of collective behavior, discoverable through its *natural* history.

The "Dirty Dozen" may be considered a fairly typical group.

13. The Dirty Dozen began merely as the result of a dozen or more fellows (from sixteen to twenty-two years of age) meeting casually on a street corner at the entrance of one of Chicago's parks and later on in "Mike's" poolroom a short distance away. Most of the boys were loafers, who spent their time swimming, playing baseball and football, shooting craps, or sitting around and talking. They liked brawls and fights, and the gang helped to satisfy these wants with less personal discomfort than might occur if one fellow alone started hostilities or tried to steal something. Of their various activities, some form of conflict seems to have been the chief.

There was war between the gang and the police, for even though the latter did not always have any particular offense for which the fellows were wanted, they did try to break up the group whenever it congregated on the corner.

The gang as a whole often came into direct conflict with other gangs. One night at the old Imperial Theater, the Dirty Dozen found themselves seated opposite the "Chi" gang, their rival in football and baseball. During the show, which was poor vaudeville, the fellows started to hurl remarks at each other. The verbal conflict grew into a near-riot, which continued until the police came.

The Dirty Dozen, however, was capable of collective action against other enemies than rival gangs. One night while the race riots of 1919 were at their height, the gang, armed with revolvers, blackjacks, and knives, started out to get the "niggers."

At Thirty-fifth and State streets, five miles or more from their own territory, and after some preliminary skirmishes, "Shaggy" Martin threw the trolley of a street car filled with colored people.

The rest of the gang, which had increased to about twenty by this time, piled on. "Shaggy," who was left alone at the back to hold the trolley-rope, was standing there with it in one hand and a billy in the other when a colored woman slashed him across the heart with a razor. Then someone hit her, and another fellow "got" her husband.

Shaggy died in the patrol on the way to the hospital. "Swede" Carlson, the only fellow the police caught at that time, said that his last words were, "What will mother say?" The gang took up a collection for flowers, but the direct result of the episode was a desire for revenge. They killed two negroes and "beat up" five more after the death of Shaggy.

The standing of each fellow in the gang was determined by competition and conflict within the group itself. Each member was trying to outdo the others in football and everything else. There was always a struggle for the leadership, which usually went to the best fighters.

"Slicker" Charlie and Ellman were for some reason or other "on the outs," and a fight was arranged to see who was better. The encounter came off in the park. Each fellow had his second, and the time of the rounds was set just as if it were a regular prize fight. Ellman, who won, mauled Charlie severely, and the latter fell into disgrace, at least in his own opinion.

This feeling of his own belittlement caused Charlie much resentment toward the victor and led to another fight in which Charlie struck Ellman with a lead pipe. The blood shot out of a big gash in his head. After they had taken him to the emergency hospital, a cop came in and wanted to know how it had happened, but Ellman would say nothing except that he had fallen and his head hit a rock. (The code of the gang was that honor forbade squealing.) With this incident the feud came to an end.

An example of conflict of the play type, which had a very tragic outcome, occurred one day in the park. About eight of the fellows went to the lagoon and piled into two tiny rowboats. It was a warm summer evening, and the bunch was feeling pretty good, so they decided to have a battle. Splashing soon led to striking with oars. The battle was raging when one of the boats went over. In it was a fellow called "Steam," who could not swim. The others struck out for the shore, but Steam went down. As soon as they discovered that he was gone, they went out and dived for him until one of them succeeded in getting the body. The fire department came and a pulmotor was used, but to no avail. Before the funeral a collection was taken up, and an expensive floral piece was purchased. The gang turned to the good for one day, and every member went to the church. Steam was never spoken of afterward, for each one of them felt a little bit responsible for his death.

Members of the gang often engaged in shady exploits as individuals or in pairs. Ellman and "Dago" were always managing to make some money in one way or another. At one time Ellman told me of the "booze" ring, for which he and Dago did the delivering. Where they got the booze I never found out, but they made $25 or $30 apiece for a night's work and gambled it away at a place which was a regular Monte Carlo, with tables for crap-shooting, and caller's chips which were purchased from the cashier.

The same pair were involved in the robbery of a golf shelter. Owing to Ellman's carelessness, he was followed and arrested. He was convicted of petty larceny and put on probation, but the police could not make him reveal the name of his pal. By keeping mum he saved Dago a lot of trouble.

The gang also enjoyed many quiet evenings. It was the rule for the fellows to meet at Mike's on winter nights to shoot pool and talk. In the summer their hang-out was on the corner at the entrance to the park. There was a tendency to stick together at all times in play, just as in other activities. They often went swimming. Every year they played football, for which they tried to keep in training, and they developed a good team. The older fellows were the leaders in their athletic activities.

One of the exploits of the gang was a migration from Chicago to Detroit when high wages were being paid to automobile-workers. They rented a house there and the whole gang lived together. Even though they were making fabulous wages, they did not save a cent, and finally came back to Chicago—broke. It was this Detroit adventure that made bums out of most of them. They had drinking orgies almost every night at their house, and the crap games took their money.

The gang controlled its individual members, particularly when the group was together. As individuals, and in other group relationships they were not so bad, but in the gang they tried to act as tough as possible. The man who danced, who went out with girls, or who was well-mannered was ostracized. Charlie used to act hard-boiled, and he even wore his cap so that it made him look tough. Ellman, who liked to give the impression that he was a ruffian, was going with a girl on the sly. When he was with the gang he was one of the meanest fellows in it, but when he went out with his girl he was very courteous, quitting his loud talk and dropping his braggadocian air.

In the last few years the gang has disintegrated. There has been a tendency for its members to be incorporated into the more conventional activities of society. The majority of them seem to have become more settled in their mode of life. Some have moved away. Even the fellows who have changed, however, are still pretty low under the polished surface. Gang habits and influences still persist.[1]

The first fact to be observed about the Dirty Dozen, a characteristic which may be regarded as typical of all gangs, as distinguished from more formal groups, is its spontaneous and unplanned origin. Unlike a college club or labor union, its beginnings were unreflective—the natural outgrowth of a crowd of boys meeting on a street corner.

Another significant mark of the gang is its intimate face-to-face relations. Sometimes its members actually live together in a place of common abode. Although many of its enterprises may be carried on by small groups, the majority of the bona fide members of a real gang must get *together* periodically if it is to continue its corporate existence.

ORGIASTIC (EXPRESSIVE) BEHAVIOR

The most rudimentary form of collective behavior in the gang is interstimulation and response among its own members—motor activity of the playful sort, a "talkfest," the rehearsal of adventure, or a "smut session." It may be mere loafing together. It may assume the character of a common festivity such as gambling, drinking, smoking, or sex. It is in this type of behavior that the gang displays and develops at the outset its enthusiasms, its spirit, its *esprit de corps*. If it behaved only in this way, how-

[1] Manuscript prepared by a former associate of the gang.

ever, it would remain a merely orgiastic or festive group such as the "Fusileers."

14. The Fusileers were college fellows with a few congenial friends and some women attached, who stuck together closely for two or three years. They were bound together by ties of sincere friendship and by common standards of conduct. Several of them were fraternity men, but they dared not let their "brothers" know of this relationship. They were hard drinkers and rounders, and they wanted complete freedom from traditional morality.

college fellows

The chief activities and interests of the group were of the festivity type. The first year they held frequent parties on the south shore at the home of one of the members whose parents were away for the summer. One autumn, two or three nights a week, they collected at the Smiths' before starting out in their cars to make the rounds of the cabarets. The Smiths, who were a middle-aged couple, liked to have the crowd come to their home to sing and dance and bring something along with them to drink. It was absolutely necessary that there be plenty of liquor; otherwise the party did not feel in good spirits.

There was an unwritten law among the men not to interfere with each other's women, and this was carefully observed, for what was one girl more or less? The girls were, for the most part, well-to-do and moved in the best society. College women were tabooed because there was nothing in it for the boys. They went with girls who smoked, drank, and had about as loose morals as their own. The wilder the women were, the better they got along with the Fusileers.

In order to protect the reputations of their women and themselves they started to look for a flat where they could continue to carry on their parties unmolested by society and its conventions. The rendezvous must be located in a tough neighborhood where the people were used to wild, drinking orgies. Finally they managed to secure a six-room furnished apartment where the occupants of two or three other flats were in the habit of giving similar parties.

There were two classes of members: those who lived in the hang-out and those who just helped to finance it. One member acted as the bookkeeper and took charge of collecting the funds. Another was acquainted with the policeman on the beat, who was brought in several times for a few drinks. The sergeant in the territory was treated likewise; so they had almost complete protection. Another member was acquainted with many politicians around town. They did not need to worry, therefore, about the down-town police or the detective bureau.

They could furnish their own musicians and entertainers for their parties. These festivities were very much cheaper than cabaret excursions and lacked none of their attractions. The boys cooked most of their own meals, giving regular dinners occasionally. If any of the group got too drunk to go home, there was always room to sleep somewhere. The idea was such a success that there was a party almost every afternoon or evening for the first three weeks. During this time they consumed over thirty gallons of wine alone. Later on, however, they settled down to a couple of parties a week. They had their own initiation, grips, and similar contrivances. Besides, they composed their own songs and poems. When they were not singing, they were having a dancing contest or some other special stunt. These affairs would continue most of the night. [2]

Although this group developed spontaneously, was unconventional in its behavior, and possessed tradition and a natural structure, its chief activity was exploiting the senses rather than linear action and conflict. It was primarily a feeling, rather than an action, group. It sought to avoid hostile forces, whereas the gang ordinarily welcomes a fight. This is quite a common type of social group, of which many examples have come to the attention of the investigator. [3]

THE GANG AND THE MOB

When the gang becomes inflamed it may behave like a mob. Moreover, it may become the actual nucleus for a mob, as is shown by the Dirty Dozen's invasion of the Black Belt. The superior organization, solidarity, and morale of the gang give the mob an unwonted stability and direct its excited activities to greater destruction.

[2] Manuscript prepared by a member of this group.

[3] The origin of the sect has been attributed to a certain type of orgiastic group. "Just as the gang may be regarded as the perpetuation and permanent form of the 'crowd that acts,' so the sect, religious and political, may be regarded as a perpetuation and permanent form of the orgiastic (ecstatic) or expressive crowd." (R. E. Park and E. W. Burgess, *Introduction to the Science of Sociology*, p. 872.)

The less active elements in the mob, on the other hand, and even the mere spectators, give moral support to or provide an appreciative audience for the more active nucleus—the gang. This is well illustrated in the case of the Chicago race riots of 1919, when gangs frequently served as nuclei for mobs.

15. The mob in its entirety usually did not participate actively. It was "one" in spirit, but divided in performance into a small active nucleus and a large proportion of spectators. The nucleus was composed of young men from sixteen to twenty-one or twenty-two years of age. Sometimes only four would be active while fifty or one hundred and fifty looked on, but at times the proportion would be as great as twenty-five in two hundred or fifty in three hundred. Fifty is the largest number reported for a mob nucleus. . . . .

The fact that children were frequently a part of mobs is one of the thought-provoking facts of the Chicago riot. . . . .

Though the spectators did not commit the crimes, they must share the moral responsibility. Without the spectators mob violence would probably have stopped short of murder in many cases. An example of the behavior of the active nucleus when out of sight of the spectators bears this out. George Carr, negro, was chased from a street car. He outstripped all but the vanguard of the mob by climbing fences and hiding in a back yard. This concealed him from the rest of the crowd, who by that time were chasing other negroes. The young men who followed Carr left him without striking a blow, upon his mere request for clemency. In regard to the large non-active elements in the crowds, the coroner said during the inquest, "It is just the swelling of crowds of that kind that urges them on, because they naturally feel that they are backed up by the balance of the crowd, which may not be true, but they feel that way." . . . .[4]

ACTION AND CONFLICT IN THE GANG

To become a true gang the group as a whole must move through space (linear action) and eventually, as has been shown in the preceding chapter, must meet some hostile element which precipitates conflict. Movement

[4] Chicago Commission on Race Relations, *The Negro in Chicago*, pp. 22–25.

through space in a concerted and co-operative way may include play, the commission of crime,—such as robbing or rum-running—and migration from one place to another with change of hang-out or resort—for example, the migration of the Dirty Dozen to Detroit or of the "Ratters" from Toledo to Chicago.

Conflict, as already indicated, comes in clashes with other gangs or with common enemies such as the police, park officials, and so on. It takes place under a multiplicity of circumstances and assumes a variety of forms, of which, perhaps, open attack and defense are the most common. Whether the gang always fights openly as a unit or not, it usually seems to carry on warfare against its enemies co-operatively. It is as the result of collective action and particularly of conflict that the gang, especially in its solidified form, develops morale.[5]

Many gangs seem capable of reflective behavior—discussion and planning, leading to co-operative action. As in the case of the individual, this collective thinking on the part of the gang seems to arise as a response to a crisis situation, and has for its purpose an attempted adjustment of the group.

DEVELOPMENT OF TRADITION AND GROUP-AWARENESS

If the gang has had any degree of continuity of experience, the collective behavior and common purposes lead to the development of a common tradition—a heritage of memories which belongs more or less to all its members

[5] Morale refers to that quality—of an individual or of a group—of unwavering pursuance of an aim in the face of both victory and defeat. Gangs vary widely in the possession of morale. For those of the more unstable type, it may be easily shattered. For those with a long history, however, which has included the vanquishing of common enemies and the acquiring of more effective organization and solidarity, morale may become very strong. As a tactical maneuver the gang may scatter before its enemies, but that does not mean necessarily that it has lost its morale; it may mean simply that it is achieving its purpose by some other method than overt fighting.

and distinguishes the gang from more ephemeral types of group such as the crowd and the mob.

Reactions of the gang's members which indicate a feeling of distinctness from other groups arise in part through the possession of this common tradition, but they are even more the result of the integrating effects of conflict.[6] In the case of the Dirty Dozen the hostile forces were "outgroups," such as competing athletic teams, rival gangs, the despised "niggers," and the police whose meddlesome interference represented the moral and legal standards of the larger community.

OTHER CHARACTERISTICS

Like its beginning, the organization of the gang is non-conventional and unreflective. The rôles and status of the members are determined, not by formal standards, reasoned choices, or voting in the ordinary sense, but through the mechanisms of interaction in social situations. So the gang represents a social order which is natural and crescive rather than enacted.

The Dirty Dozen, like other gangs, is an interstitial group, detached and free from the social anchorages or moorings which hold the more conventional types of group within the bounds of social control.

A final characteristic which the Dirty Dozen possesses in common with most other gangs is its attachment to a local territory, within which is its accustomed hang-out. Gangs like to roam about, and sometimes their exploits carry them far afield—in this case the excursions into the Black Belt and the trip to Detroit—but they usually have their home territory, with every nook and corner of which

[6] See R. E. Park and E. W. Burgess, *op. cit.*, p. 51. "Group self-consciousness," which is produced in the process of conflict, may be described behavioristically as the positive responses of a group or its members to symbols standing for the group (collective representations) such as the group name, flag, slogan, password, and grip, or some tradition representing past common experience.

they are thoroughly acquainted, which they regard as particularly their own, and which they are ready to defend against the encroachments of outsiders.

A definition of the gang, then, based upon this study of 1,313 cases, may be formulated as follows:

> *The gang is an interstitial group originally formed spontaneously, and then integrated through conflict. It is characterized by the following types of behavior: meeting face to face, milling, movement through space as a unit, conflict, and planning. The result of this collective behavior is the development of tradition, unreflective internal structure, esprit de corps, solidarity, morale, group awareness, and attachment to a local territory.*

CHAPTER IV

Types of Gangs

If conditions are favorable to its continued existence, the gang tends to undergo a sort of natural evolution from a diffuse and loosely organized group into the solidified unit which represents the matured gang and which may take one of several forms. It sometimes becomes a specialized delinquent type such as the criminal gang, but usually it becomes conventionalized and seeks incorporation into the structure of the community, imitating some established social pattern such as a club, but in reality retaining many, if not all, of its original attributes. The gang may also acquire the characteristics of a secret society. Once developed, gangs sometimes form federations among themselves or make alliances with rings or political machines. The following case shows a group passing through several of these stages.[1]

16. A crowd of about fifteen Polish lads from fourteen to sixteen years old were accustomed to meet on a street corner in front of a store. From loafing, smoking, and "rag-chewing," they turned to shooting craps, which excited hostility toward them.

"Jigs, de bulls!" someone would shout, and they would scatter. As the group grew, business men and residents regarded as a

[1] A play-group or club which attempt to imitates a gang without really acquiring its essential characteristics may be called a "pseudogang."

nuisance the crowd which blocked the way on the sidewalk, interfered with traffic on the street and hung about at night, keeping people awake with their noise. The crowd had now become a rudimentary gang.

The next step in their development was to organize a ball team to which they gave the name "Pershing Tigers." With a name, group-consciousness increased, for they could say proudly, "We belong to the Pershings!"

One night the Altons, a gang from another neighborhood, swooped down for a raid and attempted to "clean out" their corner. Bitter enmity developed, and the Pershings cleaned out the Altons' alley with rocks, guns, and daggers. With about six months of fighting the gang became fully solidified.

Observing the athletic clubs with their large-lettered names on the big plate glass windows, one of the boys suggested that the gang organize a club. The idea made a big hit, they became the Apaches' Athletic Association and rented a room in back of a store at $5.00 a month. This required dues and more members, and the roster was brought up to seventy-five. The one officer was the treasurer, who collected the dues.

The gang had now become conventionalized and had gained a definite standing in the neighborhood. Interest in the new organization was so great that suits were purchased for its ball team, and a schedule of games was secured with other clubs and gangs. A second-hand billiard table was bought for the clubroom, and the boys spent their time there with pool, dice, and cards. Interest was aroused in pugilism, and the best boxer finally became the leader of the gang.[2]

THE DIFFUSE TYPE

Many gangs, however, do not grow beyond a rudimentary stage. Their solidarity is not lasting; the loyalties of their members to each other and the gang cannot be counted on too far; the natural leaders may not be recognized definitely as such by the rest of the group.[3]

[2] Gang boy's own story and other interviews.

[3] The following case is given by William Healy (William Healy and Augusta F. Bronner, Case Study 8, Series I *Judge Baker Foundation Studies*, pp. 16-17, 15a-17a) to illustrate what he calls the "delinquent crowd." On account of its loose organization he attempts to differentiate it from the gang (p. 9a). This group possesses, however, in a rudimentary way the essential attributes of a gang. It seems better to reserve the term

17. Olaf's crowd consists of about twenty members, ranging from twelve to sixteen years of age. It was never a real gang with an organization; some of its members associated somewhat with other crowds. There were no special meetings or meeting places; the boys congregated on the street corners, or in by-places, or in the neighborhood of poolrooms. There have been no recognized leaders, although some boys have naturally had more influence than others—the boys whose exploits had been more daring or who have set them forth with most gusto. Younger boys have been recruited from time to time but not in any deliberate or formal fashion.

While they spoke of each other as belonging to the Downey Street crowd, they were boys who merely lived in the same district, not in the same street.

Not only the main but apparently the sole bond that held these boys together has been the recounting and committing of delinquencies. The latter were practically always carried out by two or more of the crowd who would then tell their adventures to the others. The idea thus acquired would rapidly spread and be acted upon. They had no other interests in common, neither secret club activities, athletics, antagonism to other gangs nor anything else. . . . .

Thieving in stores was carried on extensively, at one time by a system—groups of three or four going into a store and getting away with anything they could. The articles were distributed or sold to the other boys; there was never any systematic sharing of booty.

. . . . It was always merely a small portion of the crowd that entered into any delinquency at one time—there was no great crowd contagion, although ideas did permeate the whole group. Satisfaction was clearly obtained not only in the committing of the delinquency and through the enjoyment of the booty but also in the recounting of their adventures in delinquency. . . . .

Among these boys there has been considerable loyalty, although, again, not imposed by any agreement. The only case of

---

"crowd" for a mere agglomeration of individuals that may fortuitously happen together (as in the popular sense) or to restrict its use to that phase of group-behavior which has the peculiar mental unity described by LeBon as belonging to the "psychological crowd" (Gustave LeBon, *The Crowd*). Healy's case is a very good example of the diffuse type of gang.

"squealing" that we know of was when H gave information to the police about Olaf and M.

The psychology of such a crowd is comparatively simple and by no means belongs to the realm of the abnormal. Even with the loose-knit organization of this particular crowd, appearance in court and commitment together to X led to development of some group-consciousness and group-loyalty. The members are held together by forces so general as sometimes to be called instincts—gregariousness, imitation, rivalry, desire to appear well to one's fellows, curiosity, the love of novelty, and the desire for acquisition or possessions.

Several hundred diffuse gangs were found in Chicago, each varying in some particular, perhaps, but conforming to the general type presented above.

THE SOLIDIFIED TYPE

In antithesis with the diffuse gang is the solidified type, which is the result of a longer development and a more intense or more extended conflict. A high degree of loyalty and morale and a minimum of internal friction contribute to a well-integrated fighting machine, by means of which the gang presents a solid front against its foes.[4]

18. Shortly after the race riots of 1919, residents in the vicinity south of the stock yards were startled one morning by a number of placards bearing the inscription "The Murderers, 10,000 Strong, 48th & Ada." In this way attention was attracted to a gang of thirty Polish boys, who hang out in a district known as the Bush.

The pastimes of the boys were loafing, smoking, chewing, crap-shooting, card-playing, pool, and bowling. Every evening they would get together at their corner or in their shack near by to "chew the rag" and talk over the events of the day. The new members who were taken in from time to time were congenial spirits who had shown ability to elude the police or gameness in a fight.

A favorite rendezvous of the gang was a large sand pile near the railroad tracks. Here they had great fun camping, flipping freights, and pestering the railroad detectives. Most of them were "bumming away from home," sleeping under sidewalks or in the

[4] See documents 162 and 165. The superior solidarity of this type of gang over a formal group is illustrated in document 163.

prairies. They had little difficulty in swiping their food; the milk and bread wagons were a source of abundant provisions.

They broke into box cars and "robbed" bacon and other merchandise. They cut out wire cables to sell as junk. They broke open telephone boxes. They took autos for joy-riding. They purloined several quarts of whiskey from a brewery to drink in their shack.

Most of them were habitual truants, and they acknowledged their commitments to the parental school with great pride. Many of them had been in the juvenile detention home and the jail. Their "records" were a matter of considerable prestige in the group.

Although leadership shifted with changing circumstances, the best fighter, who "knows how to lead us around the corner and pick a scrap," was usually in command.

A high degree of loyalty had developed within the gang, and its members repeatedly refused to peach on each other in the courts. They stuck close together in most of their exploits, for their enemies were many and dangerous. They used to "get" the "niggers" as they came from the stock yards at Forty-seventh and Racine. "We would hit them and knock them out of the cars." They claim to have killed negroes during the riots. The police too were their enemies, for the "cops were always picking us up and we liked to get them going."

Their chief animosity, however, was directed against the Aberdeens, a rival gang that "was always punching our kids." They were forced to defend their sand pile on the tracks against this gang and several others, for it was not only a source of fun but a place where they could pick up coal for use at home. Many a rock battle was waged here and on the streets. They formed an alliance with half a dozen gangs for mutual aid and protection, and they counted about an equal number as their special enemies.

The Murderers had the reputation throughout the whole district of being a very tough outfit. When the other boys of the area would hear of their inroads, they would "quiet down like little birds when a hawk is sailing over them." The store keepers of the vicinity were indignant at their rudeness and thievery, and the neighbors regarded them as an awful nuisance.

It is not surprising that, with so many hostile forces about, this gang became well organized and acquired considerable solidarity.[5]

[5] It must not be concluded from the fact that most of the groups in the case-studies exhibit delinquencies, that the gang is inherently evil. It is a spontaneous group and usually unsupervised; its activities tend to follow the line of least resistance. See chap. xii.

THE CONVENTIONALIZED TYPE

The dominant social pattern for the conventionalized gang in Chicago is the athletic club. It may take other forms, however, such as dancing, social, or pleasure clubs, pool and billiard clubs, and benevolent associations or political societies. About one-fourth (335) of the groups enumerated in this investigation are clearly of the conventionalized type.

The tendency toward conventionalization usually manifests itself first at the period from sixteen to eighteen years of age. In many cases the gang takes this step on its own initiative, but often it is encouraged to do so by a politician, a saloon-keeper, or some welfare agency. In this way it attempts to achieve social standing and make its activities legitimate in the eyes of the community (becomes an accommodation group). It may adopt a constitution and by-laws, provide for the election of officers and the payment of dues, require the observance of rules of order, or take on other formal features. It often incorporates, receiving its charter from the state or buying it from some defunct organization.[6]

Beneath the external earmarks of a club, gang characteristics often persist. The result is a sort of social hybrid. If supervised and backed by wholesome influences, the gang club may become thoroughly socialized; otherwise it may function as a destructive and demoralizing agency in the community, or it may lose its vitality and enter upon a period of disintegration.

19. Our gang numbered about seven boys of grammar-school age, who were drawn together into a gang by need of protection against Mickey O'Brien, a roughneck from State Street and the neighborhood bully.

At the first encounter between the gang and Mickey, "Spike," one of our members, noting our overwhelming numbers, fingered

---

[6] Before prohibition it was necessary to incorporate in order to get special bar permits.

Photo by Author

Photo by Author   THE "MURDERERS," LITTLE AND BIG

Above are the Little Murderers playing their Sunday morning games. Below diagonally across the street from them the Big Murderers are amusing themselves. This gang (in the customary two divisions, junior and senior) received its forbidding name at the time of the 1919 race riots when it is said to have disposed of several Negroes. (See document 18.)

his nose at the enemy. After a lively exchange of words, Mickey decided he was no match for us and retreated. A few days later he saw Spike alone and chased him down an alley. Spike's whistle for help brought the entire gang from their cave in a vacant lot and Mickey was chased, caught, and beaten. After that we were all for one and one for all.

We now thought we ought to organize the gang, and held a preliminary meeting in our dugout. Bill, our ringleader, wanted only one officer, the "gang leader," a position which he thought he would be able to fill. I stood out for several officers. Finally we compromised by combining both suggestions and decided to have a captain (Bill's job), a president, a vice-president, a secretary, and a treasurer. We decided also to have a council for the boys who were not officers, and we finally appointed Johnnie, who was only a little "punk," as caretaker of the cave. Everybody was satisfied, since everybody had an office.

With our new-formed organization, which we called the "Tigers," enthusiasm waxed apace, and we built a new shack where we could cook some of our meals. The news of our success spread through the neighborhood, and we were soon besieged with applications for membership. After discussion, three new boys were initiated into our group. Then our trouble began. We had become more of a club than a gang. Discontent was brewing and two cliques were formed. Eventually the three most active in organizing the original gang were expelled, and the new members moved the headquarters to their own neighborhood. Finally the old gang came back to us, but our unity had vanished and we divided our property and called it quits.[7]

THE CRIMINAL TYPE

If the gang does not become conventionalized or incorporated in some way into the structure of the community as its members grow older, it often drifts into habitual crime and becomes completely delinquent.

20. Originating with a dozen adolescent truants in the vicinity of Halsted and Harrison streets, Joe's gang has been a solid group for over ten years. Its members have initiative and a sense of honor toward each other and those who have befriended them. They went straight for some time, owing to the efforts of teachers and social

[7] Manuscript prepared by a former member of the group.

workers, but they have now become a hold-up and beer-running outfit.

One of the members was shot by his own father. Several of them pulled off a $100,000 robbery in a Loop jewelry store. Joe drove a wagon that bombed a building under construction on the North Side. At various times members of the gang have become deeply indebted to a professional bondsman whose exorbitant charges have made it necessary for them to commit more robberies. Joe worked as a teamster, and some of the others have worked, but the whole group has gradually drifted into crime.

The gang has dealt summary justice to its own members, having killed two of them on account of internal friction. Joe was shot recently and later died from the wound, but he declined to give the name of his assassin or any other clue. The Black Hand would have dealt cruelly with his sister, he said, had he squealed. It is thought that the shooting was due to a feud with a rival gang of beer-runners. [8]

THE SECRET SOCIETY

The gang may develop the features of a secret society —secrecy, initiation, ritual, passwords, codes, and so on, —either spontaneously because these devices perform a real function in its life, or in imitation of such secret societies as it observes in its cultural environment. In the latter case, the chief motive seems to be the thrill of mystery and the prestige of the social pattern in the community rather than mutual protection. The secret rites of the Mafia and the Camorra among the Italians, or of the Ku Klux Klan and the Black Hand in this country, provide a real basis for solidarity and security against interference; but the imitations of such organizations found among boys' gangs in Chicago present only the outer trappings of the genuine secret society.

THE NATURAL HISTORY OF A GANG

The following case shows the processes of conventionalization and the assumption of the attributes of a secret society in both of the ways mentioned above.

[8] Interviews and records.

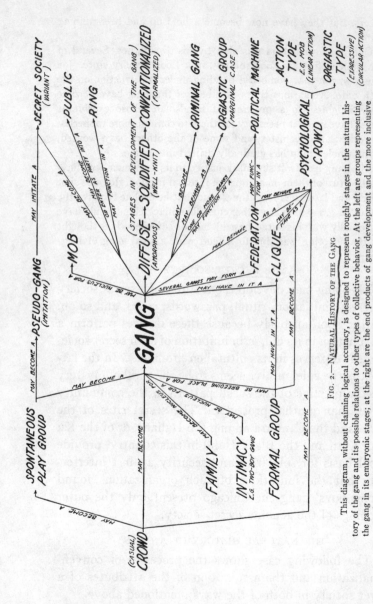

FIG. 2.—NATURAL HISTORY OF THE GANG

This diagram, without claiming logical accuracy, is designed to represent roughly stages in the natural history of the gang and its possible relations to other types of collective behavior. At the left are groups representing the gang in its embryonic stages; at the right are groups representing the end products of gang development and the more inclusive groups into which the gang may ultimately enter. The formation of what Le Bon calls the "psychological crowd," either of the action or of the orgiastic type, may characterize these groups at any stage in their development; it represents a type of recurring behavior rather than a species of group. (See chaps. ii, iii, and iv.)

21. About a dozen boys in a three-block area who had played together since childhood took the name "Tri-Street Athletic Club." A clubroom in a barn was furnished with a stove, cots, pennants, and other equipment. Although there was no initiation, there was a password and a secret handle to open the door. Dues of twenty-five cents a month were fixed, and the number of members was increased to about twenty.

The proverbial fights took place with other gangs, but our chief enemies were the Scarboros from a neighboring street. Tomato fights, mud fights, and raids were frequent. On Hallowe'en the two gangs vied with each other to see which could get away with the most stuff, but we co-operated wonderfully well to fool the police. At worst we were only "friendly enemies," and there was never that bitter enmity which existed between the gangs in the Italian section.

Our activities included football, basket-ball, and baseball in season, and we scheduled many games. In the winters there were bobsled parties ending with oyster stew at the home of one of the members; girls were usually included on these occasions. The parents knew of the gang's activities and some of them took an active interest in us. The father of one boy always brought back a possum from his hunt and put on a big dinner for the gang. The gang got out a weekly school paper, censored by the principal of the grade school. Although published for the whole school, it bore the initials of the gang—"T.A.C.," which had now become secret symbols and were also worn in monograms on our sweaters.

The T.A.C. existed for about three years. When most of the gang entered high school, a change in the organization soon took place. The new principal tried to shut out all activities and make high school a routine. The opposition of the gang was intense, but they dared not openly defy him. The result was a new organization, composed of thirteen boys, all but three of whom had been members of the T.A.C. It was called the "Hoodlums," and its fundamental purpose was to oust the new principal. It had no formal initiation or organization, but of necessity it was a genuine secret society.

The Hoodlums now became a secret political faction in opposition to the high-school fraternities, and succeeded in capturing a large number of high-school honors for our men. We put on several dances, but our chief interest was in gathering material "on the principal." We finally sent a committee to the school board and presented our case against him with such success that he had to resign. When the new principal arrived, we took him into our confidence and came out into the open. The Hoodlums now became conventionalized in the "Forum," and took up the rôle of a debating club and a high-school boosting organization. We backed all worthwhile activities, sending cars to haul the teams, rubbing the men down in the gymnasium, getting out placards, and so on. During this time we continued to function as a wire-pulling faction and the nucleus for a political party in the school.

It was a rather curious fact that we now acquired all the elaborate formulas that characterized the high-school fraternities—pledging with a period of probation, a pin, and a ritual of initiation, in which our faculty advisor at first participated. This was made up of three parts: questioning, a solemn ceremonial with presentation of a pin of our own designing, and finally a "roughneck" initiation.

The rough-neck initiation gave closer unity to the group and made each new man feel more at one with the brothers. The older men looked forward to giving it to the Freshmen, and the latter anticipated it with great eagerness in spite of the "punishment" it involved.

Contrary to the state law, there were in the high school a number of secret fraternities. Largely to combat these, rules were now passed that all high-school clubs would have to hold their meetings in the schoolrooms; they could give, during the year, only one dance, to be held in the gymnasium and to close at ten-thirty; money must be handled through the school auditor; and pledging was to be abolished. The school further decreed that each club should take up some one line like debating, art, or literature, which we regarded as "bunk" for high-school students.

After some difficulty we got permission to hold the Forum meetings in the evening, but the principal kept forgetting to leave the building open, and in disgust we finally served notice that the club was disbanded. Again we had been driven under cover, and again we became a genuine secret society, this time a local Greek-letter fraternity. The group is now a perpetual organization of from thirty to thirty-five members, with an alumni council which attempts to keep up its moral standards. All our men are pushed in school activities, in which they occupy places of prominence. Dances and banquets are frequent, and meetings are held in the boys' homes. [9]

---

[9] Interview with a former member of the group.

AGE TYPES

Somewhat loosely correlated with the type of gang is the age of gang members. This sort of grouping tends to fall within a larger geographical one.

22. A new crop of youngsters in a district plays together and the older group passes on. Here there is some intermingling, however, precocious boys tending to get into a group a little older than they are, but remaining within the same geographical boundaries. One may see as many as four different age groups playing in the same street at the same time. There are some games that nearly all the groups can play together; other games eliminate the younger groups and the older ones play them alone. The age grouping is really a smaller division within the geographical. [10]

A study of the age statistics of the gangs of Chicago indicates four general types as shown in Table I. Many

TABLE I

Type of Gang	Approximate Range of Ages (Years)	Member Referred to in This Study as
Childhood	6–12	Gang child
Earlier adolescent	11–17	Gang boy
Later adolescent	15–25	Gang boy
Adult	21–50	Gang man

gangs of a mixed type include two or more of the foregoing ranges of ages. The adolescent or the adult who has become somewhat seasoned in a life of crime is usually

[10] Unpublished study by an experienced boys' worker in gangland. The geographical grouping seems to be more important in determining the associations and loyalties of the gang than does that of age. "For, however much the older generation may have been detached by migration and movement from their local associations, the younger generation, who live closer to the ground than we do, are irresistibly attached to the localities in which they live. Their associates are the persons who live next to them. In a great city, children are the real neighbors; their habitat is the local community; and when they are allowed to prowl and explore they learn to know the neighborhood as no older person who was not himself born and reared in the neighborhood is ever likely to know it."—Robert E. Park, *et al.*, *The City*, p. 112.

referred to as a "gangster."[11] These distinctions are important because of the different characteristics of gangs of different age types. The general plan of the book will be to deal with the younger gangs in the earlier chapters and to progress to the older as the theme is developed.

Statistics for the gangs upon which age figures are available (1,213 cases) are shown in Table II giving the approximate distribution.

TABLE II

Type of Gang	Range of Ages (Years)	Number of Cases	Percentage of Total
1. Childhood.............	6–12	18	1.48
2. Earlier adolescent........	11–17	455	37.51
3. Later adolescent.........	16–25	305	25.15
4. Adult.................	21–50	38	3.13
5. Mixed.................	Wider range	154	12.70
6. Athletic or social clubs...	(Late adolescent or adult)*	243	20.03
Total gangs..........	....	1,213	100

* Athletic and social clubs upon which more exact age figures are available have been included under types 3, 4, and 5.

Childhood gangs are usually of the mischievous, neighborhood kind; they are embryonic and diffuse in their organization, being closely related to the play-group; they usually meet on the streets, in yards, or in other open spaces of the neighborhood. Adolescent gangs are usually unsupervised and semi-delinquent; they are better organized than those of younger boys, and they ordinarily have a more definite hang-out—on a special street corner, in a prairie, or in a cave, shack, or barn. The older adolescent gang often meets on the streets but usually tends to hang out in a poolroom, saloon, or store of some sort. When gangs of this type become conventionalized (probably assuming the name of an athletic club), they attempt to get some definite quarters where they will be welcome to loaf,

[11] This is the common usage in the newspapers and popular literature dealing with gangs.

or to rent a clubroom, oscillating between it and the streets or poolrooms as economic pressures dictate. Unsupervised groups of this sort commonly lead an irregular sort of life and often drift directly into criminal practices. The adult gang may assume the form of a club with definite quarters or a common hang-out; otherwise, it is usually of the criminal type, with a special rendezvous such as a roadhouse or a poolroom, or meeting by appointment.

The ordinary assumption that gangs tend to be definitely segregated on the basis of age, boys from twelve to fourteen, for example, preferring exclusive association with other boys of the same ages, is not readily supported.

23. The gangs of this region seem to be organized on the basis of physical ability rather than size or chronological age. In one group the oldest boy is fifteen and in second-year high school, while the youngest is only eleven. The eleven-year-old can play baseball and other games better than the older boy who is rather clumsy. If this older boy were at all clever, his size would permit him to enter an older gang which uses the same street.

In one of these gangs there has been a boy quite small and younger than any of the others, who could put on the boxing gloves with a boy nearly twice his size and handle himself very creditably. Another small boy, however, in the same gang cannot fight or do anything strenuous because of a bad leakage of the heart, yet he, too, is a member in good standing. [12]

A wide range of ages is indicated in 154 cases in the present study. A gang of older fellows includes a few young adolescents or even a little boy or two, or vice versa. If numbers are sufficient, a differentiation may be made by the boys themselves, on the basis of age, into "midgets," "juniors," and "seniors," or more often just "juniors" and "seniors." In these cases, however, the younger groups still retain an intimate relationship to the older. In conventionalized gangs, a definite rule with regard to age is customary; this, however, is usually not

[12] Unpublished study by an experienced boys' worker in gangland.

enforced, or if it is, boys of the barred ages may still be hangers-on, "fringers," or an affiliated group. The older gang often likes to use the younger boys, who can make themselves serviceable in many ways, and many times it seems to enjoy the rôle of protector or patron.

PART II

Life in the Gang

Introduction

The problem of dealing with the boy can be stated very largely in terms of his leisure hours. Ordinarily school and work, either at home or elsewhere, fill a large portion of his day. The period after school or work, vacations, and periods of unemployment—spare time—are the real problem.[1]

The most important agency in directing the spare-time activities of the boy is the family. In the under-privileged classes, family life in a large number of cases—either through neglect, misdirection, or suppression—fails to provide for or control the leisure-time behavior of the adolescent. School, church, and the recognized agencies of recreation, which might supplement this lack, are woefully inadequate to the need in gang areas. The boy with time on his hands, especially in a crowded or slum environment, is almost predestined to the life of the gang, which is simply a substitute, although a most satisfactory one from the boy's point of view, for activities and controls not otherwise provided.

The problem is greatly intensified in gangland areas by the allurements of already existing gang tradition and gang activities. Once a boy has tasted the thrilling street

[1] Compare Henry W. Thurston, *Delinquency and Spare Time.*

life of the gang, he finds the programs of constructive agencies insipid and unsatisfying. Gradually the gang usurps time usually given to school and work, and, by supplanting home, school, church, and vocation, becomes the primary interest of the boy.

The lure of the gang is undoubtedly due in part to the fact that the gang boy is in the adolescent stage which is definitely correlated with gang phenomena. Although this period has no exact limits for any individual, it includes broadly for the boy the years from twelve to twenty-six. It is a time of physical and social development—an interstitial period between childhood and maturity. Its duration is generally marked by conflicts consequent to the attempts of the growing personality to adjust itself in its larger social milieu which represents a new world for the emerging child. If these new needs for expression are not provided for by the conventional agencies, they will be met in other ways.

It is just here that the gang functions for the boy. Even in the disorganized areas of life in a great city, the young child, necessarily dependent, is incorporated in the family or some other child-caring institution. Girls, too, are usually much more carefully supervised and protected in these regions.[2] The adult man, also, even though he has passed through the adventures of gang life, usually marries and "settles down," or becomes otherwise articulated in a conventional group. The adolescent of the underprivileged class, however, is particularly prone to the gang mode of life because he finds in the gang the types of behavior which appeal to him and which are not provided in an effective way by the conventional agencies.

From the standpoint both of spare time and of adolescence, therefore, the gang is an interstitial phenomenon which almost ideally meets the demand for types of activity

[2] For example, the Italian system of chaperonage for girls.

which particularly appeal to the boy. It is proposed in Part II to present a picture of some of these activities which make life in the gang.

CHAPTER V

The Quest For New Experience

How to break the humdrum of routine existence—this is a problem for the boy. It is the problem of life generally and a great deal of human energy is expended in the flight from monotony and the pursuit of a thrill. "Our leisure is now mainly a restless search for excitement."[1] William I. Thomas has classified the various forms of behavior of this type under the caption, "The Wish for New Experience."[2]

The quest for new experience seems to be particularly insistent in the adolescent, who finds in the gang the desired escape from, or compensation for, monotony. The gang actively promotes such highly agreeable activities as rough-house, movement and change, games and gambling, predatory activities, seeing thrillers in the movies, sports, imaginative play, roaming and roving, exploration, and camping and hiking.

The gang, moreover, stimulates the boy to an even greater craving for excitement. His adolescent interest in

[1] See Robert E. Park, *et al.*, *The City*, pp. 117–18.

[2] See William I. Thomas, *The Unadjusted Girl*, pp. 4, 5. This together with his three other wishes—for security, for response, and for recognition—may be thought of as class terms for four persistent types of human behavior. Reasoning backwards, we arrive at the wishes conceived of as fundamental human needs.

that which thrills becomes reinforced by habit; ordinary business and pleasure seem tame and dull in comparison with the adventures of the gang. Habituation to this type of life in adolescence goes a long way toward explaining behavior in the young-adult gangs and even of the hardened gangster.

25. When I first moved into the neighborhood I met two brothers who took me one night with the rest of the gang—about thirteen boys eleven to twenty-two years old. We stayed out till nine, pitching pennies on the corner. They showed me their hang-out up in a barn, where there was an electric light, and we began to stay out till two or three every morning.

We used to bring up pop and candy to eat, and play cards. It was a big room, with furniture and everything. The people had stored an old dining-room set, a library table, a kitchen table, and an army bed up there. We had to go up a ladder, through a trapdoor. It was lots of fun. It was not really a club, just a hang-out. Some of the big fellows got to bossing it, and we called them the "Bimbooms." Then they called the whole gang the "Bimbooms."

We loved baseball and sometimes we would all play hooky from school to go to a game. When we had our own team, we called it the "Congress Athletic Club."

On the corner, we would pitch pennies and then it got to be quarters. We played Rummie and Seven-and-a-half for money. I wanted to learn how to play Stud-poker, but no one would teach me. Oftentimes we shot dice for pocket-trash. Sometimes when we were hollering and playing games, the flying-squad would chase us away. The horse-cop would run us like anything, but we were too fast for him. Then he'd throw his club and we'd throw it back again at his horse's feet to make him prance. We'd call him "Old Mickey Cop."

In the wintertime, we'd hitch boards to street cars, and it was a lot of fun to see the fellows hit a switch and get spilled off. I never liked to go to Union Park with the family, but to go with the gang on the "L" platform and blow up pigeons through their beaks or smash stolen eggs in the kids pockets.

We used to keep pretty much to ourselves, and if another gang got fresh with us, a couple of guys would go down and get the Winchesters to come up and help us. One gang of fifteen or sixteen kids would try to run us off our corner just to be smart. They had a double-barreled shotgun, which they would load with rock salt. And when it hit you, would it hurt! You tell 'em, boy!

We built a fort in a vacant lot on the corner to keep them from shooting us. Then they'd throw rocks and knock the boards off, so they could hit us. They would usually come around raiding about three times a week. We had beebee guns and a 22-rifle, in which we shot blanks to scare them, but we might have shot something else if we'd had it.

I like to fight, and I took training at a down-town gymnasium with "Kid Joe." Several of our gang belonged down there. I won medals for boxing.

The wish I'd like to have most in the world is a big club, with all kinds of sporting equipment.[3]

ROUGH-HOUSE

Sheer physical activity of a random sort is characteristic of gang behavior. The gang boy is not afflicted with "spectatoritis," which someone called the great American disease; for he likes to be in the thick of the play, and the bigger the mêlée, the better he enjoys it. With the gang, he is as full of energy as an electric dynamo.

27. There was not much equipment for this gang to use and not much supervision. The most accurate description of the behavior of the twelve or fifteen boys who usually hung out together is pandemonium. The noise was deafening. Only once, in several weeks' experience, did I get them quiet enough to say a few words. They were constantly chasing each other about the room, in and out of doors, and around the block. Everybody seemed to be hitting everybody else or striking out in all directions at the same time They could not hold steady long enough to play a game of pool; at about the third shot, the balls would begin to fly off the table. Agility was at a premium, and lucky was he who escaped injury. Eventually the pool balls began to fly across the room, with bad results to the plaster.[4]

This ceaseless activity without apparent purpose or direction, this chaotic expenditure of energy, may be regarded as a form of "milling" typical of the gang.

[3] Gang boy's own story.

[4] Observations by the author.

MOVEMENT AND CHANGE

Behavior in the gang often takes the form of movement and change without much purpose or direction. Almost anything which possesses novelty suffices—until its newness wears off. Activity may lead in the direction of delinquency or anywhere else, so long as it keeps the gang boy "going." A surprising instability of interest is often manifested, and new contacts and alliances are made with amazing rapidity.

28. I was supposed to go to school, but Eddie said do I want to come wid him. I went wid him. We met Mike and went to the "Boy." I do not know his name, but Eddie had seen him out in South Chicago. The Boy, who was about sixteen, had been in St. Charles. When we met him he was working in a wienie shop on Sixty-third. We were about twelve and thirteen then.

The Boy brought us some buns, and then we went to Jackson Park. On the way back we went to a show. When we came out, we bought some candies. We slept that night with the Boy, in a little shed. The next day we spent in the park. About four o'clock that afternoon, we helped the Boy, but we left the door of the store open so we could come back later. In the evening we went to a show. About midnight we met the Boy and came back and robbed the store. We got about $46 in there. Then we went back to our shed to sleep.

The next day we all went to Twelfth Street, where we bought tennis slippers, four hats, four mouth organs, some cuff buttons, some bananas, and some soft drinks. The Boy always held the money. Then we went down town to a show. Afterward we bought some candies. Then the Boy bought himself one of them there collars [Van Heusen].

The Boy had a train ticket and we went to Forty-third Street on the Illinois Central. We got tired of sitting down, so we got off there and walked to Sixty-third. The Boy bought a package of cigarettes. We went to Jackson Park. The Boy had some guff [golf] sticks and we started playing around on the links. Then it was about eight o'clock, and we went to the show again. We bought some candies.

That night we robbed another wienie store where the Boy had worked.

The next day we went out to Jackson Park again and went boat riding. We stayed in the park till noon, picking up guff balls and making tips for finding them. We was wid another boy out there. Mike stole the guff clubs on us and ran away back to South Chicago. We went boat riding in the afternoon, and that night we went to a show on Sixty-third. That night we slept in the same shed again. The Boy had a big trunk full of stuff there.

The next morning we sneaked out and went back to Jackson Park boat riding. We went to the guff grounds again and got balls and sold them. We started out looking for stores to rob that night. In the afternoon we went to another show. That night we tried to break in the door of a store. The boy took a rock and tried to break the lock, but he couldn't. Finally the little boy grabbed it and broke through. We went in and got cigars, cigarettes, a searchlight, and a gun. We found a lot of ice-cream, but most of it was salty. We spilled all the cones out of a big box. Then we took all the gum, candy, and a lot of O'Henrys. Went back to our shed. We smoked and ate candy the whole night.

The next morning we bought two loaves of bread for breakfast. We went boating again. In the afternoon we went to White City and spent $6.00. We came from there to a restaurant and bought some meat. After playing around on Sixty-third, we went to a show. Then we went again to our shed to sleep. Our beds were some old coats and paper trash. . . . .

The next morning we were up early and jumped from the shed. We went to Commercial Avenue and bought some wienies, coffee, and pop. We tried to get boats on Calumet Lake but had to come back. We hung around Commercial Avenue till about noon and then went to Eighty-ninth Street, where the Boy shot off some bullets. We went back to Commercial Avenue and bought some pie and coffee. Then we went to a quarry at Ninety-fifth Street to play, and finally came back to sleep in a shed by the Boy's house.

That night we robbed a grocery store. We got some money, a gun, some canned shrimps, candies, cigars, cigarettes, stockings, cuff buttons, and bananas. We slept in the store on a shelf till about five o'clock in the morning, and then got out through the back. Then we went to the Boy's brother's shed, where we fetched all the stuff. We went out again and got ourselves some eats. We went to a movie show. Then we went out to the quarry again to ketch minnies with a little hook and bait. That night the Boy gave his brother a box of cigars. When his brother found he was sleeping in the shed, he asked him why he did not come home. Then his brother took all the stuff from the shed into the house and kept it. That night we went and tried to rob an A. and P. store. We were hungry and did not have nothing to eat no more. When we got in we found we'd made a mistake and it was a barber-shop instead of the grocery.

Finally, me and Eddie and the Boy went back to his brother's shed to sleep, and Johnnie went to his own shed. In the morning Johnnie came early and waked us and said that a man from the police had been around there. The boy got his brother's pay check, took it to the bank, changed it, and kept the money. Then we bought eats and candies. We also bought a bar of soap and went to the quarry to wash ourselves. Then we took a hike to the Calument River.

When we were out there, two policemen went by in a flivver. They stopped and asked us what we were doing. They knew the Boy; for they had been looking for him a long time. So the policemen robbed the Boy and found his revolver. They took it and tried to shoot into the air, but it had no bullets and was broke. Then they robbed us and got all our stuff, dice, cigarettes, and $6.00. They took us to the station, where they finally brought Eddie and Johnnie. And that was the end of our sport.[5]

GAMES AND GAMBLING

Games and gambling afford another form of thrill and relief from dullness and routine. Most popular in the gang are games involving action, rivalry, and chance.

Games of chance, like many athletic sports, may be regarded as one form of conflict behavior involving risk. In gambling the gang simply follows a social pattern prevalent among all ages in gangland.

29. A man in one of the newspaper alleys had a paper game with horses on it and powder strips. You would light it, and the horse on the strip that burned out first would win. The boys would bet on these horses. The man who was doing this was just a bum who hung around down there. The cops would not see the games. When the watchman would swing his stick and chase the kids out, they'd wait a little bit and then begin all over again. Another

[5] Gang boy's own story.

fellow had a board with six lines on it. It had spaces with numbers in them. You would put your money on the space you thought would win and then shoot three dice. If you won, you would get twice the amount on your space. The kids lost a lot of money this way.[6]

Crap-shooting, or "indoor golf," which has been called the African national game, is learned by gang boys, both white and colored, as soon as they are old enough to handle the dice. Since it is a favorite sport on Sunday mornings, the boys often call it "Sunday School." Losses sometimes mount to several hundred dollars on a single game. Raffles constitute a popular way of raising money.

The formation of pools, to be given the winning side of a baseball game, is a common custom among the gangs. Betting—on elections, on races, on athletic contests, or on anything else where chance is involved—is a favorite pastime among the older gangs.

PREDATORY ACTIVITIES

Stealing, the leading predatory activity of the adolescent gang, is as much a result of the sport motive as of a desire for revenue. It is regarded as perfectly natural and entails no more moral opprobrium for the ordinary gang boy than smoking a cigarette. "C'mon, let's go robbin'," is the common invitation. The response might be, "Naw, too tired," or "Too busy," but never, "T'ain't right." Unless under conventional pressure, these boys do not regard such delinquencies as misconduct.

30. I asked Jimmie if his was a tough gang. After his indignation at the question had cooled, he resumed his usual good-natured smile.
"Well, what does your gang do, then?" I ventured.
"Oh," came the naïve reply, "We go robbin' mostly."[7]

Two types of things are usually stolen: those that the

---

[6] Gang boy's own story.

[7] Interview with a gang boy.

Photo by Author

A STREET GANG AT "SUNDAY SCHOOL"

Shooting craps (the boys call it "Sunday school") is the favorite Sunday morning occupation of the gangs. This row of houses illustrates the dominant type of housing in gangland—frame cottages, built up from the street, usually with room for a family underneath the stairway. Several of these cottages may be placed on a single lot, so that no yard space remains for the children.

boys can use and enjoy and those for which there is a ready market. Thievery in the gang takes a great variety of forms.

31. Our gang started by robbin' the fruit peddlers. A kid would ask for a peck of potatoes and then run with the basket. Then when the peddler chased him, the other kids in the gang would strip his wagon.

One day we robbed watermelon. We would spread it around and let the other kids in on it. We could not do anything with eighty watermelons, but it was fun robbing them.

We would go over the Red River for swimming. We'd loaf at the boathouse, and one day we copped a motor boat without knowing how to run it. When we ran out of gas we got picked up by the police.

We robbed the Jews on Maxwell Street. We'd go into a china store and ask how much a plate was and then drop it. Then the Jew would throw plates. My mother sold some suits to a Jew. The gang followed in a Hudson and robbed the suits.

We used to go robbing at a wholesale grocery. Five of us went there one night; we had been in twice before. We knew there was money in the safe, but we was afraid to take it because the safe might have 'lectricity. So we filled a big bag with sardines, matches, candles, etc.[8]

Burglary is a common type of gang enterprise.

32. My gang used to go out nearly every night looking over stores to decide which ones to make [rob] on Sundays. We would select the gamest in the gang to do the job. If we took the whole gang it would look funny; and besides there would be too much noise and running around the store.

In most cases when we went robbing, somebody would ditch or stool on us. Then if a store happened to be robbed in our neighhorhood, the cops would always grab one of the gang for it. We got away with it a lot of times without getting caught.

I was shot through the wrist once [shows scar], but only some real good members of the gang [inner circle] ever found out I was hurt [shows pride at having been wounded].[9]

Breaking into merchandise cars and general thievery from the railroads is also quite common in the gang.

[8] Gang boy's own story.   [9] Gang boy's own story.

Robbing drunken men, variously known as "jack-rolling," "rollin' de bums," "rollin' de dinos," etc., is a universal practice among the gangs. The little boys like it because of the ease with which they can handle their victims. The big boys are attracted by the large sums which drunken men often carry. Sometimes the victim is knocked down and his bank roll taken away from him; or a little boy lures the "bum" to an appointed place, a bigger boy puts his arm around the man's throat from behind, while a third boy goes through his pockets. A gang sometimes respects racial lines in jack-rolling, and to carry on such enterprises in some other gang's territory is likely to precipitate a war.

Much in the way of vandalism accompanies junking and robbery; there is usually an utter disregard for the conventional rules set up to protect property.

33. Our gang used to go robbing stores almost every day. When trucks would come along, we'd jump on and throw the stuff off. Sometimes we'd raid ice-cream wagons. If the driver saw us, he would jump off and give us a shag. If he caught us, he would usually kick us in the pants and let us go. When we wanted to steal a bicycle, we'd jump into the chains, destroy the brakes, or file the lock.

We'd go in a store robbing a poor old lady. We'd ask her for an empty box and steal everything she had while she was gone. Or we'd all take an apple and start eating; then we'd say we did not like the fruit, throw down a nickel on the counter, and run out with a lot more stuff.

We did all kinds of dirty tricks for fun. We'd see a sign, "Please keep the street clean," but we'd tear it down and say, "We don't feel like keeping it clean." One day we put a can of glue in the engine of a man's car. We would always tear things down. That would make us laugh and feel good, to have so many jokes.[10]

34. This type of activity seemed to be the particular delight of one gang of whose depredations the officers of the Baltimore and Ohio Railroad complain bitterly. Not only do the boys carry off

[10] Gang boy's own story.

merchandise from the cars, but they wantonly destroy it. In one case they scattered meal all over a car with damage resulting to the amount of about $500.

The social settlement whose corner was the favorite rendezvous of the gang was a frequent object of vandalism. During one whole summer the chief interest of the gang seemed to be in breaking windows. They would also break locks and damage property on every occasion. As a result, the equipment of the settlement was usually in a very dilapidated condition. The boys would indulge in perfect orgies of rough-housing in which all the furniture, especially boxing gloves and pool cues, figured. On one occasion when one of the boys found that the cards with which they were playing belonged to the settlement, he started to burn them one by one in a little bonfire of matches which he had made on the sidewalk.[11]

Activity of this sort often has a special purpose. It may be indulged in to satisfy a grudge, "to get even." When it takes place as the result of a "general soreness against the world," it may be regarded as a kind of juvenile *sabotage*. It may be practiced in order to get a shag (enjoy the thrills of a chase), to demonstrate marksmanship or some other skill, or to provoke the usual responses enjoyed by the practical joker at the expense of his victim.

COMMERCIALIZED RECREATION

All forms of commercialized recreation capitalize the wish for variety and thrill. One of these is the poolroom. A few years ago a study was made of four hundred Chicago poolrooms, indicating pretty well the activities indulged in, in such places, by the gang boy or young man who frequents them.

35. Gambling was observed in 108, or over 25 per cent of the poolrooms visited. Poker, dice, gambling wheels, baseball pools, and betting on billiard games were the favorite forms. On Twenty-second Street in the old vice district, twelve minors under eighteen years of age were illegally present in a poolroom where gambling went on in connection with the games. In a hall on Sixty-third Street, six minors were seen manipulating a gambling-machine, at

---

[11] Interviews and observation.

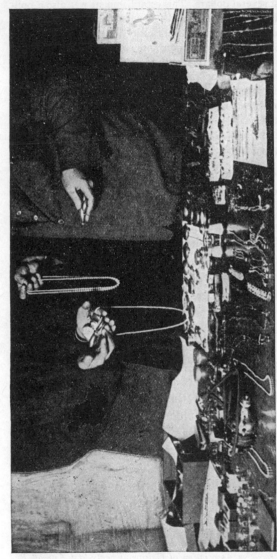

GANG LOOT

Here is the loot (in process of being sorted by police officials) recovered from a single predatory adolescent gang, which had been engaged in extensive thieving exploits. The picture shows the great variety of articles collected, including two dozen watches, twenty-seven cravat pins, half a dozen necklaces, an equal number of rosaries, two or three dozen rings, a dozen or more bracelets, a dozen brooches, opera glasses, watch chains, cigars, lorgnettes, and a miscellaneous assortment of other articles including an electric vibrator. Stealing is one of the major activities of the undirected gang or gang club. (See documents 30–34.) Yet these boys are fundamentally wholesome and only require a redirection of their energies into socially approved channels.

which they lost several dollars. This establishment was also a polling-place, and voting-booths had been deposited for an election. In nineteen halls immoral or disorderly conduct was noted. On the West Side, acts of perversion were suggested to the investigators by a young boy. On the South Side, overt immoral conduct by the proprietor and a woman was witnessed. In scores of places, indecent verses appeared on the walls and show cases. The language of patrons was frequently obscene and profane.

Liquor was illegally sold in four halls. In two places whiskey was purchased, while in the other two, bottled beer, on which appeared the original labels, was sold.[12]

In spite of the curfew regulation of the ordinance excluding minors from poolrooms, and of the friendly cooperation of the Illinois Billiard Association in enforcing the law, gang boys still manage to hang out in or before poolrooms. The data of the present study show fifty-two gangs meeting regularly in poolrooms, and there are undoubtedly many more. The leaders or patrons of older gangs are often the owners. One of the city's most notorious groups, which has terrorized a whole community for years, has as its rendezvous a poolroom owned by one of its leaders. In another case such a hang-out was nicknamed "The House of Crime." It is said that the majority of Chicago's holdups are planned in places like this, which are often raided by the police in search of criminals. The influence of the older poolroom gang was manifest in the case of Itschkie's "Black Hand Society."[13]

Other forms of commercialized amusement which have a prominent place in the gang boy's world are carnivals, arcades, amusement parks, and vaudeville and burlesque theaters. In these places, gang boys come in contact with a questionable class of people, see salacious

---

[12] *Bulletin,* Juvenile Protective Association, September, 1919. See also, *Juvenile Protective Association of Chicago Twenty-first Annual Report,* 1921–22, p. 13.

[13] See document 188.

pictures, hear vulgar and indecent jokes, and become familiar with numerous gambling devices.

THE GANG BOY AND THE SPORT WORLD

In the realm of sports the gang boy is most completely assimilated to the dominant social order. He knows the standing of the big ball clubs, follows the world-series, and has a special admiration for the wrestlers and the "pugs" (pugilists). Jack Dempsey, "Charley" White, and "Strangler" Lewis and local boxers are often his heroes.

Sports and athletics provide the gang one quite wholesome and very popular form of new experience and escape from ennui. They are the mechanisms through which secondary conflict is substituted for the primary type.[14] Indoor baseball or playground ball is the most popular sport among the gangs, primarily because it is easy to play in the small spaces of congested neighborhoods and is less dangerous to life and property than "hard" ball. Welfare and commercial agencies in the city have been able to deal extensively with the gangs by organizing this interest and forming leagues.

Other sports enjoyed by the gang are swimming, skating, fishing, football, basket-ball, wrestling, and boxing. Of these, football and boxing are the most popular. Football is of intense interest because the conflict it involves is personal, direct, and dangerous. The same is true of boxing, which represents the nearest approach to fighting that has social sanction and which can be carried on in a very limited space within the gang's own hang-out. Almost every gang has its pugs, and a flattened nose, a cauliflower ear, or an otherwise battered "phizz," like the scars of student duels in Germany, are marks of distinction. It is curious to note that the Polish boxers often

---

[14] See document 107.

assume Irish names in the ring, and that the Irish some-times take English ones.

LOAFING

In the absence of an opportunity for active excite-ment, the gang resorts to loafing. The loafing gang, like Mr. Micawber, is always "waiting for something to turn up" and spends its time recounting its adventures, rag-chewing, telling dirty stories, indulging in low horseplay, or annoying passersby. It is likely at any moment to cease its loafing rôle, however, and embark on some enterprise if opportunity arises.

STIMULANTS

The use of tobacco in every form is a universal habit in the gang. It is not uncommon to see little "punks" of five or six "dragging" at a cigarette or puffing a big cigar. The use of snuff is very common; a gang of boys in knee pants, for example, all kept their supplies in improvised tin boxes which they carried in the knees of their knicker-bockers. One important element in the fascination which smoking holds for the boy is that it is ordinarily contrary to parental wishes and hence is a sign of emancipation from all the restraints of home control. It gives a feeling of self-direction and independence which is very agree-able to the adolescent.

In the consumption of alcoholic beverages, the gang is simply following the customs of most of the immigrant groups from which the gang boy usually comes. The par-ents have their own stills and drink at home; the young men of the neighborhood follow suit; and the boys imitate their big brothers.

The secret of the gang is not that it initiates new inter-ests; the impulses to which it gives expression are so ele-mental and immediate that they are bound to find an out-let somewhere. It is not that the gang gives a direction and pattern to impulses that might find expression elsewhere; its movements are altogether too random and ill defined. The gang's patterns of activity are determined largely by the environment and the patterns that it discovers in the world about it.[15] *The fundamental fact about the gang is that it finds in the boys who become its members a fund of energy that is undirected, undisciplined, and uncontrolled by any socially desirable pattern, and it gives to that energy an opportunity for expression in the freest, the most spontaneous and elemental manner possible, and at the same time intensifies all the natural impulses by the process of cumulative stimulation.*

[15] See chap. xii.

CHAPTER VI

The Rôle of the Romantic

Adolescent fancies cast over the world—too often trite and ugly to the adult—the rosy light of novelty and romance. Even what has become most commonplace to the sophisticated, holds a genuine fascination for the gang boy. He sees in a broken sewer a sea on which sails the Spanish Armada. A sour basement becomes an ogre's cave; a dank areaway, a glorified castle. To him the piles of rubbish in the city dumps or the mud hills along the drainage canal are mountain fastnesses, while stretches of wasteland become prairies of the Golden West. He hoists the "skull and crossbones" over an old boiler as a perfect pirate ship. He digs an Ali Baba's cave in the forest preserve and is discovered only when he brings in a bit of spring water to be tested by the city bacteriologist.

45. Visions of treasure islands, Spanish galleons, and pieces of eight flitted forever for ten young freebooters last night when two policemen lodged them in the juvenile detention home. The leader of the gang, who is only fifteen, had found a cave in the river bank near Racine Avenue, organized his band, and started out to fly the Jolly Roger against the walled cities along the drainage canal.

Cutlasses and marlin spikes were needed, not to mention a revolver or two, so the boys looted an army and navy goods store in the vicinity Sunday night. Monday night they stocked up with ice-cream cones and candies from a convenient confectionery. They devoted Memorial Day to plundering a grocery. All they lacked was the pirate ship. They were to have seized that last night. "And at the rate they were going," said one of the coppers, "they would have had a whole fleet before the end of the week."[1]

While gangs vary in this respect, one boy who responds imaginatively will liven up the most sodden group.

46. I lived on the lower side of town, where the "tough-mugs" were. Being more imaginative than the rest of the gang, I amused them with my fancies and furnished the idea for many an adventure. I used to listen by the hour to the tales of a circus performer, who told me of a mysterious rope cave located along a neighboring cliff. This spot became enshrined in our imaginations as the quintessence of romance, and to discover it became our greatest ambition. We got a man to show us the place where it was supposed to be. I organized the boys like Alpine explorers. With a clothesline about our waists tying us together, we scaled the cliff. At last we discovered the cave, and there, sure enough was the old rope hanging out, just as the circus man had told us. We dug the recess deeper, and made it our rendezvous. We never succeeded in finding the hidden treasure, but we had a wonderful time up there.[2]

IMAGINARY CHARACTERS

Not only does the gang boy transform his sordid environment through his imagination, but he lives among soldiers and knights, pirates and banditti. His enemies are assigned special rôles: the crabby old lady across the alley is a witch; the neighborhood cop becomes a man-killing giant or a robber baron; and the rival gang in the next block is a hostile army. Sometimes he creates companions where they are lacking.

47. My pal and I belonged to the Silent Three. The third member, who made us a gang, was a very terrible and mysterious personage. He was really the dominant figure in our triumvirate although he was entirely imaginary. We had a cave in which solemn conclave was held. Secret ceremonies of the most diabolical charac-

[1] News item.

[2] Interview with a former member of the group.

ter took place there, including cursing and spitting on the American flag. We were at odds with the world, to which we felt ourselves superior. To protect our secrets we developed a series of symbols and writings which nobody else could possibly fathom. We also had hidden places where we buried our treasures with the utmost solemnity.[3]

Adolescence is also an age of hero worshiping; and the gang boy acts out the rôles of the fictitious or real persons whom he most admires: Robin Hood and Captain Kidd, or "the big gun around the corner"—a notorious criminal, a prize fighter, the most vicious boy in the neighborhood, or even a tramp.

To boys the tramp is not a problem, but a human being, and an interesting one at that. He has no cares nor burdens to hold him down. All he is concerned with is to live and seek adventure, and in this he personifies the heroes in the stories the boys have read. Tramp life is an invitation to a career of promise and a challenge. A promise that all the wishes that disturb him shall be fulfilled, and a challenge to leave the workaday world that he is bound to.[4]

It is heroes like these whom he may surround with a halo of glory and emulate as he grows older.

IMAGINATIVE EXPLOITS

"Be blythe of heart for any adventure"[5] might well be the slogan of the gang boy. The sport motive provides one key to the interpretation of the behavior of the gang. The imaginative interest affords another. Exploits and activities which are nonsensical or merely mischievous to the adult have an entirely different meaning to the boy in quest of adventure.

48. The boys in my gang, which numbered about fifteen, have played with each other since we were wee little fellows. One day we discovered a large chicken coop in the alley behind the home of

[3] Manuscript prepared by a former member of the group.

[4] Nels Anderson, *The Hobo*, p. 85.

[5] William Dunbar.

one of the boys. I saw immediately that it had possibilities for a clubroom, which had long been a cherished ambition of the gang. We moved in at once with such furniture as we could drag through a little three-by-four door. We became the "Polar Bears" and excited the envy of all the other boys in our suburban community. Our rivals now got busy and established a club of their own in the attic of a grocery store.

I thought I was pretty tough then. I smoked, shot with a revolver, and fought. When we had our gang fights we would make up a lot of stuff about armies. Most of the kids would stay away from home during the period of hostilities. We were interested in a lot of things beside fighting. One older boy, who was making an aeroplane, excited great admiration among us. He worked on it for four years and got everything just right. When he tried to fly it, it would not go in the air more than twenty-five feet. He used to fly along the ground. I think he was a-scared to go higher.

One day when we came back to our hang-out, we found the chicken coop nailed up. We found a new rendezvous in a basement under the old police station. We played in the old police cells and had a great time down there. We found a lot of stuff stored away, and helped ourselves freely. Among other things, there were flag-staffs, which we converted into swords for dueling.

We went to the movies about every other day, and it was from a picture that we got the suggestion for our new name—"The Alley Rats Knights of the Round Table." Our new hang-out was near a bakery where they kept a lot of pineapple. We would get it from the kegs, and a lot of peaches and other stuff, for our feasts. There were very few boys in the gang who did not steal.

In the summertime we liked to cook our food in the open. We would go out where there were not many houses and get eggs and chickens every Sunday. One time the sister of one of the boys swiped a chicken for us, and stuck it under her coat. We took it to the foundations of an old house, where we twisted its head off, made a fire, and cooked it. We ate it, although it was hardly done enough.

At harvest time we'd go to a haystack and slide down and climb around on the great piles of baled hay. We like to make little huts and we'd go out in the cornfields and build them out of the stalks, so that we could smoke without being disturbed. They are getting too many houses out there now—they spoil the prairies.

We had certain special places that we liked to go. One of these was Wasp Jones's gravel pit, where we liked to swim. There was a big bull there, and we had a lot of fun with him. We would always tie our clothes in the legs of our pants, so that if we saw him coming, we could grab them and run. One day the bull came before we got them tied up, and all seven of us had to shin it up a tree.

Another place we liked to go to was a monastery near a pond where the cows drank. After school we'd go swimming there. We called it the "Pope's pond," and I had a bicycle on which I would ride three boys, and we called that the "Pope's taxi."

Another favorite place was what we called the "Willows," near which was the haunted house. Inside, the wall was broken in big cracks and the plaster was falling off. The first time I went in, the boys tried to scare me. They slammed a door when I was in the attic. I jumped out onto the roof and got away. We liked to go in there for the man to chase us, but one day when we came he had a gun. It was a lot of fun there; whenever the plaster would fall it would scare you.

We used to flip the freights and go to the water-tower to play. I ran away twice with some of the boys. We wanted to stay on the freights, but we got caught at Waukegan and were sent home. Mother does not want me to stay out at all, but one day we ran away to Desplaines and slept there all night. We took lots of clothes with us for a long trip, but a man with a star saw us when we tried to catch a train, and told us to go back or we would be put in Parental [School]. We went back half way to Chicago, and then we got a freight that took us a hundred miles the other side of Elgin.

The gang finally got caught and sent away for a robbing expedition.[6]

The wanderings of the gang become great imaginative enterprises for the boys, for they are exploring the mysteries of worlds which are new to them. The leader of a gang of adolescents, who were hiking west from the city, told the rest of the boys they would soon reach the Mississippi. All of them, with the exception of "one big Swede," knew that they would not succeed in doing that for they had not come to Joliet, but they got a great thrill out of pretending, just the same, and they all hurried so that they could reach the great river, "where the covered wagons went through," before nightfall.

[6] Gang boy's own story.

NIGHT

The best time for the romantic exploits of the gang is at night. "The night hath a thousand eyes," and they are all winking their invitations to boys to come out and play. Danger and adventure lurk in every dark corner. Opportunity for daring is increased a hundred fold. Under the mantle of darkness the gang can do its mischief and make its escape.

A common complaint of parents is that the gang boy stays out at all hours of the night. In certain areas, like South State Street, Maxwell Street, and South Halsted Street, it is a frequent observation that the boys actually suffer from lack of sleep, so great are the night attractions of those regions.[7]

49. It got too dark to continue gambling at Rummie on the street corner, and the gang started to move. After several unsuccessful attempts to "shake" me, they gave it up and permitted me to range about the neighborhood with them. It was a warm evening and children were swarming under every light. We went first to see an oil fire, which had been burning all day. I wanted to proceed farther, but one of the boys said, "Don't go that way, that's niggertown; it ain't safe!"

Then we wandered through dark alleys toward Maxwell Street. The boys kept running hither and thither, giving each other the slip in the darkness and emerging at unexpected places. When we got to the market, we purchased "polly" seeds [roasted sunflower seeds, tasting something like pistachio nuts].

After several trips up and down the crowded business street, it was decided that we should eat chop suey, that is, if I agreed to pay for it. I wanted the boys to go into a Chinese place and sit down at the tables, but this seemed quite a foreign notion to them.

"Oh, you want to go where de dukes are," said one of them. "Dat's where de rich people go—where you have to go in and *sit down!* Not me!"

Then there followed a great flood of protestations from the gang. They'd take their chop suey in a bucket and eat it in the open, or not at all.

After our feast we continued from one place of interest to an-

[7] See documents 55 and 56.

other. When I left the gang, it was very late, but I was convinced
that the adventures of the night had just begun.[8]

THE REALM OF ADVENTURE

Every gang has its own domain, which may be conceived best in terms of the imaginative world in which the
gang boy lives. This is a realm of adventure centering in
the hang-out, which the gang boy regards as his castle.
The area immediately surrounding this cherished spot is
home territory, beyond whose borders lie the lands of the
enemy and the great unknown world. In addition there
are special playgrounds of the gang where the boys find
unusual opportunities for amusement and adventure.
Most of the activities of the group have a definite relation
to this geographical division of its world.

THE GANG BOY'S CASTLE

The hang-out is the hub of the gang boy's universe.
It is a place to loaf and enjoy good fellowship. Exploits
are planned and loot is divided there. Boys sleeping away
from home frequently find in it a haven where rest and
food may be obtained. It is also an asylum from officers
of the law. Whether it be a cave in a mud hill, a prairie,
a deserted shack, or just a street corner, it is dear to the
gang boy's heart and is to be protected against marauders
at all costs. It is his palace and citadel combined, and
from its turrets he looks out and sees in all the dreary
raggedness of the slum a world full of adventure and
romance.

In the present investigation, data with reference to
the hang-outs of the gang were secured in 1,288 cases.

50. Approximately 726 gangs have their hang-outs out of
doors; 535 of these are street gangs which usually meet on the
corners. In many cases they choose their vantage points because of

[8] Observations by the author.

Photo by Author

Photo by Author

RENDEZVOUS

Above is a bit of the "city wilderness" which served as a camping ground for the "Tent Gang." (See document 57.) The bridge over the reserve canal links territories of rival gangs and is often the scene of pitched battles. Gangs of adolescent freebooters burrow into the mud-hills along the canals in these areas of "no-man's land."

Below is the "broke-down" cave of the Rinkus gang. The hole at the right of the picture was formerly its castle, but the police or an enemy gang came through one day and "broke it down."

proximity to such interests as ballgrounds, garages, moving-picture theaters, poolrooms, fire departments, stoneyards, roundhouses, and swimming pools. Others select their meeting places near some business which may afford victims for teasing, or chances to "cop" supplies; viz., fruit stores, groceries, drug stores, saloons, breweries, and railroad tracks.

Alleys are found to be the favorite rendezvous of 24 gangs; more fortunate are 44 others that meet in open spaces like vacant lots, fields, and prairies, which afford better opportunities for games. Ten of the out-of-door gangs frequent athletic fields, church yards, or the frontage along canals, rivers, and the lake. In 102 cases they meet in or near parks, playgrounds, schoolyards and social settlements. Nine gangs hold forth under bridges, viaducts, and the elevated tracks.

While all gangs like the open and most of them roam about on occasion, nevertheless this study reveals 562 whose chief hangouts are indoors. There is hardly a street gang that does not aspire to have, be it ever so humble, a clubroom of its own. Eight are content with caves, holes and dug-outs; 24 boast shacks, shanties, sheds, and huts; 4 dwell in barns; and 22 reside in basements. Thirty-one gangs have their headquarters in homes, cottages, flats, or storerooms of one description or another. In some cases they are welcomed in a business place which may enjoy their patronage; thus there are 30 hanging out in barber shops, candy stores, soft-drink parlors, delicatessens, cigar stores, hotels, and lunchrooms.

Some of the social influences which play upon the gangs may be inferred from the fact that 3 meet regularly in bowling alleys, 6 in saloons, 7 in dance halls, and 52 in poolrooms. Our investigation indicates that 368 of the 562 gangs which have indoor hangouts have the use of some sort of clubroom, either rented or donated, but the exact nature of these accommodations is not specified. Most of this group are gangs of the so-called athletic club type, which rent quarters or have them furnished by politicians and others dependent upon their patronage.

HOME TERRITORY

The home territory, usually the immediate neighborhood in which the boys are living, may extend for a block or two in crowded sections or may cover the whole local community in the sparsely settled suburban areas. The boys know every foot of ground, every nook and corner, of this region which they regard as exclusively their own and will defend valiantly against invaders.

In some cases the gang has very definite ideas as to the boundaries of its home territory. Just as among nations borderline disputes sometimes precipitate disastrous wars, so gangs may be mobilized and led to battle on the same issue.

ENEMY TERRITORY

Beyond the frontiers of the gang's home territory lie the domains of the enemy. Rival gangs hold sway in these regions.

51. The group to the east of us, we called "Snodgrass' bunch," though it was commonly known as the "Fifty-seventh gang" because of the number of the block. Snodgrass was the leader, and the gang was composed of about six boys, all from that block. They met any place in the summer and by appointment in the winter, though Brady's barn was the favorite hang-out. They went in for athletic games, gang mischief such as getting shags and hitching, and occasional arguments with our group.

The "Fifty-nines," on the other side of us, we usually called "the next block gang." They were the least closely organized of the various groups. Their activities were much the same as the Fifty-sevenths, and their habitual meeting place was in the shed in back of their leader's home.

The Ontarios lived on the street of that name, and were fairly good friends of ours. They met in a shed, and we exchanged amities and occasional hostilities across the alley. They drew their gang from several blocks, and had about ten boys, altogether. They were a little older than our bunch and played a good deal of pool in the attic of the home of one of the boys. They had an athletic club in the shed.

The Park Avenue gang was the toughest. Park Avenue was the business street, and these fellows lived above the stores; they hung out back of the grocery for which their leader delivered goods after school. They were about seven in number and indulged in a great deal of mischief. We exchanged hostilities with them often but never came to actual blows but once.

The last of the groups was the Catholic gang. Our gang was Protestant, and these Catholic boys from the north, coming through our territory on their way to school, made us their enemies. They had a remarkable disregard for other people's property, and we first became provoked at them when they got the habit of picking up souvenirs when they went through our yards on their way home. We had many battles with them, and often chased them out of our block.[9]

To the narrow outlook and inexperience of the adolescent gang boy, unforeseen dangers lurk in these outside regions. Many of the groups of smaller boys never stray beyond their own neighborhood, although as they get older their horizon gradually expands. In enemy territory the authorities and the police are more formidable; these regions, moreover, are often in possession of other races, nationalities, or social strata; they are decidedly unsafe, particularly if a boy is alone.

52. If you come into the neighborhood of the Wolves, who have their rendezvous in the Black Belt, they stop you up and the first thing they ask is, "What's your name?"

Then, "Where do you live?"

If you say you live on Fifty-fifth Street, they say, "Don't you know you haven't any business here?"

Biff! and you like to never get out alive![10]

Nor are the dangers to be encountered in enemy territory confined to the adolescent gangs. The same thing applies in general to the older groups. Individuals from rival areas are often stopped and held up.

53. A group of Bridgeport people went for a picnic, in automobile trucks. They had to pass through Cicero on the way. Cicero gangs stopped some of the machines and took money, pop, and edibles. In retaliation four cars of young men from Bridgeport made a raid in Cicero. Any time they heard of a Cicero man coming to Bridgeport they would mob him. Gangs in both regions were involved, and the police had to put a stop to it by picking participants up and putting them into the "paddy" wagons.[11]

[9]Manuscript prepared by a former member of the group.

[10] Gang boy's own story.   [11] Interview.

THE UNSEEING ADULT

It is hard for the grown-up with all his responsibilities and practical necessities to retain an understanding of the boy's imaginative outlook on life. Unless he is an "adolescent hold-over," he becomes too thoroughly conventionalized and incorporated in the social machinery of his community. He loses sympathetic touch with youth and becomes a scoffer at the precious dreams and sentiments which are such an essential part of boyhood. On this account he rarely has a complete understanding of the boy.

Autobiographical materials (life-histories) are coming to have a prominent place in the scientific literature of child study. It is being recognized that methods of dealing with behavior problems of children must be evaluated chiefly in terms of their effects upon the internal attitudes and sentiments of the child rather than his immediate external behavior and the formal theories underlying such methods. *Such materials as have been collected indicate how differently children respond to situations from the ways in which adults respond to the same situations and from the ways in which adults expect the children to respond.* The additional development of this type of material will serve to illuminate the whole field of juvenile delinquency and make methods of dealing with problem children more intelligent and more effective.

The "channels of communication," as Jane Addams points out, between youth and the adult are often closed.

54. "There is great difficulty in keeping open the channels of communication between the younger generation and those of us who go back to the mid-Victorian or early Victorian in our experiences." . . . .

Then when we come to the crime wave, "one is very much bewildered." Miss Addams cited two incidents in support of the point that "here again the channels of communication are closed." One was that of a fourteen-year-old girl thief who could not believe that an understanding interrogator had not herself had experience in crime. The other was that of a girl brought into the Juvenile Court—a girl who had just stood at a corner, had been asked by a man to take a ride in his automobile, and had been out all night. A social worker remonstrated that she had stood on corners but had never been asked to take such an automobile ride, and the girl said, "Well, just chase yourself to a looking-glass and you'll find out why."

Miss Addams told several other incidents illustrating how difficult it is to comprehend their views when one tries to talk with some of the boys of today. She told of five boys "in one neighborhood who had stolen a tire from a car of a teacher." The teacher said that he would not prosecute them if the boys paid him $15.00. The boys said: "We only got $2.00 for the tire; why should we pay $15.00?"

"A boy of sixteen in our club boasted that he had $6,000 in the bank. His bank book showed that this was so. He said he had earned it by driving a "booze wagon" twice a week from Chicago to Joliet. He got $200 a trip because there was so much danger from hijackers. He had saved his money, had gone to a university and was quite sure his $6,000 would more than put him through. There again it was hard to make the boy understand. He cited, as with bootleggers, the men supposed to be buying, and he "painted all with one brush."[12]

Although so much of the gang boy's life is fanciful, it often has the utmost reality for him, and many times he does not distinguish between what is real and what is not. He interprets his own social situations in his own terms and with the utmost seriousness.

To understand the gang boy one must enter into his world with a comprehension, on the one hand, of this seriousness behind his mask of flippancy or bravado, and on the other, of the rôle of the romantic in his activities and in his interpretation of the larger world of reality.

[12] Report of an address on "The Spirit of Youth Today," *City Club Bulletin*, December 28, 1925.

CHAPTER VII

Playgrounds of the Gang

The playgrounds of the gang are areas where gang boys find unusual opportunities for amusement and adventure, not offered in their home territory. The most important of these are certain streets, the canals and the river, the lake front, the Loop, the newspaper alleys, the amusement parks, the forest preserves, and the railroad tracks.

PICTURESQUE BUSINESS STREETS

Two business streets kaleidoscopic in their movement of life and with numerous possibilities for petty thievery along their crowded thoroughfares are South Halsted and Maxwell.

55. South Halsted is an area of excitement and mobility. The quarter is too congested for privacy, and the ordinary taboos of social intercourse are largely absent. Even the passer-by may observe the intimate life of its residents.

In one of the Greek coffee-houses one may see a wedding in plain view of the public. There is no room for it at home, and the coffee-house is equipped with a stage and three musicians. Here thirty guests of a nuptial party are regaling themselves. Everybody is there, from "granny" down to the youngest.

A little farther along a horse has keeled over on the sidewalk. Somebody from the crowd is massaging its abdomen. "What's the matter?" we inquire. "Why, the horse has a belly-ache," is the matter-of-fact reply.

Stolen goods are being disposed of in a restaurant where an excited crowd is hunting bargains. This is a neighborly sort of place, with someone playing a piano at the back of the room.

Cheap movies abound, and the gangs travel from one to another.

A "wild wop," crazed with moonshine, dashes madly from a side street, followed by a crowd of his countrymen who are attempting to restrain him. They catch him, but he breaks away, and starts after a woman with a small and demure male escort. The little man surprises the crowd by knocking the giant into the gutter with a heavy blow well planted between the eyes. The wild man jumps up and starts running again, with his friends in noisy pursuit.

An additional chapter of a Greek gamester's feud is enacted openly. A man seats himself on a doorstep. An unknown assailant, thought to be a retainer of the murdered "King George," a gambling chieftain, shoots him with a rifle fired from a second-story window on the opposite side of the street. Incidentally a few stray bullets pass through a plate-glass window where some innocent social workers are having a conference.

Picturesque gypsies go hither and thither in their bright calicoes and gaudy beads. Many "parlors" have been established for fortune telling and palm reading. Romantic tales are related, too, of gypsy love, gypsy gold, and gypsy hate, and occasionally the "kings" of the tribe air their quarrels in the city courts. It was in one of these lairs on Halsted Street not so long ago that a father sold his fifteen-year-old girl to the highest bidder, for the sum of $1,660.

At another place a great crowd of people jam the sidewalk. "What's the matter here?" we ask. "Oh, a lady shot herself right in her belly-button!" comes the answer. "Her husband has a crippled arm, and they have had some trouble with their daughter." Sights and stories like these are an everyday matter with the children, who are usually the first to be attracted by any disturbance.[1]

Gangs are attracted from all directions by the picturesque and lively sights to be found on Maxwell Street and not infrequently come long distances to tease and rob the Jewish tradesmen.

56. The Maxwell Street Market, which stretches for about five blocks along Maxwell and centers at Halsted, is the great Rialto

[1] Observations by the author and others.

of the poorer class of Jewish tradesmen. Begun in the nineties, the market has expanded until today it is said that $1,000,000 worth of business a month is transacted there. Investigation has revealed, too, that thousands of dollars worth of stolen goods have been sold each year through numerous "fences" [receivers of stolen goods].

The market extends between low, dilapidated tenements, the first floors of which are used as stores and shops of all descriptions. The sidewalks and streets are lined with stands and carts, from which every conceivable commodity is sold—from "kosher" meat to moonshine stills. What space is left in the middle of the street is crowded with an unending throng of pedestrians and some few vehicles, struggling through the surging mass of bargain-hunters.

Weary old men and worn young children stand behind the little carts. As an observer was jotting down a few facts beside one of the fish stands, he heard a weak voice from a boy of fifteen, "What statistics are you taking down? Write my name there too— I want my name in the paper." As he was passing by another stand, a tired-looking little girl remarked, "I know what you are doing, you want to know about human people in the Ghetto."

In the streets, piled high beside the little carts, are crates containing anything from live poultry to eggs and oranges. In the stalls or dumped right out on the pavement are all sorts of wares— hardware, toys, trinkets, fresh fish and fowls, groceries, shoes, and furniture. It is an endless display of an endless variety of things.

The Jewish tradesmen who conduct the business of the market are very enterprising and eventually they usually move out of the Ghetto to more prosperous communities. Occasionally a storekeeper becomes overeager for business, and resorts to "pulling." A complaining witness in one of these cases tells his story to the court:

"I didn't need no suit, but he grabs me by the arm, drags me inside, and tells me if I don't take advantage of a bargain sale and buy a suit he'll crack me in the eye. I told 'im those suits would be all right for guys that carry umbrellas and he hit me."

The air is filled with the odor of fresh fish and garlic, and there is a ceaseless din—noise of victrolas, parrots, men crying out their wares, women calling to each other, hens cackling, roosters crowing, and babies crying, all at once.

Old men and women in the costumes which they have worn for generations look like pictures from some old copy-book. An old patriarch stands beside the little charcoal oven where he roasts corn or bakes potatoes. His gray beard reaches almost to his knees, his long black overcoat sweeps the ground, and his cap is pulled tightly over his ears.

On another corner we see a group of children gathered about a big farm-wagon to watch a fake Indian-charmer give an exhibition. In the middle of the street, beneath a large umbrella, sits an old man having his toenails cut. A man in a green coat, a pack on his back, comes along with little birds that "pick out your fortune." Occasionally gypsies pass to and fro, adding color to the scene.[2]

RIVERS, CANALS, AND LAKE FRONT

The wastelands and prairies adjacent to the city's numerous canals and slips, along the various branches and forks of the Chicago River, and near the unimproved portion of the lake front make ideal "camp grounds." Good hiding places for games are found here and boating, wading, and swimming even in polluted waters attract the gang boys.

57. The Tent Gang, which grew out of the Tigers' Club, had about fourteen boys, from fifteen to seventeen years old. We decided the best place to pitch our camp was a waste space by the Illinois and Michigan Reserve Canal.

We had blankets, a jug for water, two chairs and a table, a bench, a deck of cards, and some dice. We brought our fishing-tackle and bathing-tights—if we could find any. We had lots of eats stored away in the tent, for some of the boys had been working and they would buy stuff. We got a lot of canned goods from the railroad cars. Sometimes we would go robbing, but I always got caught; I only got away with it a couple of times. We'd get bread from the bread-boxes in front of stores; we had duplicate keys. This was a common way of getting food when we were bumming from home.

The Tent Gang was Dago and Polish, and our leader, "Bowlegs," was the oldest and brainiest kid in the gang and was with us everywhere. He led us all up and down the canal, looking for adventures. We went fishing and swimming too. Whenever we'd get a shag [get chased], we'd hide along the canal. The watchman from the Santa Fe would always shag us and shoot a couple of times into the air, but he could never catch us for there was always plenty

[2] Observations by the author and others.

Photo by Author

Photo by Author

FASCINATING STREET LIFE

The many gypsies who have moved into the South Halsted Street area constitute a colorful element in gangland. They carry on their ancient customs, even to child-selling, in their fortune-telling booths and palmistry "parlors." (See document 55.) Below is a group of children on Maxwell Street. The street educates with fatal precision. These informal aspects of education are far more vital in the life of the child than the conventional types. Children in these areas are usually prematurely sophisticated.

of good places to hide. Sometimes we got in trouble for robbing or breaking windows. We used to fight the West Siders, who lived north of the canal, and who were mostly Bohemians.

We only got to keep our tent about three weeks, for one rainy day the squads [police] came through and broke it down. The whole gang was there and they wanted to know who owned the tent. Most of the gang was sent to the Parental [School for truants] for bumming school. What was left of us hung out at a street corner after that, to wait till our pals came back.[3]

Gangs like the "Hillers" live like cliff dwellers, in caves among the mud hills formed by the excavation of the canals. These regions are usually gang frontiers and borderlands, which are often the scene of bitter conflict by rival claimants. Like the gullies of Cleveland or the wharves of New York, they are neglected areas that constitute a sort of no man's land. Not infrequently squatter families in shacks or house boats defy all the minions of the law. Lawlessness is common among them and litigation is often necessary for eviction. In these regions gangs which escape social control may lead an irresponsible or criminal life.

58. The "Mudlakers" built themselves a shack in one of the hills thrown up in digging the old Illinois Lockport Canal. This was a rough bunch, with about forty members, aged sixteen to nineteen, and mostly Bohemian in nationality. In case of an offense in this neighborhood, they were always the first whom the police suspected. A few of them worked, but some were always loafing. Most of them had police records.

All of them gambled. Some of them were expert crap-shooters and would clean up as much as $40 in an afternoon by means of loaded dice. They engaged in a good many fights, usually fistic. They used to cause trouble by setting the wooden bridge on fire at Lawndale Avenue. They would also break windows and break into school buildings. In one case they stole pencils, ink, story-books, and light bulbs, and ripped the telephone off the wall trying to get the nickels out. They also broke up the furniture.

[3] Gang boy's own story.

Later in their development, they rented a room in a cottage and called themselves a club.[4]

The undeveloped portion of the lake front has limitless opportunities for swimming, fishing, gambling, and unsupervised play. The "McMullens" attracted attention by burning a fiery cross there. Another gang stoned a man almost to death when he remonstrated with them for scaring the fish away. In a clash on one of these unpatrolled beaches the race riots of 1919 had their origin.

THE LOOP

The Loop (Chicago's central business area) with all its crowds, its bustle, its excitement, and its bright lights, attracts gang boys in twos and threes, but usually not the gang as a whole. There is too much danger of suspicion from watchful eyes. The two portions of the Loop most frequented by the boys are the South State Street district and the newspaper alleys.

60. South State Street is fundamentally a man's street, and its business caters largely to the transient element in the masculine population. It is the playground of Hobohemia as well as of the gangs.[5] It is the haunt of foot-loose country boys and lonely sailors. Gang boys, little Arabs of the street, may be seen at night wandering about in twos and threes. Streetwalkers pass quickly along, glancing furtively from side to side. Cheap jewelry stores run auction sales, at which raucous-voiced spielers crack jokes at the expense of sleepy hobos. The swinging doors of the missions beckon to the sinful or despairing. There is a penny arcade showing the more spicy pictures, like *Milady's Bath*, for a nickel. A tattooing parlor has many customers and puts the eternal stamp of an anchor, a spread eagle, or an undressed woman on a brawny arm or a hairy chest, for a very modest sum. Pictures of naked girls loom on all sides in front of the cheap burlesque theaters, where men only (and boys) may see the latest Bowery beauties specializing in legs and shapes and tights (or lack of them).[6]

[4] Interview.   [5] Nels Anderson, *The Hobo*, pp. 7, 8.

[6] Observations by the author.

THE NEWSPAPER ALLEYS

Wherever a chance for excitement is coupled with the opportunity to pick up an easy living, the gang is doubly sure to appear. This has been the situation in the "alleys," really distributing rooms, of some of the down-town newspapers. Here is a focus of great mobility, which has long had a disorganizing effect upon boys.

61. Into each of these two distributing rooms came nightly, during the time of the inquiry, from forty to eighty men and boys. They began to arrive at about 6:00 P.M.; and while they waited for the 9:45 edition they gambled, fought, drank, boasted, and swore the time away. . . . . .

Among the alley lodgers and frequenters, our investigator found runaways from all parts of the country: from New York, from Ohio, from Oklahoma, from Montana, from California. Seven youths had "bummed" to Chicago from the West. A homesick Italian boy who had run away from Buffalo and wept intermittently for several days was sent home by the Juvenile Court. There were also many Illinois boys who had run away from Pontiac, St. Charles, the Parental School, and other correctional institutions.

Abandoned space under the sidewalk and the opportunities for eluding capture offered by adjoining low buildings made the "port of missing boys" a natural refuge for those who wished to escape the inquiries of their relatives, the truant officers, or the police.

In both the alleys indecent stories prevailed. . . . . Two of the frequenters of the alleys, men in charge of news stands, openly boasted of their success in acting as panderers for streetwalkers. . . . . Indecent songs were sung.

There was much thieving among the men and boys, both inside and outside the alleys. . . . . Young boys offered bargains in articles stolen inside the department stores. They would go into the stores in groups, and while one of their number made a trifling purchase, the rest would elbow goods off the counter to the floor, and get away with it to the alley.

Gambling was a regular practice in the alleys. . . . . The boys often lost so much in gambling that they were obliged to stint themselves in food the next day.

Many of the boys drank heavily. This was undoubtedly caused in the case of those who lived in the alleys by an insufficient, irregu-

lar, and improperly balanced diet. . . . . The filthiness of most of
the boys in the alleys was extreme. Many of them were verminous.
. . . . Few of the boys were above begging for money, clothes, or
whatever they needed.[7]

As a result of special policing, boys under sixteen were
kept out of the news alleys for a time. The stories of
several gang boys, procured in connection with the present study, however, indicate that these places still harbor
floating youth and that as yet the gangs have not forsaken
them. Many boys have been observed loafing in the alleys, in one of which a crap game was in progress in a
small court directly behind a policeman's back.

PARKS AND FOREST PRESERVES

The playgrounds and the parks are often used by
gangs, and gang boys frequently go *en masse* for over-
night hikes or camping expeditions to Fox Lake, the
Desplaines River, and the various forest preserves adjoining the city.

The forest preserves, like the river and canal regions,
tend to become areas of escape from social control and
may shelter squatter families as well as gangs, all living
according to their own inclination.

63. About twenty of the Woodstreeters used to go out to the
forest preserve to camp. I bought a tent from my uncle for $15,
for which he had paid $179. It was big enough for about eleven
boys to sleep in. We did lots of fishing out there, and there was an
old German who used to swear a lot because he wouldn't get any
fish. His son got a big eighteen-pound carp. We'd go swimming
and rowing too. We'd take a boat a fellow had, use it, and then
put it back.

When we got hungry we used to go around to the farmers'
orchards and strip their pears. Each boy would take a hundred-
pound potato bag, and we'd load these with apples and pears to
carry home. Sometimes we'd go robbin', breaking into stores and
box cars in the freight yards. One time we found a little cave by
the river with human bones in it. My brother found in a shed the

[7] Elsa Wertheim, *Chicago Children in the Street Trades*, pp. 5-7.

body of a man with his arms and head off. When we heard about these things they would scare us, but we liked it.[8]

The forest preserve sometimes provides a hiding place for a criminal gang.

64. Three fellows and a girl, all happy-go-lucky nomads whose only home for the last several weeks had been an army tent in a forest preserve, were forced to pitch camp in the Hudson Avenue police station late Saturday night. They were charged with operating an extensive automobile theft scheme, in which more than fifty high-priced machines are said to have been stolen from Grant Park and the Loop during three months.

Before their arrest the wandering quartet had pitched their tent in the forest preserve at Eighty-seventh Street and Western Avenue. Two policemen who have been traversing the region for several days made the arrests.

The stolen cars taken to the camp were remodeled and repainted in the silence of the forest. The leader of the gang, who was the "star-salesman," disposed of the revamped machines. Twelve cars were recovered by the police.

The girl, who asserted proudly that she was the sweetheart of one of the men, was the housekeeper, and looked after the tent while the rest of the gang were in the city.[9]

THE "SITUATION COMPLEX"

The structure and behavior of a gang is molded in part through its accommodation to its life conditions. The groups in the Ghetto, in a suburb, along a business street in the residential district, in a midwestern town, or in a lumber community vary in their interests and activities not only according to the social patterns of their respective milieus but also according to the layout of the buildings, streets, alleys, and public works, and the general topography of their environments. These various conditioning factors within which the gang lives, moves, and has its being, may be regarded as the "situation com-

[8] Gang boy's own story.

[9] News item.

"PRAIRIES" WHERE GANG BOYS PLAY

The boys call these neglected open spaces, numerous in gangland, "prairies." That they are full of rubbish and discarded objects only makes them more interesting as play-grounds. Below is shown the ball diamonds of the Rinkus gang on property being held for industrial purposes.

plex," within which the human nature elements interact
to produce gang phenomena.

A change in the setting of a gang is likely to result in
an alteration in its program of activities.

66. The Bearcats, who are a mixture of four or five nationalities, meet in an old tenement. Their activities are sports and games,
teasing drunks, and stealing fruit, melons, and chickens, which
are available in the neighboring countryside. They did not begin
to shoot craps until the new sewer from Gary into the Calumet
River spoiled their fishing and swimming hole.[10]

The *man-made* factors in the gang's impersonal environment are of equal importance in their influence upon
the location and nature of its activities. In New York,
where boys have such restricted play space and where the
tenement provides the chief form of housing for the poor,
adolescent gang life differs from that in Chicago. Chicago,
comparatively young and free from tenements, sprawls
over a large territory and most of its congested areas have
many ramshackle buildings and hide-out places for the
gangs. Railroads and sources of junk, such as empty
houses, alleys, and rubbish dumps, also condition the life
of Chicago gangs in important respects. A blind street, a
hemmed in or isolated housing situation, a group of dwellings fronting on an inclosed court or private street, or a
large number of flats above the first story in an exclusively business area like South State Street give a particular
trend to the group life of the boys living within their con-
fines. These are but a few of the many cases where technic situations condition the gang; illustrations of the
working of this principle are to be found in the various
case-studies presented throughout the book.

[10] Interviews.

CHAPTER VIII

Junking and the Railroads

An activity of the gang which provides ample opportunity for excitement and revenue is the gathering of junk. Junking is representative of the intimate relationship existing between the activities of a group and its immediate physical, technic, and social environment.

67. . . . . The junk business was seen to have passed through successive stages, changing in form until it became stable in three types—the wagon, the retail shop, and the wholesale shop. . . . . The wagon peddler comes into direct relation with the boy and represents the chief point of contact between junk-dealing and juvenile delinquency. There are between 1,700 and 1,800 of these wagon peddlers in Chicago. In the past five years they have doubled in number, while the retail junk shops have increased only 50 per cent.[1]

One important factor in the situation is the presence of numerous junk-dealers of whom many are anxious to buy from boys.

68. Frank said he rode with his father when he went collecting and that "sometimes on the North Side as many as twenty-five boys come to the wagon to sell things—rags, brass, and bottles. On the West Side, sometimes three to five boys sell things to my

[1] Albert E. Webster, *Junk Dealing and Juvenile Delinquency*, an investigation made for the Juvenile Protective Association of Chicago by Harry H. Grigg and George E. Haynes.

father in a day. . . . . They come to the house from six o'clock in the evening on until eight." Frank said that his father never required the boys to bring any written paper from their parents.

Junkmen sometimes actually instigate robberies on the part of the gang boy or his group—a direct encouragement to delinquent habits.

69. A dealer lent a saw to a gang of boys on the Northwest Side and instructed them to saw out the lead pipes in a vacant house and bring them to him. Both the junk man and the boys were apprehended and taken into court.

In a newspaper report, the existence of a "robber band" operating in three cities was indicated. The confession of a member— only twenty-one years old—named a West Side junk man as the head of the band. The report stated that the junk-dealer regularly met the young fellows in a poolroom on Twelfth Street, where the robberies were planned and the assignments given out. According to the police, the value of loot from Chicago robberies alone during the past sixty days amounted to over $100,000.[2]

Junking may be one of the first steps in the gradual process leading to the complete demoralization of the gang boy. The distinction between picking up some discarded object to sell and appropriating the unguarded property of others can hardly be very clear to the adolescent in a gangland environment. Experience in junking also affords some knowledge of the technique of crime such as familiarity with fences, learning to recognize merchandise cars, etc. Junking, in other words, becomes a directly educative process in the wrong direction.

SOURCES OF SUPPLY

Opportunity to sell junk is one important element in the situation. Opportunity to procure junk to be sold constitutes the other. While the alleys and the rubbish dumps contribute material for this purpose, the chief sources of supply are empty houses and the railroads.

[2] *Ibid.*, p. 36.

70. Anthony, a fifteen-year-old youngster, with three companions, broke into an empty house. In cutting out the lead pipe, they did $200 damage, but the junk-peddler who purchased the loot gave the boys only $1.50 each. The dealer was afterward arrested for receiving stolen property. This gang also robbed freight cars.

A gang of nine boys entered an empty flat above a theater on the Northwest Side, picking the lock with a button hook. The flat, which was steam heated, was made their rendezvous. Here they loafed, smoked, and planned robberies. No railroad yards were visited, but the attention of the gang was concentrated on holdups and junking vacant houses. Jimmie, a fifteen-year-old member, entered an empty house, removed the lead pipe, and sold it for $3.00 to a peddler. His experiences, like that of scores of other boys, ended in a court and commitment to an institution.[3]

THE RAILROADS

Plundering merchandise cars has become so flagrant that the railroads employ special watchmen and police whose best efforts seem almost futile in coping with the problem.

71. Five of my gang would go on a car-robbing expedition at once. Two would watch to give "jiggers" on either side of the track, while the other three of us would break the seal on the car. We'd usually try to get into a green seal car because that kind has merchandise and lots of cigarettes. It is a heavy offense to break government seals, but we always wanted to get good stuff. We wouldn't take suits because they had names in them, but we'd get lots of chickens and other stuff to eat and wear. I had a five-bushel wagon which we would load up with our "haul." Then we'd take it around and sell it to our regular customers. Lots of private families stock up that way. We'd get caught plenty of times, but the railroad police would often let us go. They robbed too, "betcha," when they were small. When kids get started this way, they go right on. They take the blame for each other. "I never saw a guy who never stole yet!"[4]

The mere accessibility of railroad tracks indicates the

[3] *Ibid.*, pp. 40–41.

[4] Gang boy's own story.

importance of the technic environment in determining the direction of the gang's activities.

72. That a significant relation exists between juvenile junking and railroads has already been indicated. Twenty-eight out of the 100 boys studied were accustomed to secure junk from railroad yards or tracks, and 22 had at some time taken it from railroad cars. It has also been shown that in the case of 86 boys, 48, or over 50 per cent of them, lived less than 6 blocks from the tracks, while the average distance from the railroad for the entire group was only 5 9/43 blocks. This accessibility was thought to have an important bearing on the practice of securing material from railroad yards and cars.[5]

JUNKING IN THE GANG

Practically every gang in the areas where these opportunities exist goes "hunting with a gunny-sack" when in need of revenues. The investigation of the Juvenile Protective Association, which included a study of 100 delinquent boys committed by the court to an institution, showed that 88 of them made it a practice to collect and sell junk,[6] and that 75 of the total number belonged to boys' gangs, practically all of which were unsupervised.[7] The study of gang boys for the present investigation showed that most of them went junking on occasion.

73. Tino's gang was engaged in robbing the railroad cars. They would take a hammer and break the seals. Tino borrowed a horse and wagon from a married friend, telling him he was getting apples to sell from South Water Street at $2.00 a barrel. In reality he procured them and other commodities from the merchandise cars. The gang would back the wagon up, load it, and peddle the loot. Tino got half the profits. He became paralyzed in the arm as the result of being shot by a watchman, but he was never caught.[8]

74. A gang of five boys, who hung out in a poolroom in Chicago, operated along the Belt railroad as far as Hammond, Indiana. They were from fourteen to nineteen years of age and Polish, Irish, and Italian in nationality. They would board a mov-

[5] Webster, *op. cit.*, p. 36.   [6] *Ibid.*, p. 13.
[7] *Ibid.*, p. 17.   [8] Interviews.

ing freight train and with a rope ladder go over the side and break into a car. The stuff they wanted would be thrown from the train, picked up by their confederates and taken back to the city to be sold to the owner of the poolroom where they hung out.[9]

A gang which becomes organized around junking as its chief interest is likely to develop into a semi-criminal group, acquiring a special technique for securing and disposing of its loot without the interference of the law.

75. A gang of about six young Lithuanians living together in a lodging house are professional brass thieves. They take the brass bearings or journals from the trucks or journal boxes of the railroad cars. To accomplish this feat, considerable expertness is required, for the car must be jacked up to relieve the weight that holds the journals in place. The rolls themselves weigh about ten pounds apiece. The gang works in twos and threes on cold nights in winter when there are few watchmen about. In the summertime they ship out of the city or work about the ragshops for the junk dealers.[10]

THE ATTITUDE OF THE PARENTS

The attitude of the parents is often one of condonement and even encouragement of the boys in their stealing from railroad tracks. In some cases the families of the boys act as receivers for the stolen goods.

78. A gang of from six to ten boys about fourteen years of age hung about on Jefferson between Twelfth and Sixteenth streets. They were involved in at least nine burglaries of railroad cars. The parents of all the boys, who lived in the immediate vicinity of the tracks, were arrested and fined, but only about $150 worth of stuff was recovered. Nine different railroads were involved in the case.

Most of the loot was taken to the homes and disposed of through the parents. Cases of electric irons, which had been obtained by the boys six years before, were found in one of the homes. Fifteen yards of stolen linen was found in a cradle under an infant, and the mother of the baby was wearing stolen shoes. Dozens of

[9] Interview with a railroad detective.

[10] Interview with a railroad detective.

cases of salmon, cartons of cigarettes, and boxes of shoes stolen three or four years before were discovered.

Among other things recovered, were a hundred car seals, which were used as a means of covering up merchandise car breakage. The boys did not know how to discriminate between the seals of different roads, however, and put those of the New York Central on cars routed over other lines.[11]

The general point of view of the parents in these communities seems to be that thievery from a railroad is not wrong because it is a big corporation. Whole neighborhoods sometimes engage in stealing from the tracks.

79. The whole neighborhood turns out to steal from the cars at Western and Twenty-fourth. The juvenile officers are lenient in this connection, because they know how much a part of the neighborhood mores this has become, and they do not blame the children for following the pattern of the group. The mothers do not understand English and this increases the difficulties encountered by the railroad police in dealing with the situation.[12]

A gang activity closely akin to junking is fuel gathering, which, especially in the case of coal from the railroads, seems to be a neighborhood tradition in most immigrant communities near the tracks.

Familiarity with opportunities for delinquency is an important factor.

83. The leader of the Conkey gang, composed of fellows from seventeen to nineteen, had been stealing from the tracks since he was twelve. He and the other boys lived near the railroad and got used to riding the cars.

The group had a system worked out for merchandise stealing. They would board the cars just outside the yards in the southwest clearing. On the way to Hawthorne they would pry open the door of a merchandise car and throw off the loot, which would be gathered up by a confederate with a horse and buggy. He would haul the stuff to the home of one of the members where it would be disposed of.

[11] Interviews with railroad detectives.
[12] Interviews with railroad detectives.

One of the boys had been a switchman during a strike; another had been a railroad clerk and knew how to identify a merchandise car. Some of the men to whom the goods were taken were car inspectors for the railroad. Most of the loot, however, was sold to four other railroad employees, who bought shoes, pants, linen, and other commodities at one-eighth of the regular price.[13]

The data with regard to junking and the railroads afford another illustration of how elements in the situation complex turn the gang's activities in a particular direction. Not only is the impersonal environment favorable to the development of junking and consequent delinquency on the part of the boys, but the more directly social environment which includes junk dealers, fences, and attitudes of parents, property owners, and police now enters into the situation. All these factors working together furnish opportunities for types of behavior which may ultimately lead to more serious demoralization.

[13] Interviews with railroad detectives.

CHAPTER IX

Gang Warfare

The gang is a conflict group. It develops through strife and thrives on warfare. The members of a gang will fight each other. They will even fight for a "cause," as when a Chicago gang of some note sent a number of young men down into Oklahoma to help a former governor in his struggle against the Ku Klux Klan. Gangsters are impelled, in a way, to fight; so much of their activity is outside the law that fighting is the only means of avenging injuries and maintaining the code.

92. Jimmie, the leader of the gang, is a bad actor. He would kill a policeman, if necessary, to get away. Most of the bunch are getting rounded up now, on account of their robbing expeditions. The greatest sport of the gang was fighting, and Jimmie would lead the boys to battle on the least pretext.

One Fourth of July the bunch had a big fight with Danny O'Hara's gang. We had about two hundred on our side, and there were about as many there for Danny. Danny got hard with Jimmy and told him that he was trying to start a fight or something. First Jimmie busted Danny in the nose, and then the whole gang started fighting. We had the traffic blocked on the boulevard for a long time, and finally the patrol wagons came, but they did not get any of the gang.

We had wars with lots of other gangs. We fought the Deadshots, and there were about a hundred in the fight. Jimmie got bounced on, and when he saw our enemies were too big for us, he beat it.

We fought the Jews from Twelfth Street, but they had too many for us. They're pretty good fighters. We knew they had more than we did, so we went down with clubs and everything.

Another time we went to Garfield Park to lick the Thistles. We had only about seventy-five guys. They had said that they could lick Jimmie and the rest of the gang, and right away he wanted to go down there to fight them, but he got beat up as usual. There were too many of them for us, and half of them were men about twenty years old.

We also had a war, starting over a baseball game at the park, with the Coons from Lake Street.[1]

THE STRUGGLE FOR EXISTENCE

In its struggle for existence a gang has to fight hostile groups to maintain its play privileges, its property rights, and the physical safety of its members. Its status as a gang among gangs, as well as in the neighborhood and the community, must also be maintained, usually through its prowess in a fight.

Gang warfare is usually organized on a territorial basis. Each group becomes attached to a local area which it regards as peculiarly its own and through which it is dangerous for members of another gang to pass.

94. There are a number of gangs in the vicinity, the two most prominent being the Marshfield and the Gross avenue gangs. Ashland Avenue is the dividing line between the territory of these gangs and if one boy crosses into enemy territory he does it at some peril. Armed invasions are not infrequent.[2]

The older gangs engaged in the illicit liquor business also have their own territories within which they may receive certain police or political protection, and over which they often wield political control.

THE GANG FEUD

Gangs of the semi-criminal type composed of older boys and men engage in a struggle for existence which

[1] Gang boy's own story.   [2] Interview with a social worker.

takes the form of frequent and bitter feuds. The beer-runners' wars are usually of this sort. Not only does the desire for revenge for injuries once sustained enter into such situations but there is also a definite wish for the security of certain economic interests vested in the exploitation of some illicit business.

95. An internecine warfare within the ranks of the gambling, beer, and booze overlords of Cicero got definitely under way yesterday when one faction tried to dynamite the Hawthorne Park Inn, owned by a recognized leader of another of the controlling groups.

Sixteen sticks of dynamite, linked by two-inch fuses, were placed under a section of the inn at nine o'clock in the morning. The two men who lighted the fuse were seen. One of the employes of the place plucked the fuse before an explosion could take place, while the others gave chase to the vandals and captured them. They were engaged in beating them into unconsciousness when the Cicero police arrived.

During the past week the owner of the inn received four 'phone warnings to close his business.[3]

The original causes for such a war may be forgotten and an extended feud may develop between hostile gangs. Anger, hatred, and thirst for revenge are continually stimulated by repeated insults and aggressions. A killing by one side calls for a killing by the other.

96. One of the most vicious gang wars on record occurred between the Rats and the Jellyrolls, two notorious St. Louis gangs. It lasted over a period of years, resulted in many killings, and assumed such acute form at one time that the whole city of St. Louis was aroused to indignation.

A man reputed to be the brains of the Rats gang under its old leader, a constable, was entrusted by the latter with bringing up some booze from New Orleans. He came back, however, with neither the liquor nor the money, saying that the vessel and her cargo had been sunk in the Mississippi. It is said that the constable did not believe this story, and as a result his lieutenant deserted to the Rats's bitterest enemies, the Jellyrolls.

[3] News item, *Chicago Herald and Examiner*, August 23, 1924.

Not long after this event the Rats's leader was murdered and the Jellyrolls received the blame. The Jellyroll lawyer, who was supposed to have hired the assassins, was now marked for death and dispatched by the Rats's firing squad. The most dangerous man in the Jellyrolls, who had been wounded in a skirmish, now took every opportunity to taunt the Rats. He was next executed and found with twenty-six bullet holes in his body.

The next step in the war was the wounding of the Rats's leader by Jellyrolls who sneaked up on him in a curtained car. This so enraged him that he gave out a list of sixteen Jellyrolls who were to be hunted out and killed. The gang could not find the Jellyrolls immediately, so they shot up the leader's home. The Maxwelton club, the hang-out which the Rats had established on a country road, now took on the appearance of an arsenal; $50 a day was spent for the ammunition used in target practice. Two gangsters, imported by the Jellyrolls from New York, were shot by the Rats. A little boy was crippled in one of the affrays, and the gang made up a purse of $500 and gave it to him.

The warfare finally became so desperate that the president of the board of police commissioners and the chief of police, unable to cope with the situation by ordinary methods, had a conference with the Rats's leader and the whole gang in their hang-out and warned them that the war would have to stop or the state militia would be called out. The leader of each side signed an agreement to end the war. The Rats merely laughed at this procedure and were told that while they were to stop hunting the Jellyrolls, they were to shoot them on sight. After the truce was signed the Jellyroll leader was spied on the street and the Rats' "redhots" notified. The result was that a cousin of the intended victim and a Missouri state representative with whom he was talking were both killed; the Jellyroll leader saved himself by stepping into a doorway. The Rats merely laughed off this double murder as a miss, and hostilities were continued but with less vehemence owing to the fear of public action.[4]

CRISIS IN THE GANG

The common enemies against whom gangs struggle include rival gangs or alliances of gangs; members or

[4] A condensed statement prepared from various sources, but chiefly from an account of the Rats gang by Ray Renard published in the *St. Louis Star* from February 24 to March 31, 1925. Renard, a former mem-

groups of different races or nationalities; the police; railroad detectives; school authorities, such as principals and truant officers; storekeepers and officials of businesses upon which the gangs prey in one way or another; and neighbors or parents. The relations of a gang to these hostile forces can best be interpreted in terms of the cycles of war and peace, of conflict and accommodation, which they undergo.

The periodical equilibrium between the gang and its social environment seldom lasts long. A slight indignity, a casual clash, the breaking of a window, or the discovery of some new source of revenue or pleasure creates tensions and unrest which precipitate a crisis. One gang picks on individual members or little boys belonging to another.

97. We used to fight three other gangs with bricks. Some one of them boys would hit one of ours. Then the boy that got hit would come and tell us and we would start fightin'. Sometimes one of us would get hurt with a brick and then we would stop and go away. We would be afraid of trouble if anyone got hurt.[5]

An invasion of a rival gang and the stealing of supplies calls for a return raiding trip and finally an open battle of retaliation.

Gang feuds arising in some such way may result in bitter hatred and hostility lasting for years. Occasionally the family feud is carried over into the quarrels of the boys.

98. Miss X, principal of a school of 2,500 pupils in the heart of the Italian district in New York, states that the boys in this neighborhood begin ganging very early. There are many feuds between rival gangs, the origins of which are probably due to family influences. The young gangsters often carry dangerous weapons, and there are serious encounters going to and from school.[6]

---

ber of the gang, made his confession while serving a sentence in the Atlanta penitentiary.

[5] Gang boy's own story.   [6] Interview.

99. A juvenile vendetta yesterday sent Tony ———, ten years old, to the county hospital with a knife wound in his side. The police believe the stabbing was done by a fourteen-year-old boy in the same neighborhood. It is alleged that the two boys have long been enemies, their animosity resulting from a family feud.[7]

By a process of summation repeated crises are precipitated, each a little more serious than the preceding. Unrest is fomented and tensions are increased until the consummation of the series is reached in some event that attracts community attention or necessitates the intervention of the authorities. Such was the case in Chicago's North Side jungles, where the "Drakes," the "Spauldings," and the "Westerns," Polish gangs known collectively as the "Belmonts," joined together to fight the "Elstons," composed of Irish and Swedish boys making up the "Big Hill" gang north of the railroad tracks. Minor clashes between these two groups had taken place for two years before the final crisis was reached.

100. Edmond Werner, fifteen, self-styled leader of the roving Northwest Side gang which carries the cognomen of the "Belmonts"—and pockets of darnicks—prefaced his story of the gang fighting between the Belmonts and the Elstons, which Saturday resulted in the death of Julius Flosi, eleven, with this bitter statement today.

He told me of the innumerable battles of fists and bricks which have been staged for the possession of the lonesome bit of railroad trackage at California and Elston avenues, in the last two years, and describes how, when the two gangs realized the impotency of bare knucks and ragged stones, each turned to firearms.

In the show-down scrap Saturday between Werner's Belmonts and the Elstons, Flosi was killed by a bullet from a 22-caliber rifle. He was an Elston.

"Dey picked on us for two years, but even den we wouldn't a shot if 'Stinky'—the big guy and the leader of the Elstons—hadn't jumped out of his dugout in a coal pile Saturday and waved a long bayonet wid a red flag on one end of it and an American flag upside down on de udder and dared us to come over de tracks."

[7] News item.

Werner and six other Belmonts are in cells as a result of Flosi's death, and an eighth is being held until the police find his brother. Four are at the Shakespeare Avenue station.[8]

PRIMARY CONFLICT

The conflict which follows a crisis in the gang is usually of the primary type: The gang, for the most part, falls outside the influences of the laws and customs which are designed to provide methods of negotiating difficulties. Gang warfare is ruthless.[9] "Treat 'em rough and tell 'em nuttin'!" is the slogan of a Chicago gang leader of fifteen years. The treatment of prisoners held by the gang is often brutal and inhuman: severe beatings are commonplace; and in one case a gang, using a penknife, peeled strips of skin from the back of an unfortunate captive and rubbed in salt before releasing him. Fatalities are only too frequent in clashes between rival gangs.

101. Thomas Kelly, eighteen, died at the German Deaconess Hospital early today from a skull fracture which he suffered when he fell in an alleged gang fight at Root Street and Union Avenue.

Stockyards police were called by neighbors when ten or more young men engaged in a fight. At the approach of the patrol wagon, all but Kelly fled. He was found unconscious, his head on the curbing.[10]

The law of the gang in its wars is "an eye for an eye and a tooth for a tooth."

102. A stripling with a gun took the law out of the hands of the New York police today and wrote a dramatic finis to the career of Jack Kaplan, alias "Kid Dropper," notorious gunman and leader of the East Side "Dropper" gang.

The gangster chief, on whom the police had been trying to fasten something for months, swaggered at noon from the Essex

[8] Unsigned article in Jack Robbins' Scrapbook, dated October 27, 1919.

[9] The machine-gun became the standard weapon of Chicago gangs in their internecine warfare in 1926.

[10] *Chicago American*, September 4, 1923.

Market Court. He had just defeated the latest effort to connect him with the shooting of two members of a rival gang. . . . .

A slim figure that had been lurking behind the cab straightened up, drew a pistol, and fired through the back window of the cab. The Dropper slumped in his seat with two bullets in his head. He and his assailant were taken to the court building, where Kaplan died in a few minutes.

The man who did the shooting made the following statement in reply to the questions of the police:

"An eye for an eye and a tooth for a tooth. If I hadn't gotten him, he'd have gotten me.

"I met the Kid about eight months ago. He was friendly with all his gang until a few weeks ago, when I got a note from his bunch saying the Kid would have to get $500. How could I give it to him? I'm a poor man, working for $25 to $30 a week."

The attack on the Dropper may have saved the lives of several policemen and possibly innocent bystanders, for in the round-up made by detectives in the crowd that gathered after the slaying, half a dozen armed members of the Dropper's gang were taken.[11]

PROCESSES OF ACCOMMODATION

Occasionally gangs agree to a conventional substitute for the more primary form of group conflict, in the nature of a joust between two individual champions selected by their respective retainers.

103. The West Division Street district was for a time terrorized by two rival gangs who alternated their thieving raids on the local merchants with pitched battles. The police were helpless to control the situation.

When group fighting proved unsatisfactory the leaders made a truce and held a parley. They decided to take matters in their own hands and fight it out for the gangs, just the two of them. Backed by their respective gangs they made application to use the hall of the Northwest City of the Boys' Brotherhood Republic for the purpose of the scrap which was to constitute a decision for both gangs.

The intercession of a few grown-ups averted the combat, however, and a peace was negotiated.[12]

[11] *New York Times.*

[12] Abridged from an article in Jack Robbins' Scrapbook.

Outsiders who have a real interest in boys, and who are possessed of considerable tact and patience, are sometimes successful, through diplomatic negotiation, in bringing about an accommodation between enemy gangs.

104. As a result of a number of complaints of fighting, a probation officer assigned to discover the reason, found that the gangs on two streets, Ninth and Tenth avenues, were engaged in incessant warfare, endangering the safety of outsiders and destroying property. In spite of many arrests the feud had continued.

The probation officer, after a good deal of preparatory work, gained the confidence of members of both gangs and called a conference to negotiate a treaty of peace. A large number of boys gathered in a school auditorium where the proposals of the probation officer for peace were carried with uproarious enthusiasm. Suspecting that something was wrong when two gangs could agree at once on so many resolutions, the probation officer inquired how many boys were from Ninth Avenue and found that not a single boy belonging to the other gang had attended the meeting.

It was found upon investigation that the Tenth Avenue gang, believing the meeting a trap set by the Ninth Avenues for their undoing, had failed to attend. After some further work to secure a better understanding on both sides, a treaty of peace was actually signed by both leaders. The warfare was ended and gradually the boys learned to mingle and even to fraternize with their former enemies.[13]

Through conventionalization the gang may become accommodated to society (socialized) and may assume a recognized place in the larger community. As an athletic club or other acceptable organization, it may associate and co-operate with other recognized groups in the community; or it may lose its identity and be assimilated into some larger social unit.

In most instances, however, assimilation does not take place and accommodation is usually far from complete. Genuine accommodation is often lacking and conventionalization represents merely a compromise with the

[13] Abridged from Franklin Chase Hoyt, *Quicksands of Youth*, pp. 114–17.

social order in an effort to gain security and prestige. The old gang traits persist, while the formal acquisitions are largely superficial.

ALLIANCES AND ENTENTES

Like nations, gangs are prone to form federations for defensive and offensive purposes. These larger groups also tend to pass through general cycles of war and peace, conflict and accommodation.

105. I was with the Shielders in their war against the Dukies. There were about seventy-five Shielders and they would all bum school at once just to fight. The Dukies went to the Mark Sheridan and the Healey schools, while most of the Shielders went to the Ward School. There were several gangs on each side.

Hostilities would begin when some of the Shielders would cross the tracks into the enemy's territory and start a fight. Then when the Dukies caught one of the kids alone, they would hit him, and he would get their big gang after them. The battles took place over the tracks or under the viaducts and rocks and coal were used as missiles. The flivver squads would interfere to stop the fighting when it got too hot.

One time there was a nigger on the Shielders' side. He had a big razor and was going to kill one of the Dukies when a copper shot and killed him. He did not mean to kill the boy, but there was peace after that for a while. The fighting has begun again now in spite of warnings by the police.[14]

SUBSTITUTES FOR CONFLICT BEHAVIOR

For uncontrolled pugnacious behavior can be substituted conventionalized but exciting forms of rivalry which divert interest and energy from the more brutal kinds of fighting. In such cases primary conflict is replaced by secondary or the purely "play" type, mollified by protective rules and ethical standards, a substitution which is one criterion of social progress in general and of socialization of the gang in particular.

It is usually possible to crystallize the bellicose propensity of the gang into some sort of athletic team which may

[14] Gang boy's own story. See document 115.

be pitted against its rivals. Undirected athletics, however, particularly if a pool is at stake, may end in a free-for-all fight, and a gang often undertakes its revenge as an aftermath of a fair fight. In this way, secondary conflict as determined by the rules of the game breaks down and is followed by the primary type.

106. At the park we had a big gang fight, which grew out of a baseball game with the colored guys from Lake Street. The score was a tie, but it was getting dark and the niggers did not want to play no more. They started a fight about the money that was up on the game—ten dollars on each side. We thought we'd beat them up, but we did not like to try it on their own grounds. The next day when our leader heard about it (he was not at the baseball game), he went right over to Lake Street. He got bounced on the first thing and knocked out in an alley. Then the niggers hid in ambush, and we could not find where they were hiding. A few days later we got even with them when they came swimming in Union Park. We got some of them in there and nearly drowned them.[15]

CONVENTIONALIZATION OF CONFLICT

In the following case social direction of the behavior of the gang has made of it an accommodation group.

107. About seven or eight boys living within a radius of two blocks started in school together, and by the sixth grade the group was further increased by four new boys. The gang was formed as a result of nutting expeditions, camping trips, and such deviltry as is usual among youngsters. In the sixth grade we started a football team, and the natural leaders, Steve and Rocky, did the organizing. This leadership held in general for all the years we were together.

Among the earliest associations of the gang were those of our field meets. Whenever there was a big track and field contest either at the high or the normal school, the boys living in our section of the city always put on their own meet in a handy vacant lot. We proceeded to get letters, but that was almost as far as the organization of the South Sixth Street Athletic Club went.

When, during our sixth-grade year, we were able to beat the grade-school teams, we began to think that we were a pretty good bunch, and group-consciousness developed. During the rest of the

[15] Gang boy's own story.

grade-school years and through high school we were able to keep the gang intact. The greatest incentive to pass in school was to keep in the class with the gang. When we entered Teachers College, competition was keen, and not all of us made the team, but by the end of the third year eight of the old bunch were playing regularly, or were at least on the squad.

Following the selection of the squad by the coaches the incoming men of our old bunch were initiated into a senior social organization called the "Funnel Gang." This group was unorganized but had three or four recognized leaders. The initiation consisted simply in taking the new man along with the group and trying his nerve on party refreshment raids, or perhaps in having him sing to the best of his ability a number of ballads late at night in front of the principal women's dormitory.

The gang was a unit not only during the football season, but throughout the whole year. Steak roasts, roller skating parties, sleigh rides, and other social or quasi-social functions were regular affairs of the team as a whole.

The emotional solidarity of the gang is illustrated by the following incident: During a game "Cookie" was deliberately "kneed" by an opponent. The effect was instantaneous. A cold-blooded rage that made every man play to kill came over us. Not a word was said, but a feeling of unity of purpose (for revenge) dominated the group.

Every time a man pitched into an opponent he had the feeling of getting satisfaction for a personal injury. Feelings of physical pain were almost wiped out by the dominant sentiment. I came out with three broken fingers and never knew when I had hurt them.

The solidarity of the group was greatly augmented by the conflict situation in football. There was a decidedly pleasant feeling in combating the out-group with our own side. This did not come from the feeling that the "bleachers" were watching, for no one thought of the crowd except in the most detached sort of way.

In 1917, when war was declared, none of us entertained the idea of enlisting. As the situation became clearer, however, and men began to leave for the camps, we began to talk over the matter among ourselves. Always the discussion was what shall *we* do? Whatever we did, we knew would be done as a group. At the end of the season Steve suggested that we enlist as a body (the whole team), and leave at once. Some wanted to join the marines; some the army; but a vote decided on the navy. In order to stay together, we went to the Great Lakes Naval Training Station and enlisted as a group of apprentice seamen, even though some of us could have received ratings had we been willing to quit the others.[16]

THE CONFLICT CYCLE

The cyclical process of interaction, pointed out above, in which there are alternating periods of conflict and accommodation may now be stated more fully.

The situations underlying most human relationships, if analyzed far enough, will probably prove to be of the struggle pattern. Even man's play tends to take this form. Life is a struggle not merely for existence, but for the gratification of all human desires. Every group, as well as every person, is a self-appropriating organism attempting to wrest from its environment the fullest measure of satisfaction. Although tastes are directed toward a variety of different "goods," rarely is there a sufficient amount of any one of these for everybody who desires it. The supply of any tangible or intangible thing which meets a human need (with the exception of a very few "free goods") is limited, and struggle is the inevitable consequence. Society may be regarded as a complex system of accommodations in which these competitive relations are defined, standardized, and rendered stable.

As a result of this struggle, all human relations tend to undergo cycles of conflict and accommodation that have definite stages of development and consummation.

This notion of the struggle pattern of life provides a valuable key to the explanation of the gang—its behavior, its relations within the larger framework of social life, its structure, and the status of each of its members with reference to each other.

WAR AND PEACE

It is important to distinguish warfare from mere mischievous or predacious behavior. When there is war there

[16] Manuscript prepared by a former member of the group.

is an issue. The war is carried on, partly because it is exciting and gives free play to impulses otherwise controlled, but its outcome is presumed to settle the issue.

In this warfare there usually grows up a code; when the battle is fought under the rules, that is to say, in the manner that is regarded as usual and expected, it tends to assume regulated ceremonial character.

Then arises the notion of permitting the leaders to fight it out. This is the beginning of accommodation, but now there results a struggle for precedence and prestige. A ball game may be fought with much the same motives as a battle, but rules and standards, not necessarily formulated, grow up. Presently the outside world, the larger group, is invited in to act as arbiter: to see fair play and to define the rules.

Under these conditions struggle tends to assume the form of regulated play in which the interests are merely subjective—superiority, prestige, etc. It may take the form, however, of a political struggle in which the interests are real rather than ideal.

This is the point at which the outsider representing the public and the community may play a rôle. He may function in the direction of regulation of conflict in the interest of the larger community. *The temptation of the outsider, however, is to make the whole struggle innocuous and harmless and so to deprive it of any real meaning.*

CHAPTER X

Race and Nationality
in the Gang

The gang in Chicago is largely, though not entirely, a phenomenon of the immigrant community of the poorer type. Of the 880 gangs for which data have been secured

TABLE III

RACES AND NATIONALITIES OF GANGS IN CHICAGO

Race or Nationality	Number of Gangs	Percentage of Total Gangs
Mixed nationalities.....	351	39.89
Polish.................	148	16.82
Italian................	99	11.25
Irish..................	75	8.52
Negro.................	63	7.16
American—white.......	45	5.11
Mixed negro-white......	25	2.84
Jewish................	20	2.27
Slavic................	16	1.82
Bohemian.............	12	1.36
German...............	8	.91
Swedish...............	7	.79
Lithuanian............	6	.69
Miscellaneous.........	5	.57
Total.............	880	100

as to race and nationality, only 45 are given as wholly American; while 63 are negro; and 25, mixed colored and white. Of those remaining, 351 are of mixed white nationalities, while 396 are dominantly or solidly of a single nationality group. A few of the members of these gangs are foreign born, but most of them are children of parents one or both of whom are foreign-born immigrants.

Comparison of the percentages of gangs of foreign extraction, made up dominantly of one nationality with the

TABLE IV

GANGS OF SINGLE FOREIGN NATIONALITY IN CHICAGO*

Nationality	Number of Gangs	Percentage of Total	Population of Foreign Extraction†	Percentage of Total Foreign Extraction
Polish.................	148	37.37	318,338	16.4
Italian................	99	25.00	124,457	6.4
Irish..................	75	18.94	199,956	10.3
Jewish................	20	5.05	159,518	8.2
Slavic................	16	4.04	77,309‡	3.9
Bohemian.............	12	3.03	106,428	5.5
German...............	8	2.02	431,340	22.2
Swedish..............	7	1.77	121,386	6.2
Lithuanian...........	6	1.52	44,065§	2.3
Others...............	5	1.26	363,501	18.6
Total gangs dominantly of one nationality........	396	100	1,946,298	100

* The members of these gangs are largely the sons of foreign-born parents.

† The figures for the population groups of foreign extraction have been derived from the census tables on mother-tongues of foreign white stocks as affording the best basis for comparison, with the exception of the Irish figure, which was necessarily derived from Census Table 9 (p. 926) on country of origin of foreign white stocks. See U.S. Census 1920, Vol. II, *Population*, pp. 1006-11.

‡ This figure includes Slovak, Russian (including some Russian-speaking Jews), Ruthenian, Slovenian, Serbo-Croatian, and Bulgarian stocks.

§ This figure includes Lettish stocks.

percentages of persons of each ethnic stock in the total population of foreign extraction in Chicago indicates that the Polish, Italian, and Irish furnish many more gangs than might be expected from their population groups, while among the Swedish and Germans there are relatively few gangs.

That these figures do not give a fair estimate of the contribution of each foreign stock to Chicago gangs is evident from the fact that there remain 351 gangs of mixed nationality in which the proportions of the various stocks are unknown.

TABLE V

NEGRO, FOREIGN, AND AMERICAN GANGS IN CHICAGO

	Number of Gangs	Percentage of Total	Chicago's Boy Population from 10 to 24 Years of Age Inclusive	Percentage of Chicago's Total Boy Population from 10 to 24 Years of Age Inclusive
American (native white parentage).............................	45	5.26	83,075	25.70
Negro.......................	63*	7.37	12,202	3.77
Foreign extraction.............	747	87.37	227,501	70.39
Other races than white or Negro.	00†	0.00	416	.14
Total....................	855	100	323,194	100

* The twenty-five gangs of mixed negroes and whites are necessarily omitted.
† A number of Chicago Chinese are members of tongs, which are very similar to gangs. The number of such groups is not known.

A comparison of the percentages of gangs of negro race and of white foreign and native extraction with the percentages of boys (ten to twenty-four years old) of these groups in Chicago shows that the gang is largely a phenomenon of the immigrant community; that the negro population of the city provides more than its share of such groups; and that the native white population of native parentage, which has 25.70 per cent of the boys, contributes only 5.26 per cent of the gangs. The small contribution of the American element is further emphasized by the fact that large portions of the forty-five gangs returned as American are undoubtedly of foreign extraction.

OLD WORLD ANTAGONISMS

Chicago has the character of a vast cultural frontier— a common meeting place for the divergent and antagonistic peoples of the earth. Traditional animosities are often carried over into gangs and color many of their conflicts in Chicago.

It should be pointed out at the outset, however, that conflict between gangs is organized primarily on a territorial rather than on a racial or nationality basis.[1] Regardless of race, fighting goes on over the imaginary lines along streets, alleys, canals, rivers, railroad tracks, and elevations, which constitute boundaries between gang territories. In the bitter Hamburg-Canaryville wars participants on both sides were largely Irish.

108. If you've ever lived back of the yards, you've heard of Hamburg. And, of course, if you've heard of Hamburg, you've heard of Canaryville.

Hamburg ran from Thirty-first to Fortieth. And south of Fortieth was Canaryville. The deadline was the old street-car tracks. No Hamburg lad, unless he thirsted for a fight, crossed the dead line. Vice versa for the Canaryvillians. But sometimes—on Saturday nights—there was mutual thirst. And the broken noses and black eyes that were seen the following Sunday were too numerous to count.

That was sheer boyhood stuff. The political aspect was found in that other noted feud that raged between Tom Carey's "Indians" and Mike McInerney's gang—Mike, the old gray wolf as they called him in the days when he trained with Roger Sullivan. Carey's bunch ruled west of Halsted. Mike's held undisputed sway east of it.[2]

Where an area is dominantly of one nationality, solidarity is national as well as territorial, and old world antagonisms are carried over into gang wars.

Among the most bitter of these intercultural enmities transplanted from the old world is that between the Jews and the Poles. This is particularly marked during periods when the Jews in anti-Semitic countries are suffering from

[1] See chap. ix.

[2] Fred D. Pasley, "Early Days Recalled 'Back o' the Yards,'" *Chicago Herald and Examiner*, 1924.

pogroms. The two most important Jewish-Polish frontiers in Chicago are those between the Jewish settlement of Lawndale and the Polish colony to the southeast across Ogden Avenue and Douglas Park, and between the extensive Polish community concentrated about Milwaukee Avenue and the large Jewish colony extending westward to Humboldt Park. In the border strife between these regions the gangs have taken an active part.

109. An interesting collision occurred in the winter of 1920–21 shortly after the tension in public opinion over the Russian-Jewish massacres. The Poles proposed on one of their holidays to hold a parade down Division Street through Jewish territory. Jewish politicians went to the city hall in an attempt to get an injunction against the parade, but their efforts were unavailing. A gang of Jewish lads, seventeen to twenty-three years of age, then took the matter into their own hands. They armed themselves with guns and barred the way of the parade, which then chose the Milwaukee Avenue route. Members of the gang were hailed into court on account of their participation in the affair.[3]

At about the same time the WWW's are alleged to have successfully stemmed an invasion of Lawndale from the southeast by Polish gangs intent on following the example of their kinsmen across the seas and holding a pogrom in the Jewish residential area. Similar clashes are a common occurrence on the Lawndale frontier, especially in and about Douglas Park whose privileges are used by both Poles and Jews.

110. In the summer of 1921 it was rumored that a few Jewish boys had been assaulted when passing through the Polish community to the southeast. Thereupon a gang of young Jews (considered "sluggers" in the neighborhood) assembled and, led by "Nails" ———, made for the Polish district to seek apologies. They went to the street corners indicated by the boys who had been attacked and started a free-for-all fight. After a sufficient amount of physical punishment had been administered, they withdrew.

[3] Interview with a social worker.

During the period that followed clashes were frequent. One Saturday a group of Jewish boys, who were playing baseball in Douglas Park, were attacked by a gang of about thirty Polish lads. Everything from rotten tomatoes to housebricks was used for ammunition in the onslaught. The news of the affray reached the poolroom hang-outs and brought the much needed reinforcement. Men like "Nails" —— and "Nigger" —— went into the fight for revenge. A good many others including high-school boys, amateur prize fighters, and hangers-on of the poolrooms were eager for the fun of "helping the Hebes lick the Polocks." Their slogan was "Wallop the Polock!" and they rushed fifty strong to the scene of battle. Finally, policemen dispersed what was left of the Polish gang.

It was dangerous for Jewish boys to travel unprotected through Polish territory or through Douglas Park, which was a sort of "no man's land" on the frontier between the two regions. On one occasion a young Jewish boy was sent on an errand by his mother, and came back with a hole in his head, made by a broken milk bottle hurled by a hidden Polish sharpshooter.

Use of the privileges afforded by Douglas Park, which was a common meeting place of the two groups, has always been a bone of contention. There is a refectory and boathouse in the northern portion of the park, which under normal circumstances is open to members of any race or creed. During this period, however, it was a different story. Some days the Jews dominated, but when a gang of Poles larger in number approached, the former would leave. On one occasion the two gangs were of about the same size and the result was a pitched battle.

Not only did the gangs along Roosevelt Road participate in these encounters, but also the social and "basement" clubs of Lawndale found a good opportunity for sport in the "Polock hunt." A club starting out on such an expedition would almost certainly pick up other gangs and become the nucleus for a mob before it finished. Usually the Jewish boys involved were not personally acquainted with their enemies. It was enough that they were Poles, and vice versa. It was a matter of racial, cultural, and religious solidarity.[4]

Even the Orient brings its animosities to Chicago, as is illustrated in clashes between Syrian and Assyrian Persians.

[4] Manuscript prepared by a resident of the area.

111. For several years there has been an unwritten law that no Syrian Persian be allowed north of Huron Street on Clark Street. Five members of the race wandered into a coffee shop there and sat down at a table to play cards. In a short time six Assyrian Persians entered the place and saw them. They walked to the table, it is said, and remarked that the Syrians had better get off the street. At that the five Syrians started to fight. In a moment other men in the place drew knives and advanced on the battlers. Chairs were overturned and windows broken. The fight led out to the street. Finally more than two hundred had taken it up. . . . .[5]

NEW NATIONALITY FRICTIONS

When nationalities and races become segregated into relatively homogeneous groups such as immigrant colonies, antagonisms are likely to develop irrespective of previous relations in other countries or localities.

112. A gang of about twenty German-American boys, including a few Hungarians, lived in a German-Hungarian community adjacent to the northern boundary of Little Sicily in the North Side jungles. Across this boundary lived the enterprising Blackhawk gang composed of boys of about the same age, twelve to fourteen years. These two groups possessed a natural enmity for each other in which the nationality factor played a large part. The German-American gang fixed up a clubroom in a coal shed, which became a target for attacks from the invading Italians. The result of a severe stone fight was the complete rout of the German-Americans, whereupon the Italian forces seized the hang-out and broke up all the furniture.[6]

113. The industrial, railroad, and river region about Western Avenue and Twenty-sixth Street has long been a frontier between hostile immigrant colonies. Formerly street-fights, in which gangs from the rival territories took a leading part, were common in the neighborhood. They are said to have been participated in by from one hundred to fifteen hundred people. The residents of a Polish colony to the northeast, lead by such gangs as the "Hillers," who dug themselves in along the canals, would wage pitched battles with many Greeks and Italians from the southwest. A boy was shot through the heart in one of these fights.[7]

[5] News item, *Chicago Tribune*, July 11, 1922.

[6] Interview with a social worker.   [7] Interview with a park director.

CULTURE CONFLICTS AND GANG SUCCESSION

In the growth of Chicago it has repeatedly happened that one immigrant or racial group has invaded the territory of another, gradually driving out the former, only to be itself displaced later by a still different cultural or racial group. This process of invasion and succession is both personal and impersonal and involves both competition and conflict.

Accompanying this succession of communities is a corresponding succession of gangs, although gang names and traditions may persist in spite of changes in nationalities.

114. The population of the Valley [southwest of the Ghetto], beginning with the fifties and continuing after the fire of '71, was dominantly Irish. Fighting was prevalent, burglaries were numerous, and the boys of the neighborhood looked up to their leaders as the Robin Hoods or Jesse Jameses of their times. As a result the Maxwell Street police court had the highest number of cases of any court in the country with the exception of one in New York (this was in the period between 1870 and 1895).

There was one noteworthy Irish gang that began to dominate in the eighties and nineties, the M—— gang. This group, composed of twelve members between nineteen and thirty years of age, hung out at Newberry and Fourteenth streets. They had headquarters in a saloon owned by the M—— family, about which the gang seemed to center. They began, however, as a street gang; among their activities were raiding fruit and vegetable cars on the tracks and molesting peddlers. Their members included saloon-keepers, fences, thieves, and political fixers. Two or three of the M—— family have committed murder, but no one has been hanged for it owing to close-mouthedness and political influence.

The Germans began to invade the neighborhood as early as the fifties and sixties and the Jews began coming in about 1880. The Irish gangs terrorized the Germans and Jews until about 1900 when they lost their majority in the district, although they retained some degree of political control until about 1908. The Germans and Jews, who were more industrious, gradually pre-empted the better houses and became so important numerically and politically that they could make a protest against the sandbagging proclivities of the Irish. The result was that the Irish went to prison, changed their habits, or moved out, and the district became quiet about 1900.

A still later invasion of this territory has been the Lithuanian. Gangs of Lithuanian boys and some Russians have become active and the Maxwell Street district possesses a number of Jewish gangs. The Irish and the Jews have come to a sort of accommodation in the course of their dwelling together in the district. The Jew lets the Irish do his fighting and Irish women often get employment from Jews, working in Jewish homes on Saturdays. The Old World antagonism between Lithuanian and Jew, however, has been carried over and the Lithuanian and Jewish elements clash in Stanford Park, which the non-Jewish gangs call "Jew Park" and which they claim is monopolized by the Jews.[8]

A similar process has taken place in Bridgeport where the original Irish population has given way before the Germans, who are in turn being displaced by the Poles.[9]

Interterritorial feuds often become traditional, and quarrels are handed down long after the racial complexion of the regions has changed and the original causes of the dispute have been forgotten. Such is the case of the Dukies and the Shielders (together known as the "Mickies"), who occupy long strips of rival territory on either side of the railroad tracks along Stewart Avenue in the South Side badlands.[10]

115. In the earlier days when the northern portion of the Mickies' domain was Irish with a mixture of Swedes, there were nothing but cabbage patches and prairies where the White Sox ball park stands at present.

> "De furder y' go, de tougher it gets—
> I live at Toity-Toid an de tracks,
> De last house on de corner,
> An dere's blood on de door,"

has been a kind of ditty since 1898. Fighting was common among the Irish gangs of those days, who thought nothing of throwing

---

[8] Interview with a social worker, long a resident of the district.

[9] Interviews with social workers in the district.

[10] See document 105.

stones and shooting. Groups like the "Bearfoots," the "Hamburgs," and the "Old Rose Athletic Club," organized by a distillery of that name, were formed in this period, and out of them have come many vigorous politicians and some world-famed athletes.

It is said that the names "Dukies" and "Shielders" are a heritage from these older gangs. The traditional hostilities between the territories have been kept up, however, in spite of the radical changes that have taken place. The Irish and the Swedes in the northern section have given way before the Italians who are now the dominant nationality. What was formerly a Swedish church, for example, is now an Italian ink factory. When Armour Square was organized in 1906 the Dukies went in to take charge of and run the park; this brought an inevitable conflict with the Shielders. Despite their animosities, however, they have united on occasion and, as the "Mickies," have engaged in hostilities more or less continuously with the negro gangs to the east of them. The race riots of 1919 were to some extent a culmination of this warfare.[11]

THE RACIAL FRONTIER

There are two kinds of neighborhoods in Chicago occupied by negroes.[12] In one type the negroes and whites have become adjusted to each other and friction is either non-existent or negligible. In the other or non-adjusted neighborhoods there is opposition, either organized or unorganized, which often gives the area of friction the character of a frontier between white and black districts.

The most important colored-white frontier in Chicago is that on the western boundary of the Black Belt. Clashes occurred along this boundary for many years before the race riots of 1919 and they have continued since.[13]

RACE RIOTS AND THE GANG

The events immediately preceding the riot illustrate the development of a culminating crisis, while the riot

[11] Interviews.

[12] The Chicago Commission on Race Relations, *The Negro in Chicago*, p. 108.

[13] *Ibid.*, p. 115.

itself represents the following period of conflict. Throughout this period the gangs played a very important part.

116. Gangs and their activities were an important factor throughout the riot. But for them it is doubtful if the riot would have gone beyond the first clash. Both organized gangs and those which sprang into existence because of the opportunity afforded, seized upon the excuse of the first conflict to engage in lawless acts.

It was no new thing for youthful white and Negro groups to come to violence. For years, ... there had been clashes over baseball grounds, swimming-pools in the parks, the right to walk on certain streets, etc.

Gangs whose activities figured so prominently in the riot were all white gangs, or "athletic clubs." Negro hoodlums do not appear to form organized gangs so readily. Judges of the municipal court said that there are no gang organizations among Negroes to compare with those found among young whites.

The stock yards district, just west of the main Negro area, is the home of many of these white gangs and clubs; . . . . The state's attorney, ... referred to many young offenders who come from this particular district. A police detective sergeant who investigated the riot cases in this district said of this section, "It is a pretty tough neighborhood to try to get any information out there; you can't do it." A policeman on the beat in the district said, "There is the Canaryville bunch in there and the Hamburg bunch. It is a pretty tough hole in there." . . . .

Gangs operated for hours up and down Forty-seventh Street, Wells, Princeton, Shields and Wentworth avenues and Federal Street without hindrance from the police.

A judge of the municipal court said in testimony before the Commission:

"They seemed to think they had a sort of protection which entitled them to go out and assault anybody. When the race riots occurred it gave them something to satiate the desire to inflict their evil propensities on others."[14]

THE BLACK HAND AND ITALIAN GANGS

In addition to precipitating conflict between gangs, differences of race and nationality affect other phases of gang life.

[14] *Ibid.*; see pp. 11–17 for an account of the part played by gangs and clubs in the riots.

The so-called "Black Hand," for example, represents an American adaptation of an institution or at least a tradition indigenous to southern Italy and Sicily. In America it is a secret gang, whose chief purposes seem to be blackmail, private vengeance, and domination of the Italian-American community by intimidation and violence.

117. It is certainly true that the spirit of *mafia, camorra,* and vendetta, the most notorious of the Italian heritages, which developed here into the Black Hand activities, has had a paralyzing effect upon the development of Italian life. Before 1905, in New York, Chicago, New Orleans, Pennsylvania, Ohio, wherever Italians were congregated, systematic blackmail and murder produced a feeling of insecurity and terror unfavorable to all constructive activity.[15]

The Italian community had no power of organization to combat a practice which was traditional and operated like one of the laws of nature. The Italian press got as much news value as possible out of the situation, and threw the blame on the Americans, claiming that they admitted too many Italian criminals and that the American police and court system were defective in comparison with the Italian. But gradually as the practice became epidemic, affecting all classes of Italians and involving Americans also, the Italian community and the American police were forced by public opinion into an alliance which succeeded in abating the evil.[16]

Although no detailed study of this problem has been made, there are many indications that numerous secret Black Hand gangs ply their trade in Chicago. Twelve murders were attributed to Chicago Black Hand groups for the first six months of 1925. One informant who has long lived in "Little Sicily" declares that there have been three hundred Black Hand murders here in the past forty-five years. To speak about the Black Hand is bad form

[15] Robert E. Park and Herbert A. Miller, *Old World Traits Transplanted,* p. 241.

[16] *Ibid.,* pp. 248–49. For the story of the reform movement, see pp. 250–57.

among the Italians,[17] but the educated Italian slyly winks when he tells the investigator that there is no Camorra in Chicago.

The Black Hand often takes advantage of Italian family solidarity in levying its blackmail tribute. Its victims may be driven to yield to its demands or to commit crimes for it for fear that their sisters will suffer abduction and outrage.[18]

The police take a rather fatalistic attitude toward this type of killing on account of the lack of co-operation by those who might give information.[19] The general code of gangland is one of silence even with regard to one's own assailant; the gangster prefers to get his vengeance in his own way. It seems to be a matter of national habit with southern Italians in Chicago not to see or hear anything which could throw any light on the commission of a crime; and this undoubtedly is a matter of self-preservation, as well as the result of a desire to keep these matters out of the hands of American police and court officials.[20]

Another Italian institution, of Corsican origin, which to some extent has been transplanted to America, is the vendetta. This is similar to the blood-feud in the Kentucky mountains, in Montenegro, among Greek gambling factions in Chicago, and elsewhere. The ritual of the ven-

[17] *Ibid.*, pp. 247–48.

[18] Interview with a teacher in a gang area.

[19] This attitude of resignation on the part of the authorities was somewhat modified when in February, 1926, the federal government through its Bureau of Immigration began a drive to deport all alien gangsters, directing its efforts particularly against the Sicilian criminal element in Chicago. This move came after a venire of three hundred men had been exhausted in a futile attempt to get a jury in a murder case in which Italians were defendants. It was said that fear of future vengeance at the hands of the gang deterred the veniremen from serving on the jury. The method of deportation was adopted because of the supposed magical effect of a similar drive in stopping tong wars.

[20] See Marie Leavitt, "Report on the Sicilian Colony in Chicago" (manuscript), quoted in Park and Miller, *op. cit.*, p. 248.

P. & A. Photo

A GANGSTER FUNERAL

Chicago's supposed "crime wave" has been widely advertised through the spectacular aspects of gangster funerals. The photograph shows the great crowds which attempted to get a glimpse of the $10,000 casket of a gang leader assassinated by rival gangsters. Fifteen thousand people sought to attend the funeral, which is said to have cost $100,000; twenty-six truck-loads of flowers banked the grave. The gang, objecting to newspaper photographs on this occasion, seized cameras, smashed plates, and assaulted photographers.

detta, it is said, involves the dipping of the hand into the blood of a murdered kinsman, prior to a campaign of vengeance.

The name "Black Hand" is often copied by adolescent gangs of all nationalities, because of its diabolical connotation.[21] The vendetta, too, is enacted in juvenile gangs. The burial customs of the Italians, whose costly funerals confer prestige, are carried over into the elaborate rites conducted for murdered Italian gangsters.

The Italian system of chaperonage is another instance of an immigrant custom that has a bearing on the gang. Italian girls above twelve years of age are not permitted on the streets or in the company of members of the other sex outside of the family unless accompanied by a female relative. When they reach marriageable age, they are married off to approved suitors. In this way many of the problems of the boy during the same period are avoided. There is no possibility of the entrance of Italian girls into gang relationships, because they are so thoroughly incorporated during adolescence into the family structure. The boys, on the other hand, are free and on the cultural frontiers the gang comes to occupy an important place in their life. Sex hostility and morbid sex practice in some Italian gangs have sometimes been attributed to this rigid system of chaperonage which prevents wholesome contacts of Italian boys with girls of the same nationality.

THE TONGS AS CHINESE GANGS

Although tongs are said to have existed and to have arisen first in the Straits Settlements, most observers agree that the tongs are the product of the Chinese-American community; and some say that they originated in California and Nevada at the time of the Gold Rush.

[21] See the story of Itschkie's "Black Hand Society," document 188.

119. To start with, practically all Chinese tongs that resort to the use of gunmen are merely blackmailing organizations. Self-respecting Chinese don't belong to them. Contrary to general belief, the tongs are an American product. They did not come to us from China. They originated in California and Nevada during the early Gold Rush, and had their inception in the theory that might makes right.

The meaning of the word tong is "protective society." For a yearly fee, one tong will guarantee protection to its members against any enemies they may happen to have in a rival tong. As a side issue of their protective operations, most tongs exercise monopolies either in gambling, slave dealing, drug smuggling, or some similar line.

All tong killings are paid murders and all tong gunmen are paid killers. In order to maintain prestige, the tongs maintain a regular pay-roll for killers in peace time. Because the officials of the tongs involved in the killings put up the price for these killings, they are more responsible for the murders than their paid killers, who get out and do their bidding. Every tong murder committed is with the full knowledge of tong officers, and for every murder they pay out cash. . . . .[22]

120. The tong, which is as American as chop suey, started when California, in the Gold days, needed plenty of Chinese labor. It began as a benevolent association or a trade union or a social club. Then tong men found they could make money by intensive organization, plus hatchets. The idea spread through the years and the tongs grew because even the most peaceable Chinese would rather perish at the hands of fellow-countrymen than be saved by asking the white man to interfere.

How many tongs there are in America few men know, if any man. New York has had three big ones, but there have been traces of others here now and then.[23]

There can be no question but that the tongs function in the Chinese-American community in much the same way as do the more indigenous criminal and semi-criminal

[22] Sergeant Jack Manion, head of the Chinatown squad, San Francisco Police Department, quoted in the *Literary Digest*, December 13, 1924, p. 13.

[23] ———, "New Style Highbinder Fights Tong Wars Today," *New York Times*, October 19, 1924, p. 4.

gangs of our great cities. Even the Chinese have recognized the relationship of the tongs to American groups. A Chinese official in San Francisco makes the following statement:

121. The man who runs a tong is usually an old man, of course, born in China, but about half the men in tongs are young men. They would correspond to your Ragen Colt gangs, I think.[24]

The tong in America is a symptom of disorganization in the Chinese-American community; or it may be thought of as an attempt to organize in defense of certain interests, chiefly illegal in their nature.

122. Somewhat different from the highbinders, are the "fighting tongs." They were organized for the most part about 1870 when the Chinese in California were being attacked. They have become traditional defense organizations which may have been partly patriotic in their origin, but which now function in helping the Chinese when they get in trouble in this country, for example, when they have to go to court. The original patterns for them began in the United States. They were district, rather than family organizations. The On Leongs, who control the Twenty-second Street district in Chicago, were the first to come and are the richest group in this country. The Hip Sings, who control the South Clark Street area and who came from the mountainous regions, are a younger and a poorer group.

The trouble in the most recent Chinese tong war, which involved the whole country, was that a certain On Leong wanted to be president of the tong. Failing in this, he bolted to the Hip Sings, where he built up a group of gunmen.

About one-half of the Chinese in San Francisco are alleged to be members of tongs. The tongs get their chief income from some form of illegal business, fleecing their own countrymen rather than members of other races. Their members are engaged in or are accessory to traffic in dope, smuggling Chinese into this country, dealing in Chinese slave girls, and gambling. It is said that all Chinese gamblers are tong men, necessarily so from the standpoint of protection. Since the tong is often a blackmailing organization, it is somewhat analogous to the American-Italian black hand, which

[24] Interview with a Chinese official, San Francisco, October, 1924, by Winifred Rauschenbush.

P. & A. Photo

TONGMEN

Such Chinese tongs as the Hip Sings and On Leongs, which have carried on extensive and fatal warfare with each other, constitute what corresponds to gangs in the Chinese-American community. The tongs are essentially interested in promoting and protecting illegal activities such as trade in slave girls and opium, as well as blackmailing. (See documents 119-23.)

preys upon wealthy Italians. The Chinese, however, are more helpless than the Italians in a similar situation because American customs and institutions are even more foreign to them, and there is
no superior authority to settle their disputes, which cannot be
handled without great difficulty in American courts.[25]

It is thought by some observers that the so-called
"Highbinder" tongs developed out of the fighting tongs.
This is analogous to the growth of the American gang of
professional thugs and gunmen from a group first developed in conflict and then gradually turning to crime and
attracting criminal elements to it.

123. It is not possible at the present time to say what the
origin or history of the present highbinder tongs has been.

Newspaper records show that there were feuds and killings at
a very early time. As there has always been illegal business of one
kind and another, it may be assumed that these killings were, for
the most part, between underworld characters.

It is quite clear that through the creation of fighting tongs
composed of young men who represented the interest of a district
or family association, but not directly connected with it, an attempt
was made to keep the feud confined to something like a soldiery.

The highbinder tong probably arises where this "soldiery" becomes professional in character. Some clever business man, dealing
in the more profitable and illicit forms of business, who was also
what is known in a Chinese village as a bully, must have seen the
advantage to be gained by terrorizing a city community with his
gang of professional soldiers, as the bully terrorizes the village with
his gang of hangers-on.[26]

This cursory examination of the Chinese tongs indicates their generic relationship to the gang: their origin
in a conflict situation and subsequent professionalization
to carry on or protect some illicit business. The tong
represents a cultural frontier, for Chinese social organiza-

[25] Largely from an interview with Winifred Raushenbush, an authority on the Chinese in America.

[26] Winifred Raushenbush, "Preliminary Notes on the Organization
of the Chinese in the United States" (manuscript).

tion is inadequate in so foreign an environment as America. It represents a moral frontier as well in the case of the highbinder tong, which operates through blackmail and thrives on illegal enterprises which escape American social control.

GANGS AMONG OTHER NATIONALITIES

Among the Irish, fighting has been described as a sort of national habit. Bricks are popularly known as "Irish confetti." The Irish make good politicians and good policemen. It is said that the Jews own New York, but the Irish run it. Irish gangs are probably the most pugnacious of all; not only do they defend themselves, but they seem to look for trouble. Irish names are the favorites for Jewish and Polish "pugs" who assume them for prize fighting. Irish athletic clubs are probably the most numerous and most vigorous in Chicago.

There is probably a historical as well as the stereotyped temperamental explanation for the "chip-on-the-shoulder" attitude of the Irish. It is a culture complex.

124. Our immediate ancestors, fathers and grandfathers, felt the iron heel upon their necks in their early lives, and in our childhood we were fed with stories of eviction, landlord oppressions, and religious persecutions which sent us to bed night after night in fear and trembling lest before morning some Englishman should get into the house and snatch the children away in chains and slavery. Growing older we went into the world and met, more often than not, petty persecutions at the hands of those who did not understand us and the things we held sacred. We saw in it all, translated to this side of the Atlantic, the same spirit of persecution which drove our fathers from the land of their birth, and we have come to manhood carrying chips on our shoulders because of the things which men have done to us on account of our race and religion [27]

The Jews, in contrast with the Irish, do not form gangs so readily. Their family and religious life, even

---

[27] Herbert A. Miller, *Races, Nations, and Classes*, pp. 108–9. Quoted from the letter of an Irish president of an American school board.

among the poorest classes, is better organized and provides more adequately for the activities of the boy.

It is partly for these reasons that Jewish gangs are not formed except under conditions of relatively great disorganization or pressure (such as Polish opposition). Jews are not as great fighters with their fists as the Irish; they prefer to carry on their conflicts with argument, to which they have necessarily been restricted in those countries where anti-Semitism has flourished. Hence, a debating society makes a great appeal to Jewish lads. Adolescent Jewish gangs are predatory rather than combative in type. In spite of their general backwardness in physical combat, however, their freedom from external control has led them to respond to the hard, rough life with which they have been confronted in the West Side wilderness, and there they have developed several older gangs such as the WWW's and the TTT's than which there are no "tougher" in Chicago. About one fourth of the membership of the WWW's is composed of professional prize fighters, and more than once this gang has struck terror into the hearts of overaggressive Polish groups. Jewish leadership of gangs of other nationalities, dependent on wit rather than physical prowess, is not uncommon, although Jewish boys probably more often follow an Irish leader.

DEMOCRACY AND AMERICANIZATION IN THE GANG

Of the 880 gangs upon which data are available as to race and nationality, 396 are dominantly of single nationalities, while 351 are of mixed nationality. While gangs of the former type often carry into their quarrels Old World feuds and antipathies, it is a striking fact that where conditions are favorable to intermingling of different nationalities, there is extensive fraternization in the same gang of boys from these diverse and often antagonistic groups and races.

125. "I never ask what nationality he is," declared a Lithuanian gang leader of thirteen years. "A Jew or a nigger can be a pal of mine if he's a good fellow."

"Aw, we never ask what nationality dey are," said a Polish gang boy. "If dey are good guys, dey get in our gang. Dat's all we want."[28]

The obliteration of race and nationality distinctions in the gang displays a primitive sort of democracy that cuts through conventional discriminations in the same economic stratum. Gang antagonisms are more likely to arise between groups of different economic levels. This is suggestive of the old hostility between "town and gown"—the town roughs and college boys. The "rich kids" are usually given some sort of opprobrious epithet by the gangs, such as "sissies," and they in turn retort with "tough-mugs."

126. One day the boys in our crowd were riding their bicycles in a poorer section of town on the other side of the creek. Some of the boys of that part of the town came out yelling "candy kids" and began throwing stones. They so far outnumbered us that we soon retreated. The next day we gathered in all our friends and returned to the neighborhood where a rough-and-tumble battle took place. We were victors on that occasion, but the incident was the beginning of a feud between the "candy kids" and the "soup bones," which lasted well through our high school days.[29]

In Eugene O'Neill's play, "All God's Chillun Got Wings," the point is made that children know no color line, at least in those sections of a city where different races grow up and play together. This is quite evident in the adjusted black and white neighborhoods in Chicago, for colored and white boys are quite at home in the same gang. The negro invasion into the Ghetto in Chicago has been marked by fraternization of Jewish and negro boys.

[28] Interviews with gang boys.

[29] Manuscript prepared by a former member of the group.

127. About 10,000 southern negroes have recently come into the Ghetto region. Here they are paying $12 a month for quarters formerly rented for $8 but now too dilapidated for Jewish occupancy. The Jewish landlords are making a good thing of it, for the negroes even make their own repairs.

The negro boys brought in by this migration are being received in a friendly way by Jewish boys, and Jewish gangs are now fraternizing with the negroes.[30]

Such facts show how superficial are the barriers of national and racial hostility which keep these groups apart, when there is real community of interest.

THE CULTURAL FRONTIER

A superficial conclusion might easily be drawn from the statistics presented at the beginning of this chapter that the immigrant peoples of the city are responsible for gangs and all the problems related to them. Such an inference would be entirely erroneous. Native white American boys of the same economic and social classes as the children of immigrants enter into gangs just as readily, but their identity is lost because of the vastly greater number of the children of foreign-born parentage in the regions of life where ganging takes place. It is not because the boys of the middle and wealthier classes are native white that they do not form gangs but because their lives are organized and stabilized for them by American traditions, customs, and institutions to which the children of immigrants do not have adequate access. The gang, on the other hand, is simply one symptom of a type of disorganization that goes along with the breaking up of the immigrant's traditional social system without adequate assimilation to the new.

At home the immigrant was almost completely controlled by the community; in America this lifelong control is relaxed. Here the community of his people is at best far from complete, and,

[30] Interview with a resident in the district. See also chap. xvi.

moreover, it is located within the American community, which lives by different and more individualistic standards, and shows, as we have seen, a contempt for all the characteristics of the newcomers. . . . .

There is, of course, violation of the traditional code—breaking of the law—in all societies, and there is at present a general problem of demoralization in the regions from which our immigrants come, particularly where the peasant population has come into contact with the industrial centers or practices seasonal emigration (as from Poland to Germany); but the demoralization, maladjustment, pauperization, juvenile delinquency, and crime are incomparably greater among the immigrants in America than in the corresponding European communities.[31]

The extensive demoralization which exists in the Polish-American community is a good example of the cultural frontier which provides fertile soil for the development of the gang. Intense pride of nationality, which has sometimes been described and explained as an "oppression psychosis,"[32] has often led the Poles in America to concentrate their energies on the development of Polish spirit and patriotism at the sacrifice of adjustment to American society.[33] There is a high degree of disorganization in Chicago among the poor Polish populations, which are almost entirely neglected by the influential nationalistic organizations.[34]

The second generation is better adapted intellectually to the practical conditions of American life, but on the average their moral horizon grows still narrower and their social interests still shallower. One might expect to find fewer cases of active demoralization, of antisocial behavior, than in the first generation which has to pass through the crisis of adaptation to new conditions. And yet it is a well-known fact that even the number of crimes is proportionately

[31] Park and Miller, *op. cit.*, pp. 61–62.

[32] Miller, *Races, Nations, and Classes*, pp. 32–38; 74–77.

[33] Park and Miller, *op. cit.*, pp. 227–34.

[34] William I. Thomas and Florian Znaniecki, *The Polish Peasant in Europe and America*, V, "Organization and Disorganization in America," p. 54.

much larger among the children of immigrants than among the immigrants themselves.[35]

What is true of the Poles is probably true also of the poorer classes which constitute the bulk of the population in all our area-of-first-settlement foreign communities in Chicago.

The conflict between American Christianity and Old World Judaism further illustrates a failure to harmonize divergent cultures.

128. Another issue for group organization is the matter of Christian missions established in certain Jewish areas. Rowdyism develops in connection with the mission meetings and seems to be an expression of the general resentment of the Jewish camp. A bunch of young fellows will go in and do various things to break up the meeting; for example, they will pretend they have been converted and then go out laughing. Or they will interrupt the meeting at its emotional climax and, when put out, will throw stones. Members of such gangs of rough Jewish fellows range in age from seventeen to twenty-four years. Even Jewish children in elementary and high schools have a tendency to band together to ward off discrimination.

Some of these missions are located near California and Division streets. Others are on Kedzie Avenue between Twelfth and Thirteenth streets. In the former neighborhood the Jews have established a Young Men's Hebrew Association, which may be considered a sort of outpost of their religion. [36]

The gang, then, to sum up, is one manifestation of the disorganization incident to cultural conflict among diverse nations and races gathered together in one place and themselves in contact with a civilization foreign and largely inimical to them. At base the problem is one of reconciling these divergent heritages with each other and with America.[37] If there has been any failure here, it can hardly be laid at the door of the immigrant.

[35] *Ibid.*, pp. 168–69.

[36] Interview with a social worker.

[37] See Park and Miller, *op. cit.*, for a full statement of this position.

CHAPTER XI

Sex in the Gang

The influence of sex upon life in the gang varies with the age and biological development of its members. In some of the younger gangs a girl may play the same rôle as a boy. Among the gangs of younger adolescents, there is a definite indifference or hostility to girls as such, although sex interests may be evident in various types of auto-erotic activity. The members of the older adolescent or young adult gang usually have a definite though half-concealed interest in girls. Dates and dancing become important, girls' groups may enter into alliance with the gang, and certain girls may be taken under its protection or in other cases may actually become members of the gang in their sexual capacity.

On the whole, however, it is safe to say that sex represents a decidedly secondary activity in the gang. In the adolescent group in particular, it is subordinated to the primary interests of conflict and adventure to which it is extraneous. As the gang grows older, however, sex gets more attention, in most cases ultimately supplanting the gang entirely to the extent that its members marry and enter into family relationships.

SEX IN THE YOUNGER ADOLESCENT GANG

In the gang of younger adolescent boys, the usual attitude is one of indifference, scorn, or open hostility to girls and their characteristics which are classified as "sissy."

129. The leader of our gang was what is usually termed a "hard rock." He was the leader because he was the "hardest" and because he had a strip clipped off through the hair on his head so that he might show the girls how little he cared for what they thought of his looks.[1]

Most adolescent gang boys are emphatic in denying that they go with girls: they "don't like no girls." When asked why, they give a variety of reasons: They are too young; the girls do not like them; there are no girls around; they get nothing out of it and all girls do is spend money and get them into trouble. In many cases there is evidence of sex hostility: the girls stick their tongues out and "tattle."

130. "Do you like the little girls, Tony?" I asked a boy of fifteen.

"Naw! I never love no girls. I don't want to monkey around wit' girls. Dey give me troubles. I kill de girls."

He has several sisters, so I asked him if he hates them too.

"What, should I hate my sisters? Dey don't give me no troubles. Dey're my sisters."

This attitude toward his sisters is significant of the strong family bonds of Tony's group (the Italians).

"Oder girls report me to teacher for t'rowing t'ings—snowballs. One said I jumped on her. . . . . I just push her—like dat. All de oders jump on her; she don't report dem; only me. . . . . Why don't dey go straight home?" he asked complainingly; then, to demonstrate what great trouble-makers girls are, he added, "Dey have to wait for somebody."[2]

The reasons for this group attitude against women seem to be in the main that they have interfered with the

[1] Manuscript prepared by a former member of the gang.
[2] Teacher's interview with a boy.

enterprises of the group, have weakened the loyalties of its members, or in demanding time and attention have impaired the gang as an effective conflict group. Thus gang tradition discourages any but the most casual contacts, and if a boy's clandestine interest in girls becomes manifest or overt, he is usually subjected to most unpleasant ridicule, upbraided for his lack of loyalty, or more definitely disciplined by the gang.

131. As soon as a member of our gang of high-school Freshmen showed any desire to walk home from school with girls or attend one of their parties, he was automatically dropped. If he fell from grace but once, he could sometimes be reinstated by taking a "billy wedging."[3]

Although the gang at this age affects to despise girls, it sometimes has its own code of chivalry with reference to them.

132. The boy who attempted to fight with a girl was punished by the other boys. A girl might slap a boy in the face and all he could honorably do was to dodge the second blow, or, if he was very religious, as was seldom the case, he might turn his head around and ask to have the inequality rectified by a similar blow on the other side.[4]

In one case, considerable alarm was caused among women workers in a social settlement by the fact that gang boys followed them at night. The fear was alleviated, however, when it was found that the interest of these boys was in protecting the women in accordance with the Irish idea of chivalry.

In spite of the general lack of attention to girls and women, much informal "sex education" takes place in the adolescent gang.

133. The gang developed in the boy a distinct point of view, so that he considered it somewhat of a disgrace to play with girls.

[3] Manuscript prepared by a former member of the gang.
[4] Manuscript prepared by a former member of the gang.

At this stage he would be the subject of derision if caught playing, or even conversing familiarly, with any girl except his sister. The older boys, however, became instructors of the younger boys of the gang in sex matters, and in many of them a premature interest and curiosity was inculcated. There was a large amount of obscene literature and art, which was circulated very freely among the boys, copied many times over and handed down to the next "generation" as a social legacy. [5]

In one case the chief interest of the group was in learning about sex matters. These boys were finally brought into court because of a sort of polyandry carried on with a girl in their hang-out. The dominance of this interest in the adolescent gang, however, is very rare.

THE GANG WHICH INCLUDES BOTH SEXES

How may we understand then the instances of juvenile gangs which have a girl as a member? The real explanation is that the girl takes the rôle of a boy and is accepted on equal terms with the others. Such a girl is probably a tomboy in the neighborhood. She dares to follow anywhere and she is ill at ease with those of her own sex who have become characteristically feminine. Sooner or later, however, sex differentiation arises: the whole situation is changed and the girl can no longer assume her rôle in the gang.

134. My entrance into the alley gang occurred soon after my family moved to a small town of five thousand population. I was eight years of age at the time, a small but strong and agile girl quite capable of taking care of myself and of my younger brothers and sister.

The first few days I watched the boys playing in the alley beside the church where my father was to act as pastor. One morning I found one of the boys surrounded by a delighted group of onlookers, torturing a frog. I could not countenance such cruelty, and I squirmed my way into the group.

"Stop that!" I commanded.

[5] Manuscript prepared by a former member of the gang.

The boy looked up in astonishment, grinned, and continued his activity. I sailed into him and soon sat astride his stomach, directing vicious jabs at his head.

"Say 'enough'!" I demanded. He wiggled uncomfortably and looked sheepishly at the interested circle of boys.

"Nuff!" he said, and I let him go. The next day I was invited to take part in a game of Piggy; I had made my debut into the gang as an equal.

Nearly all the boys in the neighborhood of the church belonged to the gang, the number varying from fifteen to twenty. For a short time I was the only girl, but after I had become "friends" with Marion, who lived around the corner from my home, I saw to it that she also became a member, although she was never accepted on a status of absolute equality. "Cliff," the oldest of the boys, was the recognized leader, and the gang followed him unquestioningly.

The requirements for joining the gang varied and, although never expressed, were definitely understood to include some ability in the line of physical prowess. Some contribution to the gang's welfare was sometimes sufficient for temporary membership. Forrest, whom we knew as rather a sissy, was admitted for a time because of his new football. Marion, too, enjoyed membership for a considerable period, partly because I insisted on it and was able to back up my arguments, partly because her mother was generous with oatmeal cookies, and also because she came in handy as a captive maiden when we were conducting Indian wars. She drew away from the gang gradually when I realized that she did not belong, and withdrew my claims.

The only other gang with which we came in contact was the Sunnyside gang, a group of older boys, more commonly known as "toughs," from the South Side of town.

It was in an effort to hold his own against an arrogant Sunnysider that Cliff first swore. We were rather startled, and I, being encumbered with much religious training, waited for him to be struck dead. He wasn't. He repeated the fearful words, mouthing them as though he enjoyed the taste. Art tried it, and then Glenn; and then, the gang meaning more to me than salvation, I followed suit. After that, we swore occasionally and nonchalantly but always in the privacy of our pals.

The Sunnyside gang had a meeting place, a haunted house, and from them we got the idea of establishing headquarters. Hitherto we had not felt the need, but a meeting place now became a necessity. We chose the haymow of a barn and used it for a base.

The lack of sex differences in the gang was significant. I was always accepted on terms of absolute equality. In the instance of playing Indian, as mentioned before, I was as bloodthirsty and terrible a warrior or as stalwart and brave a pilgrim defender as any of the boys. I should have been insulted to have been relegated to the rôle of captive maiden, and I doubt if the boys thought of such a thing. Marion's submission to the part is perhaps one reason why she never really belonged. I could shinny up the walnut tree in less time than any of the boys; I took my turn at bat, and played tackle or end in our hodgepodge football struggles. Girls, except Marion, were to me silly and nonessential; and I took delight in shouting derisively with the gang, "George's got a gurrl! George's got a gurrl!" when George carried Mabel's books home from school.

My personality outside the group was very different. The most uncomfortable afternoon of my life was spent at the birthday party of one of the girls in my Sunday-school class. I was distinctly out of place among the pink and blue frills. It was evident that my attitude toward the boys was quite different from that of the other girls, and that in a party atmosphere the boys regarded me in a different light from what they did in the alley. I suffered the agonies of the damned on these occasions. I sat by myself on the stair steps—and I spilled my lemonade.

My exit from the gang occurred the spring when I was eleven years old. I fell in love. It is significant that I did not "fall" for another member of the gang but for a boy who had just moved into the neighborhood. The experience changed everything for me. Boys became boys, not fellows, and I became self-conscious. I didn't understand the process or the result, but I realized that things were different. I remember that a heavy rain had left a large puddle—almost a small pond—of water in the alley. When I came home from school some of the boys were already wading.

"Come on over!" they called. A week before that time I should have dropped my books on the steps, jerked off my slippers and stockings, tucked my skirts into my bloomers, and waded in. This time I blushed furiously, flung at them a confused excuse about helping my mother, and hurried into the house. The object of my affections stood watching the gang.[6]

Another interesting case is that of a gang composed largely of girls who had transferred their interests from

[6] Manuscript prepared by a former member of the gang (the girl in the case).

sewing to playing in a large sand hill with a protruding plank. Forced to defend their play place against other gangs, they waged wars in which combat took the form of rock battles. They took the rôles of boys until they began to wear their hair up and put on long skirts.

DO GIRLS FORM GANGS?

This is a question very frequently asked, but one not difficult to answer. Gangs composed entirely of girls are exceedingly rare. Not more than five or six have been discovered in the present investigation. One of these was a group of colored girls in Chicago having baseball as their chief interest; another was organized for stealing; and the others were marginal cases, probably more really clubs than gangs.

It might seem quite plausible to say, therefore, that the reason girls do not form gangs is that they lack the gang instinct, while boys have it. This explanation lacks analysis of the problem. There are two factors: first, the social patterns for the behavior of girls, powerfully backed by the great weight of tradition and custom, are contrary to the gang and its activities; and secondly, girls, even in urban disorganized areas, are much more closely supervised and guarded than boys and are usually well incorporated into the family group or some other social structure.

The analogue to the boys' gang among girls is probably the clique or the set, but this must be regarded as an entirely different type of collective behavior. In certain groups where girls are allowed a greater degree of freedom as they grow older, there is a trend toward a type of club which corresponds to the athletic club among the boys and is sometimes affiliated with it. This, however, is not a conflict group and it does not exist in most immigrant communities on account of the close supervision to which the girls are subject.

THE IMMORAL GANG

What have commonly been reported as "immoral gangs," composed of both sexes, are probably of the orgiastic type, such as the Fusileers,[7] rather than true conflict groups. Their chief activities seem to be what are commonly called in college circles "petting, necking, and mugging," and often include illicit sex relations. Cases of this sort are not rare.

136. This was a mixed gang whose interests were immoral. The group was well organized and carried on its activities systematically. Its members met in the open fields under the stars. One of the girls was ultimately sent to the Juvenile Psychopathic Institute for examination.[8]

Special conditions may tend to develop this type of gang. A group called the "Night Riders," of which a complete account was obtained from the members themselves, was the product of a rooming-house environment. The boys and girls, living with parents or relatives in cramped quarters, were anemic and not of the type to form a rugged conflict group like those often found in the slums. The impression from such a study was somewhat similar to that obtained from seeing pale insects crawling about in the bleached grass upon turning over a board that has lain for a long time on the ground in some damp unwholesome place.

Many cases of the "petting clique" or so-called "immoral gang" have been reported in grade and high schools and sometimes in colleges. When cases of this sort get into the newspapers, as they sometimes do, they are widely heralded as "vice rings" and their sensational aspects are played up to the nth degree.

138. The main purpose of this gang was sexual, and the indications are that not only normal but many unnatural or degenerate methods of sex gratification were in vogue. The boys of the group

---

[7] See document 14.   [8] Interview with a court reporter.

were as a whole stronger or tougher than the other boys in the school, and they succeeded pretty well in dominating the rest of us and playing the part of bullies.

In seasonable weather the scene of the gang's activity was a vacant lot on the South Side, or else a half-block of meadow land east of the I. C. tracks. The lot was at one time raided by the police and a number of the group were taken, but no punishment followed so far as I am able to discover. In rainy or chilly weather the gang assembled in some deserted barn. Members of the group also managed to get together on other occasions such as a picnic to Ravinia given by members of the eighth-grade class, when five or six disappeared and did not return until time to leave for home.

Of the fifteen or more members of the gang, some seemed to be quite normal mentally and physically while others were sub-normal or worn out by excesses. There was not much conscious organization in the group, but the biggest boy was the apparent leader. The ages of the members were from thirteen to sixteen.

Most of the members of this group had bad records: some had been in the reform school; most of them had been suspended from school at least once; and others were eventually expelled. One boy was brought before the principal for flourishing a revolver on the playground. Scholastically they were below the average, but they dominated physically and in athletics, partly due to their greater size.

The only rule which the gang had, to my knowledge, was that no member should indulge in relations with outsiders. On the whole, they made no effort to conceal the nature of their activities and seemed to take pride in flaunting them before the rest of us. They possessed certain signals by which one of the boys could "ask" one of the girls while in class. These signals soon became known to the rest of us, and it is probable that even the teacher was not entirely unaware of what was going on.

The attitude of the rest of the class toward the group was largely one of disgust mingled with hatred. This was especially true of the boys, although there was a small group on the border line that looked upon the gang with admiration.[9]

Groups of this type are probably far more common than is ordinarily supposed. There is every indication that ease of obtaining parental permission for the free

---

[9] Manuscript prepared by an observer of the gang.

and unchaperoned use of the family automobile, or ready access to the cars of friends, is one of the most important elements in the situation.

CONVENTIONAL SEX LIFE IN THE OLDER GANGS

The conventional sex relations of members of the older gangs, especially of the conventionalized type such as the athletic club, usually take the form of picnics or hilarious truck parties to the forest preserves and dances.

Dances are exceedingly popular and a source of considerable income. The club dance is held in the club's own rooms or in a rented hall and is often patronized by other clubs. The dance programs are elaborate and contain a great deal of advertising by local business men and also by politicians who in addition often act as patrons, make speeches, or lead the grand march.

Gangs virtually control certain of the public dance halls of the city. The conventionalized gang may take the name of its favorite dance hall and organize an athletic team bearing the same name. The clubs often have special "pull" with the management of these halls, which may depend largely upon such patronage for their receipts. Special nights at the dance halls are set aside for particular gangs or clubs; special concessions and privileges are granted with reference to exclusiveness and the use of liquors. In return the gang protects the management from the ordinary bum or loafer and is liberal with its patronage. Clashes between gangs in or about the dance halls are not uncommon occurrences.

THE STAG PARTY

A favorite form of entertainment with certain so-called athletic clubs and gangs of similar type is the stag party. The nature of these affairs which are exceedingly demoralizing is described in a report of the Juvenile Protective Association.

140. . . . . While some stag parties are legitimate and unobjectionable affairs, others are characterized by conduct too obscene to permit description. . . . .

It is impossible to describe in this bulletin the immoral practices permitted at some of these parties which rival the extreme depravities formerly prevailing in the commercialized vice district. Only hints of certain scenes actually observed by Protective Officers can be given. Stories of the most obscene character are related by a woman to a crowd of men and boys. Indescribably filthy jokes are perpetrated by a ventriloquist with the aid of a puppet. Degrading dancing—vile beyond description—is indulged in by girls some of whom are apparently scarcely out of their teens, while a woman gives nude an unbelievably debasing dance. After these demoralizing exhibitions girls circulate through the audience taking up a collection and assuring the patrons that, "the more you put in the more the girls will take off." Then follows the climax of the evening. Women dancers appear, first singly and later in groups entirely nude and proceed to participate in a licentious debauchery in which the men near by join. The scene finally culminates in a raffle of one of the girl performers, the man holding the winning ticket being awarded the girl for the balance of the night.

The Juvenile Protective Association has concerned itself with these unspeakable exhibitions because of their corrupt effect on young boys and girls. An investigation of a dozen so-called entertainments has invariably revealed the presence of minors. At one affair held in the Loop the names and addresses of twenty-two boys from fifteen years of age and up were secured. At another "smoker" given on the West Side attended by many minors a girl of ten years and a nine-year-old boy were exhibited in a pugilistic contest refereed by the children's father. Immediately following the bout a nude woman danced. Women entertainers whose performances were most obnoxious have acknowledged in open court that they had children of their own.[10]

The frequency of this type of entertainment, which is not confined to the gangs, is not generally known since great precautions are taken to maintain secrecy and only occasionally are such parties raided.

[10] "Stag Parties," *Bulletin*, Juvenile Protective Association, Vol. III, No. 3 (May, 1921).

141. Story-telling palled on the guests at the ninety-second anniversary celebration of the Eagle Oriental club. . . . . They wanted the big attraction of the evening. It came. Eight young women began to dance while, little by little, they disrobed in time to the music, until they had nothing on but their shoes.

Police, having seen all there was to see, decided it was time to act. They admitted other policemen from outside and in a few moments the 8 women and 197 men were arrested. Yesterday the men were all fined $1.00 and costs each. The case of the women was continued for a jury trial, together with that of the announcer, the pianist, and the doorkeeper.[11]

Certain politicians, perceiving the popularity of the stag party, have not hesitated to capitalize the sex appeal and employ this sort of entertainment for political rallies attended by hundreds of men and boys.

SEX DELINQUENCIES AMONG THE OLDER GANGS

Among the members of the older gangs there is evidence of looseness and promiscuity often involving the obliging sweetheart or the clandestine prostitute, as well as inmates of disorderly houses. Some of the clubs have been accused of harboring women in their rooms, but ordinarily this practice is avoided as being too dangerous.

A peculiar form of sex delinquency in a particular gang area may be in the tradition of the groups of that community. This is illustrated in the so-called "gang shag" which is in vogue among the older adolescent gangs in a certain disorganized immigrant community in Chicago.

143. The gang shag is an institution peculiar to the gangs and clubs of this neighborhood. There are few sex perverts among the boys, but there is a great deal of immorality. This does not begin, as a rule, before the age of sixteen or seventeen.

The gang shag includes boys from sixteen to twenty-two years of age. It is a party carried on with one woman by from fifteen to thirty boys from one gang or club. A mattress in the alley usually

[11] *Chicago Tribune*, March 15, 1923.

suffices for this purpose. This number of boys have relations with the woman in the course of a few hours.

As a result of this institution and other irregular practices of a like nature, venereal disease is very high among the boys. One physician in the district has had as high as twenty boys from a single club of forty members under treatment at one time.[12]

The semi-criminal gangs and clubs of older adolescents and young men are sometimes guilty of attacks on women. The victim may be attacked incidentally in the process of a holdup or may be enticed to the hang-out of the gang.

144. The Bear Claws, composed of about fifty members ranging in age from seventeen up, had a clubroom in an old barn in the South Side badlands. Some of its members were roughnecks and sluggers and its hang-out was also frequented by pickpockets and other criminals, who lowered the moral tone of the club.

One night the man who was renting the barn to this group heard a woman screaming, "Murder, murder, they're killing me!" When he ran to the barn, he saw the members of the club running out. In the loft he found an elderly colored woman wired to the floor with her hands behind her head. Her body was covered with blood and scratches. She had been attacked by the whole group.[13]

There is a common practice among young men in Chicago, and this is by no means confined to boys of the gangs or the underprivileged classes, of picking up girls, utter strangers, on the street and taking them for a ride in an automobile. During the course of this ride it is customary to indulge in passionate petting, and often the affair culminates in the sex act. If the girl refuses, it is commonly supposed that she is put out of the car some place in the country and asked to walk back. So widespread is this practice that allusions to it have become a common joke on the vaudeville stage. Many a girl voluntarily or involuntarily begins a delinquent career in just

[12] Interview with a physician resident in a social settlement.

[13] Interview with a social worker in the district.

this manner; in some cases she is made the victim of a brutal attack after accepting such an invitation.

145. A Jewish girl eighteen years of age on her way home from work flirted with two young men and finally accepted a ride. Instead of driving her home, they stopped in front of a poolroom where soft drinks were served and coaxed her to come inside.

This was the hang-out of a gang of about seventeen Italian boys ranging in age from seventeen to twenty-one. The door was locked and the girl was attacked by six or seven of the group. The proprietor of the poolroom in the meantime called up the remainder of the gang, seventeen in all, and the girl was attacked by this number within an hour. The girl was three months in a hospital before she recovered. The men were sent to the Joliet penitentiary.

This is the type of poolroom gang that loafs consistently and whose members are always on the lookout for a way to make some easy change. They gamble and are out for any excitement.[14]

"CHERCHEZ LA FEMME"

Women have come to play an increasingly important part in the criminal gang. While wives of successful gangsters are well protected, sweethearts and paramours often take part in criminal enterprises, sometimes acting as lures, sometimes actually holding a gun and participating as any other gangster in a holdup. Robbery is no longer taboo for women, that is, for women who live in an underworld atmosphere. Since the occupations of men, formerly closed to women, have been opened to them, what is inconsistent about their entering the time-honored profession of the highwayman? They may do it for thrills; they may do it because hard pressed to make a living; they may do it simply as a matter of course; but at least it is more wholesome than becoming a prostitute.

Yet this sort of activity for women who live on an urban frontier should not occasion surprise. The frontier of the pioneer often created conditions favorable to the entrance of women into criminal gangs. Women were usu-

[14] Interview with a police matron.

ally attached to the bandit gangs that created such terror in the early days of Illinois. Then there was Kitty Kelly, as hard boiled as any member of the notorious gang of Australian bushrangers; and Texas had its Belle Star, who has been compared and contrasted with the modern Brooklyn gun-girl.

Cases of this type indicate how a woman, abandoning what are conventionally regarded as feminine traits, may play the rôle of a man in a gang and be accepted on terms of equality with the other members. It is quite possible in some of these cases that she may play the dual rôle of gangster and sweetheart, but ordinarily one part or the other seems to dominate. So well, indeed, does a girl sometimes play the gangster rôle that she may qualify for a share in the leadership of such a group.

146. A diminutive, bobbed-haired girl of twenty-one, who thrilled with pride on being told she resembled Clara Phillips, the hammer-slayer, but wept with shame at the thought of bringing sadness to her mother, last night confessed to the Evanston police that she was the brains and sometimes the brawn of a bandit crew responsible for seventy-five North Shore robberies and holdups.

—— —— is her name, but she particularly requested that it be given as "Honey," explaining that that was what "the fellows" called her. In jail with her is —— ——, while Tom —— is out on $2,000 bonds, being named by Honey as her crime lieutenants. Glen ——, whom she coyly terms her sheik; Connie —— and Roy —— are sought.

Honey mingled her story with many a "My Gawd!" and "That's the hell of it!" and resentfully explained that her arrest came when a "bunch of those damn police overheard me telling about one of the jobs I pulled."

"My gang didn't have the nerve, that was the trouble. My sheik, Glen, was O.K., but I had to steer him. But that —— ——. was yellow. One night we were waiting to pull a stickup at Ridge and Dempster and he got cold feet. I stuck my gun to his head and said:

" 'I'll blow your brains out if you try to quit now.'

"That brought him across all right.

"Glen started me on this stuff, I guess. I worked in my mother's confectionery store. I'd go out with him and sit in the car while he pulled stickups, but he didn't know how to work them, so I took charge. Then we annexed the rest of the gang and put over some swell jobs."[15]

MARRIAGE AND THE GANG

Ultimately the biological function of sex serves, perhaps, as the chief disintegrating force in the gang. Marriage is the most powerful and dominant social pattern for mature sex relations even in the disorganized regions of gangland. Consequently it represents the ultimate undoing of most gangs with the exception, perhaps, of the distinctly criminal groups of the professional type which specialize in rum-running, banditry, and similar activities. For the gang boy, marriage usually means reincorporation into family groups and other social structures of work, play, and religion which family life as a rule brings with it. The gang which once supplanted the home, now succumbs to it; for the interstitial gap in the social framework has been filled. Conventionalization of the gang indicates that this process of disintegration is not far distant. When members begin marrying there is a loss of interest and the club's charter and equipment are eventually sold or passed on to a younger group destined to repeat the same cycle.

[15] Genevieve Forbes, "Girl, Twenty-one, Tells How She Ruled Hold-up Gang," *Chicago Tribune*, January 3, 1923. This account in the main has been verified from interviews with members of other gangs and other informants. It seems, however, that Honey was the "brains," not the leader of the gang. The leader was Tom ——, "a husky bird and a good fighter." The gang was composed of about nine members ranging in age from seventeen to twenty-one. Honey was the only girl. The chief delinquency of the gang was burglary, rather than robbery. Honey was given a year's sentence by Judge Caverly, but this was suspended contingent on good behavior.

THE GANG AND THE MORAL FRONTIER

The different types of sex life in the gang, which it appears vary all the way from ordinary conventional contacts to the utmost depravity and perversion, depend, in the first place, upon the age of the group. The indifference or hostility to girls found among younger adolescents, where the sexual appetite is immature, is later strengthened by gang discipline. The most rigorous discipline, however, is not long able to suppress the sex responses which are the result of developing biological mechanisms and functions. The form the sex behavior takes depends pretty largely upon the attractiveness and general character of their other activities, the nature of their leadership, the degree of their conventionalization, the nature and prestige of the social patterns to which they have access, and the general conditions of social control in their environment.

Space forbids the elaboration of all these points. It is important, however, to indicate the great significance of the situation complex in this connection. The gang boy lives in a disorganized social world where loose sex life is a matter of common observation. Sometimes he sees it in his own home where brothers, sisters, and lodgers are all crowded into the same sleeping quarters.

Gang boys come into ready contact with the social patterns presented by vice, for gangland is largely co-extensive with these areas.[16]

The area of deterioration about the business center of the city has always provided the natural habitat for the brothels. The slum, just because it is the "scrap heap" of the community, furnishes a region—perhaps the only region within the city proper—in which this ancient and flagrant type of vice resort can flourish. The brothel, on account of its underworld business organization and its open appeal to a large public patronage, has always been the most

[16] See document 188.

obnoxious form of commercialized vice. It not only finds cover in this area of deterioration but also is in close proximity to the demand. Although the brothel in modern times has noticeably declined, giving place to a freer type of prostitution, and although the policy of public repression has accelerated this decline, yet the slum still harbors the vestiges of this institution. The most open and public type of vice resort within the city at the present is found there. The so-called "protected" and "syndicate" houses of prostitution in Chicago, which are remnants of a brothel prostitution, are in this area of deterioration.[17]

It becomes readily apparent, then, that these conditions of congestion and intimate contact with vice, coupled with widespread promiscuity which seems more or less traditional among the young men of these areas, present patterns of life to the gang and its members that easily promote sexual irregularities.

The energies and impulses of boys are much the same the world over; they are simply functions of the organism in the period of growth. They are certainly not instincts; for they are far more inchoate than such predetermined and definite patterns of behavior. The organism of the normal boy demands activity and change; puberty brings sexual promptings; rest, food, and bodily protection are among the needs of the boy. Such innate predispositions as these are generalized and flexible. They do not become specific until they are developed in particular directions by all the stimulating forces in the boy's environment.

But the boy is not to be regarded as a passive structure, receiving the stamp of his environment like a lump of wax. If he is healthy, his energies are keenly active and his wishes are often imperative; they must get some sort of expression. Yet the direction they take depends upon the environment. The boy is plastic; his energies

[17] Walter C. Reckless, "The Natural History of Vice Areas in Chicago," manuscript in University of Chicago Library, p. 157.

and impulses may be directed in a multitude of different ways. Just as the natural resources of a region or a country determine in a general way the occupations of its inhabitants, so the habitat of the gang shapes the interests of its members. The group, responding to its human environment, develops along definite lines. Its activities in general tend to follow the patterns which have prestige in its social milieu and which at the same time appeal to its love for adventure or to other wishes of its members.

Thus, life in the gang is a product of interaction between the fundamental nature of the group and its members on the one hand and the environment on the other. Neither factor may be neglected in explaining it.

PART III

Organization and Control
in the Gang

Introduction

The gang develops as a response to society. The social group of which the gang boy is a member has failed to provide organized and supervised activities adequate to absorb his interests and exhaust his energies. An active boy without an outlet for his energies is a restless boy—seeking satisfactions he cannot name, willing to experiment, curious about this and that, eager to escape whatever surveillance is placed upon him. The gang solves his problem, offering him what society has failed to provide.

Free from conventional control, the gang, nebulous as it is, tends toward organization of an elementary form. The demands of common activities and the opposition of its natural enemies—other gangs and superiors with authority—necessitates an effort to act as a unit, out of which it develops a code, methods of control, and a structure. The organization of the embryonic gang may be crude in the extreme and only partially recognized by the boys; yet a working relationship exists between the members, which makes of it a rudimentary society with a constructive tendency. Co-operation requires division of labor. Common enterprises necessitate subordination and discipline and create opportunities for leadership.

But from another point of view the gang is not divorced from larger social controls. Without formal and conventional control, yet it reflects in its activities the adult life and the customs of the particular community where it is found.

CHAPTER XII

Social Patterns and the Gang

In those interstitial sections of Chicago where neglect and suppression of boyhood combine to produce gangs, there abound adult social patterns of crime and vice which are naturally reflected in the activities of the unsupervised gang or gang club. In the poverty belt, the deteriorating neighborhood, and the slum there is little understanding of the interests of boys or the situations they meet in everyday life. So far as immigrant communities are concerned the parents were reared for the most part in rural or semirural Old World communities controlled by tradition and with few new and disturbing situations to be met. Their children on the streets of Chicago come into contact with a motley collection of diverse customs on the one hand and new situations on the other. Hence, they have needs of which their parents never heard.

The larger community of gangland is no better able to provide for the boy than is the immigrant family. While the mobility of these areas affords him a considerable range of contacts, these are in the main demoralizing. Attempts of the American community to deal with the situation have taken the form of settlements and various boys' clubs, but while the work of such agencies has been constructive, they are far too few in number to meet the needs of such a vast territory.

Hence, without wholesome direction for the most part from the home or the larger community, the gang adopts the patterns which have prestige in its own social environment, selecting those which appeal to it and setting them up to be followed by its own members in so far as the group controls them.

THE ISOLATION OF GANGLAND

Some degree of isolation is common to almost every vocational, religious, or cultural group of a large city. Each develops its own sentiments, attitudes, codes, even its own words, which are at best only partially intelligible to others.[1] *Between gangland and the conventionalized American community exists this barrier of unsympathetic social blindness, this inability of either to enter understandingly into the life of the other.* The social world of the gang boy suffers from this isolation and the boy himself lacks contacts which would help prepare him for participation in the activities of a conventional social order.

A large part of this isolation is due to the fact that in Chicago he usually lives in an immigrant colony, which is itself an isolated social world. Immigrant participation in American life is not encouraged by the American community. Contacts with Americans are usually superficial and disheartening and for the child are limited to certain official contact with school teachers, employers, or police.[2] It often happens also that the immigrant community resists Americanization in order to exalt the values of a nationality that has been oppressed abroad.[3] Hence, the

[1] See Robert E. Park, *et al.*, *The City*, p. 26.

[2] Robert E. Park and Herbert A. Miller, *Old World Traits Transplanted*, chap. iii, "Immigrant Experiences," describes the effects of American contacts.

[3] *Ibid.*, pp. 45–46.

children of the foreign born do not come into contact with the best in American life, but, when they escape parental control and follow their own impulses, become Americanized only with reference to our vices.[4]

The significance of this lack of cultural communion with the world at large can hardly be overemphasized in explaining the life and organization of the gang. Almost everything—history, geography, art, music, and government—that is the common knowledge of the schoolboy of the middle classes, is entirely beyond the ken and experience of the gang boy. He moves only in his own universe and other regions are clothed in nebulous mystery. He is only vaguely aware of them, for they rarely cut his plane. There are exceptions, of course, for some gangs are less isolated than others, but this description is characteristic of the great majority.

As a result, the gang boy does not participate in civic affairs, nor does he have much part in the life of his own isolated community. He knows little of the outside world except its exteriors. He views it usually as a collection of influences that would suppress him and curtail his activities with laws and police, cells and bars. In one way or another he is denied effective access to the larger cultural heritages of the dominant social order.

SOCIAL PATTERNS AND THE MORALITY OF THE GANG

In developing their own organization, gang boys cannot go beyond their experiences, and hence their codes and chosen activities must be studied with reference to the moral codes and activities they meet in the communities where they live. Gang morality develops from the interpretation or definition which the gang, in the light of its previous experience, puts upon events.

The definition of the situation, which in its social as-

[4] See *ibid.*, pp. 288–89.

pects represents morality, has been stated by William I. Thomas. Every self-determined act is performed in the light of the individual's examination and deliberation; this results in the individual definition of the situation. Definitions of the situation have already been established, however, by the groups into which the child is born and there is little chance to change these to meet individual whims. There is always, therefore, a conflict between individual wishes and the definitions, which have been worked out as the result of social experience for the safety of the group. Thus moral codes arise to curb the individual pursuit of pleasure. "Morality is thus the generally accepted definition of the situation, whether expressed in public opinion and unwritten law, in a formal legal code, or in religious commandments and prohibitions."[5]

The definition of the situation for the gang boy must emanate largely from the disorderly life of the economic, moral, and cultural frontiers of which gangland is a manifestation. The problem of gang morality, therefore, may be stated largely in terms of the patterns which prevail in the immediate social environment.

The mechanism by which the gang boy molds his life according to the patterns he knows by experience is not wholly one of rational choice. The process is common to all social life and is found in the adoption by children of the ways of their parents. It is the same unreflective process by which the child builds up the verbal habit organization represented in language.

Likewise, the play of children generally tends to follow the adult patterns. In Spain, for example, the boys play at bullfighting rather than at baseball, while the Ku Klux Klan has had its infantile counterpart in the play of American children.

So, also, the exploits of the gang tend to follow pat-

[5] William I. Thomas, *The Unadjusted Girl*, pp. 42–43.

terns in its own social world. The underlying principles and mechanisms of gang behavior are the same for all groups of this type, but there are sharp contrasts in the nature of gang activities in different environments. This is strikingly brought out in comparing the gangs of a lumbering community with those of Chicago.

148. In a lumbering community of about 5,000 members in West Virginia there were about a dozen gangs ranging in size from twelve to fifteen boys between the ages of ten and sixteen. Many of the boys came from what would ordinarily be termed good homes. They were not supervised, however, by their parents, who did not know what the boys were doing.

It seemed to be in the tradition of the boy life of the community to form gangs and have their cabins in the woods. The amusements of the gangs were determined largely by the fact that they lived in a lumber town. There was a good deal of rough life there; a great many log or lumber "hicks" would work three or four months up in the woods and then come into town on a big spree. The chief sports of the gangs were connected with outdoor life and the woods. Their activities centered around their cabins. We did a lot of hunting and fishing. We enjoyed performing great feats, such as long-distance walking, being able to cook well, handling an axe well, and enduring hardships. These were the types of thing that had prestige in the lumbering environment.[6]

DEMORALIZING SOCIAL PATTERNS

Demoralizing social patterns[7] confront the gang boy on every hand: they are in the streets and alleys; they come from the older gangs and clubs and from the under-world; and they are impressed by various agencies that exploit the boy and in so doing promote unwholesome or criminal activities. The result for the gang is an inevitable repertoire of predatory activities and a universe of dis-

[6] Interview with a former member of one of these gangs.

[7] Certain phases of heretofore accepted American morality may be regarded as in a confused and unsettled state. There are conflicting standards with reference to sex, prohibition, gambling, and so on. This makes more difficult a conclusive definition of the situation for the boy.

course reflecting the disorganized social environment of gangland.

For the young gang boy one type of group which not only has prestige but offers a pattern which he may follow with little adaptation is the older gang. In street and alley the younger gangs meet similar groups of older fellows. Many times they bully the smaller boys and force them to do their bidding. A little boy makes a good lookout, or can easily be put through a small window or a transom on a robbing expedition.

149. An awful tough gang composed of about sixty members included boys from six years old up to twenty. They have the little fellows sneak or climb into houses. The little boys may get caught, but it makes no difference. The big ones beat it and the little ones are released.[8]

Members of younger gangs sometimes have to pay money tribute to the older to keep from getting "beat up" or "arrested." The older groups often start the younger ones stealing, but sometimes protect them when they get into trouble. Often the hardened gangster is the object of adolescent hero worship.

The boys also become juniors or midgets and consciously ape their older brothers in numerous social and athletic clubs.

150. The O'Brien Juniors, who are fifteen and sixteen years of age, number about twenty-five. They hang in a clubroom some place back of the big O'Briens. The members are Irish, Scotch, and Swedish boys. When new ones are taken in, the initiation consists of "kicking them around." They have a first and a second leader. Their chief enemies are the Fiftieth Street gang.[9]

151. There is near the settlement a gang of little boys, seven to twelve years of age. They meet in an old basement, over the entrance of which they have placed a chalk sign "like the big clubs

8 Gang boy's own story.

9 Gang boy's own story.

Photo by Author

SOME OF THE "JERSEY MIDGETS"

This group was on its way to a baseball game several blocks from its hang-out. The gang is composed of about thirty boys, eleven to fourteen years old, mostly Irish in nationality. It calls itself an athletic club, showing the general tendency of the younger gangs to follow the social pattern which has prestige in their community.

have." They steal matches, play with fire, and smoke. They open milk bottles on back porches and sell junk to the dealers.[10]

Most adolescent gangs have an intimate knowledge of the doings of the underworld, and many of the older gangs themselves constitute a vital part of that "moral region." The areas which have been described as the empire of gangland include most of the underworld districts within their borders. The gang boy sees lawlessness everywhere and in the absence of effective definitions to the contrary accepts it without criticism. He soon learns where to buy stills, skeleton keys, and guns, which are sold to minors with impunity, either by mail or by dealers who have them on open display. The presence of junk dealers and "fences" encourages stealing.

Gang boys both young and old patronize the disorderly poolrooms which flourish in abundance in gangland. Indecent shows and penny arcades are patronized by young boys. Questionable massage parlors and hotels sometimes house young people. It is in gangland also that commercialized vice resorts seek a hiding place. Children have been found even living in such places, which are veritable "crime nests," and "playgrounds" for the city's gangster gunmen. The adolescent gang boy often undergoes early demoralization in these resorts.

Yet among adults of the gangland area, the use of intoxicants is a social habit usually brought over from the Old World. These families resent any official interference along this line.

152. An angry mob of nearly 1,000 men, women and children in the "back o' the yards" district hissed, cursed, and hurled missiles at federal dry agents during a raid yesterday.

Police from the stock yards district used their clubs to beat back the belligerent crowd that surged about a saloon where the prohibition agents were destroying twenty-eight barrels of beer.

[10] Interview with a social worker.

An automobile belonging to one of the government men was badly damaged before the police arrived.[11]

The attitude of disrespect for the prohibition laws can hardly be condemned in our immigrant groups without mentioning the same attitude among the middle and wealthy classes of the native population. Here too we find widespread violations, and it is largely this demand for illicit liquor on the part of the well-to-do that creates a real opportunity for the criminal gang and ultimately makes possible the far-reaching corruption of politics and government.

153. A group of twelve or fifteen colored boys had been hanging around the back room of a notorious black-and-tan café and cabaret in the Black Belt. Every evening they stood in the doorways and smoked and watched the patrons drink and the mulatto girls solicit white men, and listened to the orchestra play jazz music.

None of the boys worked regularly, and none lived at home. Several of them shared a room together, and the rest boarded separately at cheap rooming-houses. They were all waiting, more or less languidly, until the time should come when they might enter such places as the E—— Café with their women and get drunk. Finally one night they succeeded in persuading a waiter to bring them liquor and enticed several black girls to their table. When they had spent what little money they had and had exhausted their credit, they were thrown out of the place, amid the taunts and jeers of the patrons. They resolved, on the spot, to get more money in any way possible and just as soon as possible.

They separated into three parties and resolved on a common meeting place for the following day. When they gathered together the next morning they had between them something over eight hundred dollars in bills and silver.

It took them about two weeks to spend this money, and during this time they each bought new clothes, flashy jewelry, got drunk regularly every night, and acquired female companions. But they still stuck together, more or less, for the money had been pooled in a common fund and nobody had anything alone. Then too, each member of the gang seemed to need the companionship of the rest

---

[11] News item.

to encourage him to get more money. For several months there were numerous holdups and robberies in this neighborhood.

Finally one night, a colored boy was caught snatching a purse, and as a result the gang was rounded up. Each one had a gun in his pocket at the time of arrest, and only three had less than twenty-five dollars with them. They were well dressed and self-reliant.[12]

Gambling is encouraged in many poolrooms and bowling allies. In gangland there abound gambling dens, of which the so-called recreation halls are often merely a type. Gambling is practically a universal pastime in gangland.

There are also modern Fagins in these regions who promote delinquency in the gang by teaching how to steal according to the most approved methods, sometimes even conducting what appear to be "crime schools."[13]

154. The Dirty Dozen is a gang of boys of elementary-school age coached to steal certain definite things by a man. The boys, sworn to secrecy, will take their medicine when caught rather than tell on their employer. This is one secret of his continued success in breaking in new bunches to steal for him. Pull also enters into his comparative immunity, for while he has been in the bridewell several times, he has never been severely punished for his offenses.

These boys are taught to steal certain definite things such as hams, legs of lamb, etc. They often make raids on trucks, carrying off a carton of tobacco or other goods. One of their favorite activities is stealing silk shirts or underwear. They go out on wash day and take these articles from the clotheslines. A city prosecutor lost fourteen silk shirts, valued at $14 each, which he had received as a gift and which had been washed and hung out on a line preparatory for wearing for the first time. These boys were even taught to steal things from their own homes. In disposing of these stolen goods they had the co-operation of several adults in the community.[14]

[12] Unpublished manuscript prepared by Miss D. L——

[13] In one such case the boys were taught burglary, pickpocketing, and shoplifting. Their loyalty to their teacher was only broken when one of them became dissatisfied with his share of the loot.

[14] Interview with a social worker in the district.

The parents of many of the gang boys are themselves not averse to thievery. They encourage boys to break into merchandise cars and bring home a cheese or a sack of flour for the family larder.

155. A gang of twelve or thirteen Polish boys from seven to seventeen years of age operated chiefly after school and on Sundays, taking merchandise from the doorways of warehouses. Among their loot were electrical supplies valued at $2,500. Much of this material was recovered from their own homes, but the parents would not talk. They seem to have the idea that stealing from a corporation is not wrong.[15]

Many families in gangland are consumers of stolen goods purchased from boys who make such activities a matter of gang enterprise.

The boy's own family is also responsible for other forms of exploitation including the instigation of begging.

156. In its more serious phases the begging of children is usually instigated by adults. In Chicago we have the problem of wholesale market streets. Very often the children, who beg for everything from meat to fruit in the market streets, are given car fare by their parents to go and to return, and the food begged, or salvaged from barrels of waste, or stolen, is used on the family table. We have records of children habitually begging on these streets from homes of which their parents are the owners. No man, or woman, could possibly extract from the market men week after week the quantities of food that the children carry off in their sacks and baskets.[16]

The presence of periodic child labor among these classes also plays a part in the demoralization of the boys. Through the street trades, which are usually encouraged by the parents, the boys quickly become inured to street life. Most of the boys in gangland go to work as soon as a working certificate can be obtained

[15] Interview with railroad detectives.

[16] F. Zeta Youmans, "Childhood, Inc.," *Survey*, July 15, 1924.

(at fourteen), but parental connivance makes it possible for many of them to be employed illegally before that time.

INFORMAL EDUCATION

Many writers have conceived of education in too narrow a sense. The effective education of the boy, so far as the development of character and personality are concerned, takes place far more vitally outside the schoolroom in those informal contacts which escape conventional supervision. These are periods of freedom, and it is probably this very fact of spontaneous and self-directed activity that makes them so much more effective than the formal contacts that are presumed to be the truly educative ones. The education of the street, to which practically every boy in gangland is subject, is basic in the development of tastes and habits, ambitions and ideals. The promiscuous associations and experiences of the street, the poolroom, and similar places of meeting "educate" the boy and direct the interests and activities of the group. The gang vitalizes these influences and gives them prestige and permanence.

THE GANG BOY'S UNIVERSE OF DISCOURSE

Differences in the experiences of individuals and of groups result in what have been termed different universes of discourse,—"little languages" whose meanings depend on past experiences peculiar to the groups, catchwords, jokes, and songs linked to group memories.

The isolated life of gangland leads to the development of a distinct universe of discourse. The gang acquires its own language.[17] Like its morality, this argot, too, follows to some extent patterns in its own social world; for its

[17] The words in vogue in the gang are to be regarded as collective representations, which are important in maintaining the unity of the group and controlling its members.

language is largely a mixture of the slang of street Arabs, the lingo of hobos, and the jargon of the underworld.

Special words are usually in vogue in the gang to mislead the listener. The boys are given fictitious names; or their own names are interchanged in such a way as to confuse the police. Special commands are adopted as signals; for example, "Hruska, smoke de cigarette!" means "Pietro, run like hell, the cops are comin'!" and "Polish, duck in the water!" means "Greek, swim for the other side, someone's comin' to chase us out!" Curious, unidiomatic phrases are common: "Our cave's *broke down*," "We was *by my sister* for two days," or "Dey always *stop you up*, whenever you go tru' dere."

It is difficult for one in another universe of discourse to understand the gang boy.

159. The story is told of Dr. Charles Emerson, the famous nutrition expert of Boston, who was talking to a group of youngsters, that he asked them their favorite games. One little urchin yelled "Craps!" a pastime which was new to the speaker.

"Well," said Dr. Emerson, his face beaming, "if you will follow the health program I have indicated you will be able to play craps better than ever before."

"I'm for you!" shouted the lad.

Profanity has no stigma attached to it for the gang boy—it is the common language of his social world. Obscenity also occupies a large place in his universe of discourse. His interest in indecent literature, songs, and pictures is often stimulated by adults who "bootleg" to young people thousands of salacious photographs and obscene pamphlets. Most groups delight in dirty jokes and nasty stories, for vulgarity has a very large part in the humor and horseplay of the gang.

GANG NAMES

The names adopted by the gangs sometimes suggest their interests and activities, and at others reflect social patterns in their milieu. Certain names like the "Dirty Dozen" and "Buckets-of-Blood" seem to be traditional, not only in Chicago but throughout the entire country. Gangs are often given incongruous names by settlements or parks for whom they furnish teams. One group of dirty little ragamuffins, for example, was called the "Lillies of the Valley"; it would probably have been more accurate to call them "Lillies of the Alley." The limit in untactful and inappropriate names was the "West Side Nigger-babies' Association," suggested by a club leader for a white group of mixed nationality. This gang wanted to be called the "Black Hand Society," and their resentment at the leader's suggestion was instantaneous and violent.

Younger gangs in order to gain prestige readily copy the names of the older, which, like the "Dukies" and the "Shielders," are handed down from generation to generation in their local neighborhoods. The same thing seems to be true in New York, where the younger gangs are likely to keep alive such names as the "Hudson Dusters" and the "Gophers," without any semblance of the original groups.[18] The history of New York gangs also includes such names as the "Monk Eastmans," "Car Barners," "Yakey Yakes," "Red Onions," "Five Points," "Dead Rabbits," "Roach Guards," "Shirt Tails," and "Bowery Boys."

The gang often takes the name of some patron such as a social center, or more often the proprietor of a poolroom or a saloon, some politician who has been liberal, or a business firm which has in some way contributed to the welfare of the group. In the past names of breweries or of alcoholic beverages were not uncommon; for example,

[18] Herbert Asbury, "The Passing of the Gangster," *American Mercury*, March, 1925.

the "Nestor A.C.," the "Schlitz High Balls," the "An-heuser-Busch Regulars," etc.

Gang names often provide a means of wish fulfilment. High-sounding names give the members of the gang a certain expansion of personality, that may help compensate for their actual lack of status.

160. The "Golden Palace Athletic Club" was found to have headquarters in the basement of a dirty, tumble-down tenement house. The clubroom was also used as a wood, coal and kindling office and looked very disreputable.[19]

Names suggesting murder, blood, banditry, and piracy, on the other hand, are also favorites. The "Vultures," the "Forty Thieves," the "Murderers," for example, get a great "kick" out of feeling how diabolical they are and, hence, how superior to the world at large.

[19] Records of the Juvenile Protective Association.

CHAPTER XIII

Group Control in the Gang

Although gang activities and gang morality are, in
part at least, a reflection of the gang's disorganized social
world, they find a supplementary explanation in the conception of the gang as an elementary society, which, unhampered by conventional controls, tends to develop its
own organization and codes in an independent or spontaneous fashion. The codes of the gang are enforced upon
its members in a variety of ways—some definitely directed, others almost entirely unreflective. Thus, the
gang defines the situation for its members (illustrated in
the initiation of newcomers and "pledges" or probationers) and secures more or less harmonious group action.

THE UNITY OF THE GANG

The execution of collective enterprises and activities
necessitates harmony and mutual aid within the gang.
Effective collective action and continued corporate existence require that the gang control its members. Hence,
the group, both through planned and unreflective
methods, attempts to incorporate them, to subordinate
each to the demands of the whole, and to discipline the
unruly. Although the gang is not always unified and har-

monious within,[1] discord is usually eliminated by the conditions which collective action imposes.

This unity of the gang rests upon a certain consensus or community of habits, sentiments, and attitudes, which enable the gang members to feel as one, to subordinate themselves and their personal wishes to the gang purposes, and to accept the common objectives, beliefs, and symbols of the gang as their own. The *esprit de corps* of the gang, which is characteristic even of the diffuse type, is evident in many of its collective enterprises—in the enthusiasm of talk-fests, in its play together, its dances, its drinking bouts.

MORALE AND SOLIDARITY

A stable unity does not develop in the diffuse type of gang, however, until it becomes solidified through conflict. It learns eventually to formulate a policy and pursue a more or less consistent course of action despite deterring circumstances. Then it may be said to have acquired morale, which reinforces fellowship and enthusiasm in time of crisis.

161. One reason that such a group could stick together for years and win game after game, year after year, was the development of a "will to win" which could and did demand from each individual efforts for the group that nothing else could. Defeat, of course, was often a possibility, sometimes almost a certainty but a "quitter" was the last word. This intense desire to win, to put out all you had every minute regardless of how far you were ahead or behind was the only real religion most of the group had. This morale was as tangible an asset as can be imagined. Seldom mentioned, it was always present—a powerful factor not instilled by coach or the enthusiasm of an excited crowd, which had little effect on us. Cheering seemed (when heard) to come from a different world. The stimulus to win came from an intense inner desire which

[1] Compare Charles H. Cooley, *Social Organization*, pp. 24–25. Cooley presents in this statement an entirely too idealistic view with reference to the behavior of the average gang.

held up physical effort when every step was torture and every breath seemed the last possible effort. A particularly aggressive, daring, or skillful individual play would act as a spur to greater effort on the part of all.[2]

162. The Flannigan gang, composed of boys between fourteen and sixteen, has as its natural leader, Edward Flannigan, the best athlete and fighter in the gang. When the neighborhood recreational center advertised for boys to play on its baseball team, the whole gang reported along with other boys. It was decided to elect a captain and let him choose his team. Flannigan was elected and proceeded to choose his players all from his own gang. When remonstrated with he said that these other boys were members of other gangs, and if the social center was not satisfied with his players, the whole gang would quit. . . . .

During the winter the Railroad gang tried to use their rendezvous located in an old house near the tracks. This provoked a fight with brickbats, stones, etc., which resulted in a victory for the Flannigans. The boys were intensely loyal, standing by each other in a fight or backing those of their fellows who got into trouble. At their meetings at the center, none of the gang would express an opinion until the leader had had an opportunity to speak; then the gang accepted his opinion and voted accordingly.[3]

This superior solidarity creates a serious problem for the church, settlement, playground, or similar agency which attempts to use, to incorporate, or to supervise the gang. It is sometimes so well developed as to wreck a larger conventionalized organization in which it becomes a unit.

163. When our scout troop was organized we included in its membership the "Bureau Corner" gang of sixteen or eighteen boys, who used to hang in front of a grocery store in the winter but often built shacks down by the river in the summer time. Our first trouble with the gang was that they all wanted to be in the same patrol. (The scout troop, which is not allowed to exceed forty members, may have four patrols of not more than ten members each.)

[2] From a manuscript by a former member of the group. See document 107.

[3] Manuscript prepared by a boys' worker.

This difficulty was overcome by putting the cliques of boon companions in the gang, each in a separate patrol.

There was nothing but trouble during the two years the troop existed. The gang fairly ran things, in spite of all the scoutmaster could do. The other boys were afraid of them and were always trying to please the gang rather than the scout officials. The whole gang would absent themselves from scout meetings at once. If some enterprise was undertaken, the gang as a whole would enter enthusiastically upon it or withhold their entire support. Eventually when some of the members of the gang disobeyed orders at the summer camp, the whole gang bolted, and the rest of the troop seemed very half-hearted. Finally it became apparent that this group would have to be allowed complete control or banished entirely.[4]

The added danger of the development of a gang within a formal group creates another difficulty for the worker with boys.

164. An athletic club was formed by the workers in a certain church to provide wholesome activities for the boys. Out of this group developed a gang, which soon began to hang together outside the regular club hours. Eventually it became an auto stealing group.[5]

PLANNING AND CO-OPERATION

The unity of the group is further aided by the individual slogans, words, traditions, and so on, which are developed by the gang and which symbolize in common terms its objectives. The gang's planning must be carried on in terms of the common meanings which these symbols make possible. The name of the gang is of particular significance as a means of social control. It affords a common stimulus or value to which all members of the gang may respond with common sentiments. It is the rallying and unifying stimulus in a conflict situation. Since each member of the group is more or less identified with the

[4] Manuscript by the scoutmaster of the troop.

[5] Interview.

group name, it becomes a matter of common pride to defend and exalt it.

The extent to which the gang may achieve unity of purpose and organization for carrying out a co-operative enterprise is indicated in the following document.

165. The Boundary Gang operated along Twelfth Street in the vicinity of the railroad tracks in 1919. Composed of Polish, Bohemian, and Greek lads, sixty in all, fourteen to sixteen years of age, it was well organized and as tough as any in the city. Under the leadership of the notorious "Duffky," it had achieved a widespread reputation as a fighting organization, and woe to any boy from some enemy region that crossed Twelfth Street and got into its territory.

The Boundary Gang had heard reports of the self-governing cities of the Boys' Brotherhood Republic and they determined to apply for a city of their own. The Republic rented a small cottage for them at $15 a month. This was regarded as a temporary expedient to hold the gang. It was a clubhouse, but there was no furniture and the boys were keenly eager to have their home equipped.

It was proposed by the gang that they conduct a raffle to raise money for the needed equipment, but this method was forbidden by the constitution of the B.B.R. Whereupon, the boys took the matter in their own hands.

Five of the boys, selected by the gang, were chosen for special parts in a burglary enterprise. Money was raised in the group to outfit the quintet in new clothes; one boy would buy a necktie, another a pair of socks, and so on until five complete outfits of approved modes were collected. The boys washed, combed their hair and, arrayed in their new togs, essayed from the clubhouse as models of propriety. Two of them obtained work in a garage, two in a large department store at Twelfth and Halsted, and the fifth entered the employment of an athletic goods house, then located in the Loop.

The scheme was to loot the department store of such materials as were needed for house furnishings and the sporting goods house of the necessary athletic equipment. This was to be done with the aid of a truck and a Ford "borrowed" from the garage for the purpose. The plans for the undertaking were worked out on paper with great precision and skill, with every detail provided for almost like a blueprint, and later they were adjudged by an expert as among the most perfect of the type he had ever seen in his years of experience among criminals.

The lad who was working at the sporting goods house had cleverly concealed, in a large packing case in the basement under a layer of rubbish, sporting goods of every description—boxing gloves, baseball equipment, and even a heavy iron platform to be set up for a punching bag. This material had been gradually withdrawn from the reserve stock and secreted in the box. The boys at the department store had been no less active. They had amassed curtains, rods, rugs, and all sorts of interior equipment for their clubhouse and this was ready to be loaded at a moment's notice.

On the evening which had been selected for executing the coup, the boys at each place of business were to secrete themselves so that they would be locked in by their respective employers. A key had been made surreptitiously for a Yale lock to open the rear door of the Twelfth Street store from the inside and enable them to raise a huge steel bar. At the appointed hour a fight was to be started between two boys about two blocks from the department store on Twelfth Street; shooting was to occur; and in this manner, a certain watchman was to be drawn away from his post. Very carefully worked-out signals were then to be given by boys stationed at every eighty yards on the street, and the boys who worked in the garage were to sally forth, one with a truck bound for the department store and the other with a Ford to pick up the sporting material down town. All was arranged to work like clockwork. Every precaution had been taken to expedite matters. There were two sets of boys for loading. On the truck were ropes, wires, and other accessories to enable the goods to be loaded in as short time as possible. A large window at the side of the clubhouse had been broken out and nailed up with boards, working on a hinge, so that the entrance of the goods could be effected without arousing the suspicions of the neighbors.

Fortunately, or unfortunately, depending upon one's point of view, the two representatives of the B.B.R. who had been helping supervise the gang in its new home, got wind of the matter and reported it to the council of Main City. The elaborately worked out plan was seized, the goods were unpacked, and the scheme was declared off. Eventually, however, the funds were raised for furnishing their club; and the gang became Central City of the Boys' Brotherhood Republic.[6]

[6] Interview with Jack Robbins, General Supervisor, Boys' Brotherhood Republic.

This document indicates that the gang is capable of deliberation, planning, and co-operation in a highly complex undertaking. In this respect it differs markedly from the mob or the "psychological crowd" as described by Le Bon.[7] The gang often acts as a psychological crowd does, but it is capable of reflective behavior as well.

THE CODE OF THE GANG

Every gang tends to develop its own code of conduct, of which its members are more or less aware and which may be more or less rigidly enforced upon them. *The code of the gang is in part reflected from the patterns of behavior in its own social world, in part the result of the development of primary group sentiments, and in part the product of the individual group in its own special environment.* The following cases illustrate these three factors, as well as other points with reference to group control.

166. My gang, which had about ten members, had as its main object the stealing of ice-cream from the parties attended by the girls of our acquaintance. The leader was a hard rock.

The first principle and most important rule of the group was not to squeal on another member.

The gang swiped ice-cream, not because its members could not afford to buy this luxury, but because we enjoyed the excitement. One evening we managed to get away with a gallon can. Not having anything to eat it with, we used silver dollars and the crystals of our watches. For this escapade a fine of $25 was assessed against the member of our party who was caught and dragged into police court. He did not give our names, but we came to his rescue and paid the fine.

Another rule of the gang was that each member was to carry a package of Duke's Mixture tobacco in his shirt pocket with the tag always hanging out. That I did not smoke made no difference; I had to have the "makins" if some other member of the gang happened to want them.

We had a strict rule against any associations with girls.

Another rule was to protect the property of a widow and a

[7] Gustave Le Bon, *The Crowd*, pp. 39–67.

B. B. R. Photo

B. B. R. Photo

THE BOUNDARY GANG

Above is the Boundary gang in its native habitat in the Ghetto. It received its name because of its valiant defense of its home territory against marauding gangs seeking to cross its boundary. (See document 165.)

Below is the same gang a few years later after it had been made into a "city" of the Boys' Brotherhood Republic. This organization has done constructive work in redirecting the interests of gangs into more wholesome channels.

blind couple on Hallowe'en. We not only observed this ourselves but we kept other gangs in line also.

The gang was completely broken up by being expelled bodily from school. One of the boys had put glue on the chair of the manual training teacher. He was punished. In retaliation the gang "stacked" the high school; that is, put all movable objects together into one huge pile.[8]

PRIMARY GROUP VIRTUES

The gang is a primary group.

By primary groups I mean those characterized by intimate face-to-face association and co-operation. They are primary in several senses, but chiefly in that they are fundamental in forming the social nature and ideals of the individual. The result of intimate association, psychologically, is a certain fusion of individualities in a common whole, so that one's very self, for many purposes at least, is the common life and purpose of the group. Perhaps the simplest way of describing this wholeness is by saying that it is a "we"; it involves the sort of sympathy and mutual identification for which "we" is the natural expression. One lives in the feeling of the whole and finds the chief aims of his will in that feeling.[9]

While the nature of the gang code varies in different groups, depending upon differences in social environment and previous experiences, it tends to include in every case some form of expression of the primary-group virtues, or moral attitudes which focus about the group rather than the welfare of its individual members.

Loyalty is a universal requirement in the gang, and squealing is probably the worst infraction of the code. This conception of honor is combatted in the schools, but most boys prefer to take a beating rather than "stool" on their associates. Raising money to pay fines of its members is a common gang practice. One group had a rule that if one member was arrested, they should all get "pinched" and sent away to the same institution if possi-

[8] From a manuscript by a former member of the group.

[9] Charles H. Cooley, *op. cit.*, p. 23.

ble. The sympathetic strike is often used by the gang when any one of its members is in trouble.

While fighting to settle differences within the gang is not uncommon, fighting between members must follow the rules set up by the group.

168. Another custom that grew up in the gang association was a kind of chivalry, a set of rules governing fighting. Disputes between the members were usually settled by a fist fight duly refereed according to established rules. Occasionally a boy would put a ring made of a bent horseshoe nail on one of his fingers, but this practice was considered unfair. The boys, moreover, would not permit anything to interfere with their institutions. If a man tried to separate two fighting boys, they would both unite against him, or, if he proved too formidable an enemy, they would retire to more secluded parts and decide their differences in their own way.[10]

169. When G—— P—— and I got into a fight one Saturday morning the rest of the gang made us put on boxing gloves and fight it out. After five three-minute bouts we had both cooled down and were ready to resume friendly relations. "Fight it out" was a law of the gang, but the group determined the conditions and refereed the bouts.[11]

An infraction of this code, as applied within the gang, brings speedy and certain punishment. This may be physical or it may take the form of an ostracism which has very tragic results for the culprit.

The gang occasionally evolves special mechanisms for meting out justice. The leader sometimes acts as arbiter and his word is usually accepted as final. In some groups a serious or fair-minded boy sometimes takes the rôle of judge. One South Side gang has been in the habit for years of bringing its disputes for settlement to a certain shoemaker.

Another primary-group virtue which develops within the gang is a sort of brotherhood or mutual kindliness. This manifests itself in many forms of self-sacrifice. If a

[10] Manuscript by a former member of the gang.
[11] Manuscript by a former member of the gang.

member is in serious danger the rest will spare no pains to save his life. One boy will sometimes undergo severe hardships to aid another.[12]

170. The C—— gang won a prize of $30, which was up on a ball game with the B——s. The C——s did not know what to do with the money. The director of the park suggested taking them down town to a real show, but they answered that they did not have the clothes. They finally decided to give the money to a newly married member for a honeymoon.[13]

Special codes may be developed in a gang for the furtherance of special interests which are peculiar to that group. This is illustrated in the case of the fighting football gang (described in document 107), which adopted a specialized organization, with its own peculiar rules and taboos. *Gangs which develop specialized structures and codes for the furtherance of some interest of their own may be regarded as functional types.* Thus, groups are organized around such dominant interests as junking, sex, picking pockets, stealing, athletics, gambling, or some special type of crime. In each case they develop their own technique.

MECHANISMS OF CONTROL IN THE GANG

The individual member of a gang is almost wholly controlled by the force of group opinion. The way everybody in the gang does or thinks is usually sufficient justification or dissuasion for the gang boy. In such cases he is really feeling the pressure of public opinion in that part of his own social world which is most vital to him and in which he wishes to maintain status.[14] This sort of sanction will make almost any kind of conduct right or

[12] See document 13.

[13] Interview with a park director.

[14] See W. I. Thomas, *The Unadjusted Girl*, p. 32. One reason the individual responds to social control is that he has a fundamental wish for status, which society alone is in a position to confer.

wrong within the group. It will also make a boy one person when under group influence and quite another when apart from it.

Opinion in the gang manifests its pressure in the variety of mechanisms through which group control is exerted such as applause, preferment, and hero-worshiping as well as ridicule, scorn, and ostracism. Physical punishment is not uncommon. The leader has considerable power over his subordinates so long as he does not abuse it. Many of the influences that determine the behavior of the gang and its members, however, are unplanned and unreflective, and, as in the crowd, arise out of the very nature of collective action.

PUNISHMENT

One of the chief mechanisms of control in the gang is the fear of violence or physical punishment. In the fraternity this takes the form of "hazing," ducking in cold water, and paddling, especially for probationers. In the gang the member who has broken the code may be subjected to a beating or in extreme cases may be marked for death.

172. We had a rule in our gang forbidding swearing. Every one violating it received a kick from each member of the group. This rule was enforced so stringently that many were the sore seats the first four weeks after it went into effect.[15]

173. No one should snitch on another guy [squeal on him]. Anybody that snitched got sixty punches from each member of the gang. We would beat him up hard. My brother got it once.[16]

In the gang of the more vicious or criminal type, disloyalty is often punished by death. The notorious Rats gang of St. Louis is alleged to have murdered a number of its members who were suspected of treason or became otherwise troublesome. In such cases when a man was

---

[15] Manuscript by a former member of the group. See document 210.

[16] Gang boy's own story.

marked for death, he was executed by the gang's "firing squad." Fear of violence to one's family also acts as a deterrent from being disloyal to the gang, particularly in groups of the criminal type.[17]

176. Viana, the "songbird of the jail," a sixteen-year old member of the notorious Cardinelli gang, was a victim of the code of the gang. He might have saved his neck from the noose, had he been willing to divulge the secrets of the group to which he belonged. The remarkable hold of the gang was shown by his fear of threats against his family. The inflexible social organization of the gang required him to do as they did.[18]

RIDICULE AND APPLAUSE

Another important mechanism of social control within the gang is ridicule, commonly known to the boys as "razzing." It includes "making fun" of the nonconformer, "riding" him, teasing him, mocking him, laughing at him, and calling him by opprobrious epithets. It varies all the way from the subtlest allusions in conversation, the sliest winks and titters, to the coarsest pantomime, the crudest horse laugh, and the most stinging sarcasm. Only one who has been made the target for it by some intimate group in which he has had to live can understand its constant and merciless pressure in the direction of enforcing conformity. This is one of the chief weapons in the hands of the American fraternity and the gang of every nationality in assimilating new members.[19]

The use of epithets of derision constitutes one compelling element in razzing. The sort that are most effec-

---

[17] See also document 20.   [18] See document 230.

[19] "The fear of ridicule is the most dominant of our feelings, that which controls us in most things and with the most strength. Because of this fear one does 'what one would not do for the sake of justice, scrupulousness, honor, or good will;' one submits to an infinite number of obligations which morality would not dare to prescribe and which are not included in the laws."—L. Dugas, *Psychologie du rire*, quoted in Robert E. Park and E. W. Burgess, *Introduction to the Science of Sociology*, pp. 373–74.

tive for control are the so-called "humilific."[20] The gang
boy has his own epithets for those who fail to measure up
to his standards. The coward receives the hated appella-
tion of "yellow" or "yellow belly." The traitor is a
"snitcher," or "stooler." The boy who hangs back or is
not game is a "baby." The boy who plays with girls or
assumes any niceties of dress or behavior is a "sissie."
A real gang boy would prefer to take almost any punishment rather than to be called by one of these names; for
to be so called is an indication that he has lost caste in
the group which is most vital to his happiness. These collective representations of the gang get their meaning
from actual life situations; like the social virtues in the
gang, they are defined in interaction.

Ridicule defines what the boy must not do if he wishes
to maintain his status. There is, however, a positive
method of control which contributes to his desire for
recognition; this is applause and hero worshiping. To
gain the praise and flattery of his pals and such rewards
as prizes, preferment, honors, and leadership, the gang
boy conforms to types of behavior which are consonant
with the ideals and policies of the group.

177. We have one case of an Italian boy, R——, who in the
gang can always be counted upon to respond to an appeal for the
best for himself and the gang. Outside the gang his record has not
been so satisfactory. In the gang he is stimulated by group appreci-
ation; while without he is not.[21]

In maintaining the approval of the gang, the boy sees
himself through the gang's eyes. He is much concerned
with the interpretation the gang will put on his behavior,
and by taking the rôle of the gang or some leader, he at-

[20] See F. E. Lumley, *Means of Social Control*, pp. 292–97.

[21] Social worker's observations of a gang boy.

tempts to judge himself.[22] This process may be definitely expressed in some such terms as these: "What'll Rocky (the leader) say?" "What'll de guys say?" "What'll de rest of de gang do?" "I don't want to wear that, or do this; I'll get razzed for a month." "If the gang goes to rob a store and I do not go, they'll get sore on me."

CROWD CONTROLS IN THE GANG

The gang has been defined as the "perpetuation and permanent form of 'the crowd that acts.' "[23] One of its forms of behavior involves that peculiar "mental unity" described by Le Bon as characteristic of the "psychological crowd."[24] When the gang becomes excited, it does not deliberate rationally and it is likely to become completely responsive to the circumstance of the moment or act on almost any suggestion presented by its natural leaders.

The gang is particularly prone to the crowd type of impulsive behavior because it is a natural and spontaneous group. It usually lacks the protection of parliamentary procedure in keeping it orderly. Even the conventionalized gang often finds order difficult: its members deal in personalities; they do not address the chair; they do not, as a rule, arbitrate their disputes. The ease with which the gang enters into a mob has already been illustrated.

Another element in the gang's control of its members, as in the crowd's, is the security afforded the individual in the force of numbers, which tends to remove the

[22] Charles H. Cooley in *Human Nature and the Social Order*, pp. 152-53, describes this mechanism, which he calls "the looking-glass self."

[23] Park and Burgess, *op. cit.*, p. 872. The gang displays practically every type of corporate behavior even to the coolest deliberation and planning. Furthermore, it may develop an elaborate tradition, almost a culture of its own, and in this sense it is more like a society in miniature than a "psychological crowd."

[24] See Gustave Le Bon, *The Crowd*, pp. 25-26.

qualms that might well arise in an individual embarking upon some perilous undertaking on his own account. Thus, the feeling of power conferred by the mere force of numbers is often sufficient to quite distort the individual's moral perspective. This is what is usually meant by "gang spirit." Such an expression implies group-controlled action of an impulsive or irresponsible sort.

THE SUBTLER FORMS OF CONTROL

Interpretations by members of a gang of the more delicate and subtle changes in the behavior of other members may be regarded as important for crowd control. It is by the reading of these less perceptible signs that one person is able to respond to the sentiment and attitude of another. In a face-to-face group changes in facial expression, slight gestures, and the like, although largely in the field of unverbalized reactions, enable an individual to sense a situation instantly. Thus, they define the situation and promote rapport.

The gang, as an intimate primary group, develops an excellent basis for control through rapport. Life together over a more or less extended period results in a common social heritage shared by every member of the group. Common experience of an intimate and often an intense nature prepares the way for close sympathy—for mutual interpretation of subtle signs indicating changes in sentiment or attitude. Collective representations embodied in signs, symbols (such as the badge in a fraternity), secret grips and words, and the argot of the group, all promote mutual responsiveness in the more subtle forms of communication. Peculiarities of dress or physique serve the same purpose; for example, a peculiar sort of hair cut as identifying members of a certain gang or the wearing of certain types of blouses or ties.

This rapport is sometimes so complete in a gang (and

in a college fraternity also) that one receives the impression of interpenetration of personalities, if such a mystical conception is permissible. The consensus of habits, sentiments, and attitudes becomes so thoroughly unified in some of these cases that individual differences seem swallowed up.

178. In the close association of this group for years and years, we learned to know each other better than our parents did. Certain characteristics we made fun of habitually, yet no one else dared to do so without personal danger from the bunch. Cookie's passion for "ham and" was traditional. So much so that he claimed to eat ham and eggs in order to see what new jokes he would hear from it.[25]

179. When we would see something while walking along the street, practically the same comment was always forthcoming from each of us, so close was our sympathy. These relations were close enough that the mother of one of us was regarded practically as the mother of each of the others.[26]

These areas of intimacy have the most profound influence upon the development of personality.

The area of individual orientation may be defined both geographically and emotionally. For the gang boy there is an area of geographical range including home and familiar territory, beyond which lies enemy territory and the external world.

In addition to this there is an area of intimacy in which he has relations of close emotional dependence. He depends on this area for what Thomas calls "response." The member of the gang or of the intimate fraternity becomes absorbed in these emotional contacts. Rapport based on sympathy is set up. There results close fellowship which often involves a feeling of infinite security and even tenderness (pathos). Physical touch plays a part. This is the area of greatest familiarity.

The member of the gang (or the fraternity) is often fascinated by this new intimacy, which becomes the most vital element in his world and often comes to supplant family and all other relationships, at least for the time being. Entrance into such a group is often like discovering a new world. Primary personality is devel-

[25] Manuscript by a former member of the group.
[26] Gang boy's own story.

oped in these contacts; and as this area widens, personality is correspondingly modified. A certain part of this submergence of individuality within the group may be due to the hero worship of some individual member. The extent of the assimilation of the person indicates the degree of group control over him.[27]

THE LIMITATIONS OF GANG MORALITY

Certain writers have been somewhat too idealistic with regard to the educational value of the gang for the boy. They have emphasized the fact that the gang teaches its members the great human virtues. Some have even suggested that the gang is a desirable institution for the boy apart from all supervision. Other workers with boys have concluded that these so-called "guerrilla virtues" are a great asset to any social agency that would turn the energies of the gang into wholesome channels.

As preparation for life in a larger world, however, it is doubtful if the gang as such does enough. The gang virtues which have been so exalted as ideal patterns for humanity at large hold only for members of the in-group and the rest of the world may quite normally be looked upon as lawful prey. The sense of fair play which tends to govern relationships of the boys to each other does not extend to outsiders.

The ethnocentrism which marked the small groups of primitive life and tribal society, is also characteristic of the gang. The Greek-letter fraternity, which is akin to the gang in many respects, presents a good example of the same thing. A current attitude among members of such societies is expressed in such words as "We belong; we are the Greeks; we are the cultured. You do not belong; you are the barbarians; you are rude and untutored."

In another sense, moreover, the gang does too much; for along with the virtues, it inculcates in its members the

[27] Unpublished manuscript by the author.

primary-group vices. Revenge, which is characteristic of many detached primary groups, is the law of the gang. The amity which prevails among members of the same group is often accompanied by this antithetical sentiment of hatred toward outsiders. In extreme cases this manifests itself in the most abandoned types of retaliation and often does not stop short of murder.

Nor can the primary virtues which the gang is supposed to develop always be counted upon to hold for its own members. In many cases there is a betrayal of trust and in the criminal gang a man is never sure of his friends.[28]

186. Berney's gang which was organized about 1908 had as its hang-out the saloon of Joe Berney near Keeley and Lyman streets adjacent to where the Bosely playground now stands. The nucleus of the gang consisted of the Berney family and it included their cousins and neighbors. It had about twelve members, aged from twenty-five to thirty-five years.

Most of the members, who were gunmen, were usually occupied in quarreling among themselves. We have here a case of inverted rough stuff. They liked to use firearms, and, although they murdered two men who were not members of the gang, they usually turned their guns on each other in drunken brawls. The result was that by 1913–15, they had killed each other all off with the exception of one who died from a fall and another, the only remaining survivor, who is now a watchman.[29]

It is difficult to see how such training as the unsupervised gang can give, prepares a boy adequately for useful citizenship. The good citizen of today must possess something more than gang morality. He must live in a society where tolerance of other groups, responsibility toward them, and co-operation with them are essential to social order and general prosperity. To this end there is a need

[28] See Ray Renard's story of the Rats, *St. Louis Star*, February 24 to March 31, 1925.
[29] Interview with Mr. X, a Chicago politician.

for intergroup morality. One of our great shortcomings is undoubtedly just this failure to recognize obligations to other groups. One may be quite loyal to his own; yet he feels that he can injure and despoil out-groups with impunity. So it is that the politician, the grafter, the racialist, the religious fanatic, the chauvinist, the imperialist, and so on, are the higher exponents of gang morality: they are all Greeks and the barbarians must suffer.

CHAPTER XIV

The Structure of the Gang

When it was the fashion to make every persistent type of behavior a product of instinct, an "instinct of organization" was mustered out to explain the social order of the gang and the play group. This sort of explanation seems to be an oversimplification of the facts. It is one thing, moreover, to say that the organization of the gang is natural and quite another to say that it is instinctive. Such organization as develops is that which is necessary for corporate behavior and co-operation; it will vary with pressures and patterns outside the group, as well as with the previous experience and previous relations of the members within. The ultimate relations which are formed among members and factions within the gang, rather than a consequence of instinct, seem to be due to the internal processes of conflict and competition incident to gang activities.

AN EXAMPLE OF GANG STRUCTURE

The spontaneous social order which characterizes the development of the gang may be shown best by an example—Itschkie's Black Hand Society. This document is presented *in toto* because it illustrates many of the principles and mechanisms of gang behavior described throughout the study and enables the reader to observe the functioning of an adolescent gang as a whole—in all its varied relationships.

188. The Black Hand Society is a gang of about fifteen boys, twelve to fifteen years old, all of whom are Jewish with the exception of two Italians who are known as the "Greasers." Most of them live in the Maxwell Street community, the area of first settlement for the Russian-Jewish immigrant in Chicago. The Italian boys were admitted because of their compatibility and their residence in the neighborhood.

The real gang is a small, compact, select body around which there forms a wide fringe of more or less harmless, would-be gang boys who remain on "probation," so to speak, and serve as a protection for the central nucleus of the group. The real gang is a close, secret organization, operating on a business basis. Meetings are held in secret; plans and campaigns are formulated; tasks are assigned to members especially trained by their leaders for their particular jobs; signals are worked out; and finally—the deed accomplished—the proceeds are pooled and each member receives his due share either in cash, booze, show tickets, or personal effects and petty trinkets.

New members are chosen with great care and must often serve long periods of probation, during which the leader instructs them in the fundamentals of thievery and watches over them discerningly to see just how quickly and how well they are able to work out for themselves the fine points of the game. Thus, membership depends in large measure upon the boy's ability as a pickpocket, though this quality alone will not guarantee his acceptance.

The prospective Black Hander must also be compatible; he must go through a thorough grilling by every member of the group, in order to make sure that he is "game for anything," that he is sufficiently tough—for on these two points the members greatly pride themselves. Finally, once a gang boy, he remains, save in the most exceptional case, under the complete domination of the group, pledged to tell no secrets and to divulge no plans.

It is around the leader, often the chap of the readiest wit, that the gang crystallizes; and what he is, the gang is; what he becomes, the gang also becomes. "Clownie," the first leader of the Black Handers, was a half-wit, but he was an expert little thief, and it is he who introduced the "art" of stealing and organized the boys in this neighborhood into the Black Hand gang. Quicker than lightning, he had made his way in and out among the crowded groups of Maxwell Street market place, stealing first this, then that. He had money; indeed, everything he wanted. And there was excitement, too. Sometimes he would almost get caught; but always, just as the women in their stalls began to wrangle with him and to lose their heads in their anger, he would vanish. That was fun, devilish good sport.

Then the other boys began to envy him. First one boy was fascinated by Clownie and learned the tricks of the trade, then another, and another,—until there were six or seven confirmed little crooks firmly banded together, idolizing their half-wit leader and enjoying their new activities. That was the beginning of the gang. Clownie has long since left the Ghetto, but the gang still persists. The old plan of organization, the methods of doling out the proceeds among the gang boys, the old system of probation, and the old methods of exploiting the younger boys, together with all the reckless amusements to which he introduced them remain in all their original force. They have been worked over, indeed, and made yet more sordid under the rule of "Itschkie" and "Bennie the Jew."

Itschkie (Yiddish for "Izzie") is obviously the ring leader of the Black Hands at the present time. He comes from what is reckoned a fairly good family in the Ghetto. His parents are anxious to help him, to keep him off the street, yet no power on earth seems to be able to take Itschkie away from his gang. Many times he himself has tried to reform and he has kept stolidly away from his pals for a time—but always, just when he least expects it himself, the old longing for excitement comes back to him and he is off again, back to the gang and the growing vices which it promotes.

Itschkie is a born coward. Point your finger at him in an authoritative way, speak to him harshly, and he will turn and run. Yet, with his gang, he is a hero; among the boys of the street, he is to be admired; among the market folk, he is to be feared; among the police, he is one to be "handled with care." At "work," he is a tough looking customer, and once having put on the outer trappings of the "profession," he seems to himself to become equally tough.

His deep-set black eyes have a dangerous shiftiness and around them are big black circles—the outward signs of long nights of dissipation. His hair is matted and gummy, his face dirty and his hands black. His clothes fairly hang on him. Itschkie likes grotesque effects, and he knows the value of looking the part. He prides himself that his is not only one of the worst gangs, but indeed one of the worst looking, for the other little Black Handers appear equally disreputable. Already, at 15, he has assumed toward stealing the attitude of a life profession.

"Itschkie is a good little kid, but he has bad ways, that's all," declared Sammie, a member of another gang on good terms with the Black Hands.

"He is about fifteen," continued Sammie, "but he looks twelve. He never combs his hair. His skin is dark like an Italian's. He always has a smile on his face." Itschkie never misses a chance to go swimming, even if his bathing suit is stolen. He goes camping and hiking to Fox Lake with other members of the gang. They stay out there over night, but if it rains they come back home. Itschkie likes to be out-of-doors all the time; even in the winter he gathers his gang around a bonfire. He likes to be free and this is the main reason he will not work. He cannot hold a job. His mother says he has had every job in the Loop, and so he might as well give up trying for any more.

Bennie and "Greaser" are not unlike Itschkie, save in the one respect that they do not yet have the faculty for leadership to quite so great an extent as their young idol.

On the fringe of the gang are many younger boys who would like to be gang boys but who are not yet quick enough at the trade to make their membership pay, or who are not yet old enough to appreciate the necessity of keeping still or to enjoy all of the particular amusements in which the inner group spends most of its recreational hours.

"Joey" is one of these. He, likewise, comes from a good sort of family, but in his home during his earlier years there was considerable friction. This seems to have made a profound impression upon the child, and rather than stay in the home with his family under such circumstances he took to the streets. He is, indeed, a bright, innocent little chap who makes a "regular hit" wherever he goes, as Itschkie put it. Itschkie, moreover, was quick to appreciate the value of such a youngster as Joey, and he has succeeded in keeping him under the domination of the group without ever making of him a full member. It is in his case that we see best the subtle influence of the gang.

Joey has against him one weakness which must forever keep him out of the inner group of the Black Handers. He is a kleptomaniac, his friends say. At any rate, he will steal whatever he wants, when he wants it, regardless of the consequences which are likely to follow. To the Black Handers, stealing is a matter of time and place. It is not a mere prank to be indulged in at any time; it is an art to be used advisedly and skillfully. The gang boy who goes out on his own hook is disloyal; he must work in unison with the gang and pool his profits like a "man" and a "regular sport." Joey, then, willfully or not, is disloyal, and so he becomes the "just" victim of the exploitation of the older members of the group and has not infrequently been asked to hand over all of his "earnings" from a solitary expedition in order to make up for his unfaithfulness. This he has as often refused to do, and the result has been his dismissal from candidacy for the inner circle. On Joey's part this has meant the divulging of many a secret of the gang just at a time when that information should have been kept most quiet.

In the earlier history of the gang, the younger boys, especially those on probation, were not infrequently asked to steal things for the older boys, such as silk shirts, socks, and other personal effects. Sometimes, in return, they were paid a small sum; sometimes they were licked and sent about their own business. This is one of the things which has helped to make the Black Handers so strong, for they represented, in those days, the younger group of gangs who were forced in self-defense to become so expert in their little business that the older boys could not take advantage of them. This practice is fortunately dying out, for Itschkie does not think it is fair—he himself having suffered a good deal at the hands of these older fellows.

Stealing offers to the members of the gang about the easiest way of getting the means to satisfy their wishes. Itschkie was told that he and his gang ought to clean up a bit. He agreed. The next day or so saw more than one of his pals cleaned up, dressed in new clothes, and all the rest of it. Itschkie appeared himself in a complete new outfit. One can have little doubt as to where the money came from, for a similar thing happened only recently, shortly after the group was known to have made a raid upon one of the stores.

The stealing of candy, fruits, cameras, and similar luxuries is, of course, too commonplace to deserve special mention, for there is hardly a time when the group goes out on a spree that it does not indulge its desires in this manner.

The method of picking a pocket is unique. Itschkie has his gang divided into groups of three or four. Within each of these little groups there is one boy trained to go ahead as a sort of advance guard and to engage the prospective victim in conversation or otherwise attract his attention. Then by a series of carefully planned signals, they call up the second boy who quickly does the actual work. Meanwhile, the third boy has slipped up, taken over the valuables from the second, and made a safe get-away while the crowd is still gathering. In case of apprehension by the police, this leaves the gang clear, for neither of the two boys standing by have the "goods" on them and nothing can be proved. The police give them a good scolding; the youngsters have their sport talking back to the officers. . . . . And all is quiet again.

When the boys want money and sport, however, their most common resort is the drunken man or the blind beggar. These unfortunates offer both a source of amusement and the possibility of providing large sums of money which they often have in their possession. To knock off the man's hat and stoop to pick it up "like a regular guy," incidentally picking his pockets; or to borrow a knife and return it to his pocket rather than to the man—these are the most common methods of "getting" the blind man or the drunk.

That this is a paying profession may be seen from the fact that Itschkie on one Sunday secured $80 and that many a Sunday he has made $25 and $30. Even Joey is able to procure large sums at a time in this way and thinks nothing of a $15 or $20 haul from a promenade around the market.

Silver declares that the older practice of picking pockets has fallen somewhat into disuse. The gang does not engage in shoplifting, nor do they go into the Loop as often as they used to. They prefer the less risky business of "making" (robbing) the drunks.

One of the interesting features of this practice of victimizing drunken men is the fact that race lines are always observed. Both Silver and Sammie maintained that the Black Handers never molested Jewish people.

"They hop the poor drunken Polish fellows," said Silver. "They respect the Jews more because they are most all Jews themselves."

The dominant motive behind it all seems to be excitement. The boys get tired of the life of the Ghetto, for at best it is a sordid enough existence in those ever dirty, crowded streets. To steal a Ford and leave it on the roadside after they have had a Sunday's jaunt out of it is one of their pleasures; to pick up a few games from the clubrooms of a nearby settlement and carry them out into the alley for their friends whom the police have forbidden to enter the building; to climb up on the upper beams of the old I.C. warehouse

and see who can break the most street lamps; to beg money on the
street for their pals in jail; or to hook fruit and other goodies to
send to their friends in the Parental School or St. Charles—these
are but a few of the means by which these youngsters seek to
gratify their insane craving for a thrill or a new experience. Not
all bad ideas, either!

"Gambling,"—and the Black Handers like to call it by that
name—shooting craps, pool, dancing, movies, burlesque shows, and
all the social vices are a part of their repertoire. Without them,
they would be lost. There was a time when the gang sought the
gratification of its wishes in simple sports and stole only for a pastime. Today, under the influence of the negro influx into the neighborhood and of the Greek settlement to the north, the boys are
going to depths of which they had never before dreamed.

Joey, when not more than ten years old, gave a graphic account
of the inside of a Ghetto den and spoke with mingled admiration
and jocosity of the "vamps" that he had seen there. He described
in minute detail just how one should act, just how one should treat
"them there vamps," and of the time when he, too, could go there
unquestioned. He told of gambling and was most proud to be able
to feel that he was a really successful crap-shooter. He rehearsed
the details of the costumes or lack of costume of the actors and
actresses at the latest burlesque. . . . . That seemed bad enough.

The negro influx has brought with it a horrible increase in
prostitution, not on the white and white basis that has until this
time been known in the Ghetto, but public houses in which it is a
case of negro mixing with white. To the older boys of the community, this has undoubtedly meant a very serious lowering of their
moral standards and one is not surprised. Influences from the
Greek community, furthermore, have led the boys toward perversion.

The gang has a hang-out in an old deserted house down by the
tracks. This was called "Roamer's Inn," after a popular roadhouse
of the same name. It is an old broken-down dwelling located near
the Maxwell Street Police Station. The boys themselves have
broken out the windows in their stone-throwing contests. It is a
sort of asylum for hiding from the police, and a good place to shoot
craps without danger of interference. It is also a common loafing-
place and, as a member of the gang expressed it, a place to play
around and kill time.

Although the area is actually overrun with small show houses, there is but one movie in the neighborhood that is really decent. When there is nothing else exciting to do, Itschkie takes his gang to the movies—and there they may learn many an unwholesome thing. Joey, for one, tells us that he used to spend hours at the movies in order to see how the holdups were "pulled off," and judging from the type of thriller and "sexy" romance which forms the bulk of the entertainment, there are other attractions, too.

In the homes, gambling is a commonplace. Many a family will sit up all Saturday night over a game of cards and play on until the whole week's income is all but exhausted. Small wonder that the Black Handers also take freely to the habit. The same has been true of drink, though prohibition has lessened this difficulty to some degree. Many of the boys used to feel that they were not even tough were they not able to get drunk once in a while.[1]

THE SIZE OF THE GANG

The necessities of maintaining face-to-face relationships set definite limits to the magnitude to which the gang can grow. The size of Itschkie's group was determined by the number of boys readily able to meet together on the street or within the limited space of their hang-out. The gang does not usually grow to such proportions as to be unwieldy in collective enterprises or to make intimate contacts and controls difficult. Ordinarily, if all members are present, what is said by one of the group can be heard by all. Otherwise, common experience becomes more difficult and the group tends to split and form more than one gang. The number of "fringers" and hangers-on upon whom the gang can count for backing, however, may be larger, especially if it has developed a good athletic team.

Greater growth can be accomplished only through modifications of structure, such as those resulting from conventionalization. When a gang becomes conventionalized, assuming, for example, the form of a club, it may possibly grow to large proportions. The original gang,

[1] Manuscript by an intimate observer of the gang, and from records, interviews, and observations.

however, probably now becomes an "inner circle," remaining the active nucleus in such cases. The additional members may develop their own cliques within the larger whole or maintain merely a more or less formal relationship to the organization. In many cases such a club is the result of the combination of two or more gangs.

Table VI does not include the major portion of the gang clubs; these vary in number of members ordinarily from 20 or 25 to 75 or 100; only a few of the more prosperous clubs exceed 100 members. It will be seen that 806 of these gangs have memberships of 50 or under; these are largely of the non-conventionalized type. Most of the remaining 89 have memberships ranging from 51 to 2,000, though not all of them have been conventionalized.

TABLE VI

TABLE SHOWING APPROXIMATE NUMBERS OF
MEMBERS IN 895 GANGS

No. of Members	No. of Gangs	Percentage of Total
From 3 to 5 (inclusive).....	37	4.1
From 6 to 10...............	198	22.1
From 11 to 15...............	191	21.5
From 16 to 20...............	149	16.7
From 21 to 25...............	79	8.8
From 26 to 30...............	46	5.1
From 31 to 40...............	55	6.1
From 41 to 50...............	51	5.7
From 51 to 75...............	26	2.9
From 76 to 100...............	25	2.8
From 101 to 200...............	25	2.8
From 201 to 500...............	11	1.2
From 501 to 2,000...............	2	2
Total gangs.................	895	100.0

DIVISIONS WITHIN THE GANG

The mob—"the crowd that acts"—is never divided against itself; for if it became so, its characteristic unity would be destroyed. The gang, on the other hand, is often split into one or more cliques. A clique may be defined as a spontaneous interest group which forms itself within some larger social structure such as a gang, a club, or a political party. In a certain sense a well-developed clique is an embryonic gang which does not get detached from its social moorings, but remains incorporated within the larger whole.

Fighting in which sides are taken, is not uncommon in the gang. A bad split often leads to the formation of two new gangs, as when a Polish-Irish gang fell out over the disposal of stolen automobile tires, finally forming two new groups—one Polish, the other Irish.

189. The Trembles, so called because they made others tremble, split up into two gangs. The gang had thirty-nine members and factions formed without great difficulty. Two factions arose as the result of the stealing of a bronze figure from a social center in which the group had club privileges. One faction remained loyal to the crooks, while the other split off from the old gang; but both of them remained away from the settlement for many weeks. Eventually the part that broke off came back and reorganized as the Blue Ribbon Athletic club, taking its name from a popular brand of beer. The other faction finally came back too, organizing as an athletic club with the name of a local machine politician.[2]

With the appearance of a common enemy, however, cliques within the gang tend to disappear as if by magic.

THE TWO- AND THREE-BOY RELATIONSHIP

What has been defined as a "two-boy gang" or an "intimacy" must not be overlooked in discussing the inner organization of the gang. In this type of relationship there is generally a subordination of one boy to the other. In one instance other members of the group expressed it in this way, "Jerry is running Alfred now." Hero-worship, open or tacit, plays an important part in such cases. Sometimes the abilities of one boy supplement those of the other.

[2] Manuscript by an observer of the gang.

190. George and I were close pals, and this was the only extensive intimacy in the gang. There was one year's difference in our ages and we were much alike except that I had no imagination but was more of a plugger and got things done. I naturally idealized George on account of his fine personality and other high qualities.

We were inseparable companions through high school. We always went out together, alternating as to who should furnish the car. We took trips together two different summer vacations.[3]

In many of these cases one boy tends to become utterly enthralled by the other; and there grows up a devotion hardly to be excelled even in the cases of the most ardent lovers of opposite sexes.[4] While these intimacies usually develop in pairs (the introduction of a third person many times making for complications and friction), yet it sometimes happens that the relationship may include three boys who co-operate in perfect congeniality.

It is relations of this sort, existing before the gang develops, that serve as primary structures when the group is first formed and that shape the growth of its future organization. The intimacy partly explains why many of the exploits of gang boys are carried out in pairs and trios. The boys often prefer to have a favored pal or two associated in an enterprise rather than bring in the whole gang.

The two- and three-boy relationship is often much more important to the individual boy than his relationship to the gang. In such cases a boy would doubtless forego the gang before he would give up his special pal or pair of pals. A series of such palships, one or two of which may be more highly prized than others, are charac-

[3] Interview with a former member.

[4] The intimacy in the gang provides a satisfaction for the boy's wish for response. One boy may fascinate another and the two be completely wrapped up in one another. While attachments such as these would probably be regarded as homosexual by the Freudians, they exist in most cases without definite sex impulses and are to be regarded as entirely normal and practically universal among boys.

teristic of boys of the non-gang areas of the city and also of gangland boys who are not in gangs. In other words, under different conditions, the two- and three-boy relationship becomes a completely satisfactory substitute for the gang and the wish for recognition from a larger circle, if imperative, is gratified through membership in the family, the school, the club, and other groups and institutions to which the boy has access.

THE GANG IN LARGER STRUCTURES

Even though the gang remains a primary group it may acquire external relationships. A gang is often on friendly terms with one or more similar groups in its neighborhood; it may co-operate with these in athletic contests or even to the extent of financial assistance. In some cases federations of friendly gangs are formed for the prosecution of common interests or protection against common enemies. These may be nothing more than loose alliances, but on the other hand, the relationships developed may acquire a genuine emotional intensity.

A gang may get incorporated into a larger structure such as a syndicate, a ring, or a "republic."

SPECIALIZED STRUCTURES

When the opposition to a gang becomes sufficiently powerful or well organized, the gang is likely either to disintegrate or to become a genuine secret society. Itschkie's gang, carrying out a series of delinquent enterprises in the face of police and neighborhood opposition, evolved secret signs and other devices for the purpose of mutual protection. In such cases, too, strong opposition necessitates centralized control and severe discipline. Thus, in Itschkie's group there developed a compact body in the gang, differentiated from mere fringers and hangers-on, who could not be trusted or initiated into the gang's secrets. Furthermore, within this body was the so-called "inner circle," formed on account of the exigencies of group control and then developing the scheme of self-aggrandizement and exploitation of the other boys in the interests of the few leaders.

Special activities in the gang also require special types of organization. The members of Itschkie's gang were organized into teams, each member with a special function to perform in the pickpocketing activities of the group. Thus, when gangs acquire special functions, they develop special relations and structures to correspond. This is illustrated in the case of the criminal gang.[5]

THE FAMILY AS A GANG NUCLEUS

A family may become a conflict group and behave in many respects like a gang. This is the case with the family groups carrying on blood-feuds in the southern mountains of the United States and in other countries. One of the striking facts brought out in the present study is that a family of brothers very frequently serves as a nucleus for an adult gang; sometimes other male relatives function in such a group. The notorious UUU gang, which controlled a string of stills in the West Side wilderness, was built around a family of brothers, each performing some supplementary function in the group.

191. The McSmack family and their neighbors constituted one of the worst gangs I have ever known. The family has a police record as far back as 1898. The father was a thief; so it is not surprising that the six boys were trained similarly. They lived next to the Belt railroad and most of their depredations were committed with reference to railroad property. There was considerable contrast between the wealth of the railroad and the poverty of the McSmacks; so they had little compunction about stealing from the corporation. The father used the kids to steal and even came out with a gun to defend them.

The gang numbered from eight to twelve members, including some of the neighbors who joined them on their expeditions. From

[5] See chap. xviii.

time to time they succeeded in stealing from $8,000 to $10,000 worth of railroad property. They killed another thief with whom they had an altercation. Women probation officers were afraid to go in there. Most of the McSmacks died violent deaths.[6]

THE INFLUENCE OF IMPERSONAL FACTORS

The size, the character of membership, and even the degree of solidarity are sometimes determined for a group by the nature of its physical surroundings.

In heterogeneous neighborhoods, locality seems to be a more important factor in determining conflict groups than does race, nationality, or religion. Rivers, canals, elevated railroad tracks, and industrial properties afford the best gangland boundaries and determine in a general way lines of gang alliance and direction of gang conflict.

[6] Interview with a juvenile officer.

CHAPTER XV

Personality and the Action
Pattern of the Gang

Every member of a gang tends to have a definite status within the group. Common enterprises require a division of labor. Successful conflict necessitates a certain amount of leadership, unreflective though it may be, and a consequent subordination and discipline of members. As the gang develops complex activities, the positions of individuals within the group are defined and social rôles become more sharply differentiated. As a result of this process there arises a more or less efficient and harmonious organization of persons to make possible a satisfactory execution of collective enterprises and to further the interests of the group as a whole. This is the action pattern of the gang.

PERSONALITY AND STATUS WITHIN THE GANG

The significance of the sociological conception of personality—namely, as the rôle of the individual in the group —comes out clearly in the study of the gang.

Every boy in the gang acquires a personality (in the sociological sense) and a name—is a person; that is, he plays a part and gets a place with reference to the other members of the group. In the developed gang he fits into his niche like a block in a puzzle box; he is formed by the discipline the gang imposes upon him. He cannot be studied intelligently or understood apart from this social rôle.

THE "ORGANISM" AS A WHOLE

Each gang as a whole, and other types of social groups as well, may be conceived of as possessing an action pattern. Every person in the group performs his characteristic function with reference to others, or to put it another way, fills the individual niche that previous experience in the gang has determined for him. Lacking the group, personality in the sense here used would not exist.

Yet the action pattern which characterizes each group can hardly be thought of as rigid and static; for it must be constantly changing to accommodate losses and additions of personnel, changes in its members due to growth and increasing experience, and other changes within and without the gang.

The conflicts of the gang with outsiders and the execution of its other enterprises and activities result in a sort of social stratification in its membership. There are usually three, more or less well-defined, classes of members: the "inner circle," which includes the leader and his lieutenants; the rank and file, who constitute members of the gang in good standing; and the "fringers," who are more or less hangers-on and are not considered regular members. These three groups are well illustrated in the case of Itschkie's Black Hand Society.

The inner circle is usually composed of a constellation of especially intimate pals formed about the leader. The rank and file—the less enterprising and less capable—are subordinated to the inner circle, just as it, in turn, tends to be subordinated to the leader. Most gangs are not closed corporations, however, but have a certain group of hangers-on or associates—the fringers, who may be "kid followers" or admirers. They constitute a sort of nebulous ring, not to be counted on to go the full length in any exploit and likely to disappear entirely in case of trouble. Yet the gang usually tolerates them for their applause and their occasional usefulness. A gang in embryo sometimes forms in this fringe.

THE STRUGGLE FOR STATUS

Internally the gang may be viewed as a struggle for recognition. It offers the underprivileged boy probably his best opportunity to acquire status and hence it plays an essential part in the development of his personality.

This struggle in the gang takes the form of both conflict and competition, which operate to locate each individual with reference to the others. As a result the gang becomes a constellation of personal interrelationships with the leader playing the central and guiding rôle. It may be considered as a "unity of interacting personalities"; but it may also be regarded as an accommodation of conflicting individualities more or less definitely subordinated and superordinated with reference to each other and the leader.

It is in these very rôles, subordinate though they may be, that personality is developed. Any standing in the group is better than none, and there is always the possibility of improving one's status. Participation in gang activities means everything to the boy. It not only defines for him his position in the only society he is greatly concerned with, but it becomes the basis for his conception of himself. The gang boy might well say "I would rather be a fringer in the hang-out of the gang than to dwell in the swell joints of the dukes forever."

For this reason the gang boy's conception of his rôle is more vivid with reference to his gang than to other social groups. Since he lives largely in the present, he conceives of the part he is playing in life as being in the gang; his status in other groups is unimportant to him, for the gang is his social world. In striving to realize the rôle he hopes to take he may assume a tough pose, commit feats of daring or of vandalism, or become a criminal. Thus, his conception of his essential rôle as being in the gang helps to explain why the larger community finds difficulty in controlling him. If acquiring a court record, or being "put away" in an institution, gives him prestige in the gang, society is simply promoting his rise to power, rather than punishing or "reforming" him. Agencies which would attempt to redirect the boy delinquent must reach him through his vital social groups where an appeal can be made to his essential conception of himself.

THE PROCESS OF SELECTION

There is a process of selection in the gang, as a result of the struggle for status, whereby the ultimate position of each individual is determined. The result of this process depends largely upon the individual differences— both native and acquired—which characterize the members of the group. Other things being equal, a big strong boy has a better chance than a "shrimp." Natural differences in physique are important and physical defects play a part. Natural and acquired aptitudes give certain individuals advantages. Traits of character, as well as physical differences, are significant; these include beliefs, sentiments, habits, special skills, and so on. If all members of the gang were exactly alike, status and personality could only be determined by chance differences in opportunity arising in the process of gang activity. In reality, both factors play a part.

That physical differences are important in determining status is indicated by the fact that the biggest boy or the strongest is often leader by virtue of that fact alone, for bulk usually means an advantage in fighting. Mere size, too, may enable a bully to gain control of the gang; his tenure as leader, however, is always uncertain.

Physical disabilities often help to determine status in the gang, as elsewhere, through the mechanism of compensation. The defect in such cases serves as a drive to some type of behavior whose excellence will make up for the lowered status which the boy feels himself likely to possess on account of his disability. Compensation arises, therefore, because of the discrepancy between his possible rôle and his conception of the rôle he feels he ought to play.

196. "Al" is an interesting example of how status in the gang is determined by a physical defect. He was naturally looked upon as an inferior by most of the fellows because he was afflicted with an impediment of speech. In almost every instance where anything required nerve, however, or where he had an opportunity to show that he was all right, Al was there and fighting for a chance to prove his worth. When two or three fellows were robbing a golf shop, none was willing to break the window and crawl in. Al voluntarily took off his straw hat, placed it against the pane of glass, and smashed his fist through the window. Because Al was looked down upon, he took up pool very seriously. He got so that he was an exceptionally good straight pool player and for a long time he made his money for eats in this way.[1]

If a boy can compensate in some effective manner for a disability, it may not serve as an insurmountable barrier to leadership.

Fighting is one of the chief means of determining status in the gang; each member is usually rated on the basis of his fistic ability. In a fight to determine which of two contenders is the better, the gang usually guarantees fair play, equalizing the conditions as nearly as possible. In some gangs the best fighter is considered the leader; he can defend his title against all comers.

[1] Manuscript prepared by a former member. See document 13.

In addition to fighting, excelling in any other activity in which the gang engages is a method of gaining recognition. For most gangs this applies particularly in the field of athletic prowess, but it may apply equally to some form of daring or predatory activity. "Hardness" is frequently a means of getting prestige; usually the boy who has been arrested, has a court record, or has been put away to serve a sentence is looked upon with admiration.

SPECIAL RÔLES IN THE GANG

Besides leadership (discussed more fully in the following chapter) there are other social functions in the gang. Like leadership, these are also determined by individual qualities in the process of struggle and activity. They evolve as a result of group experience; they are determined by interaction in all of its complexities. The principal rôles in the gang are sometimes distinguished from each other as being different types of leadership.

If the imaginative boy does not have the qualities of geniality and physical force to give him pre-eminence, he may become the brains of the gang.

197. Billy was the brains of the gang. He was "educated," a high-school boy too. He would work sometimes, but not often. The kids would bring their "stuff" to him. One day we had a big fight over it when we were robbing a merchandise car; we had cigarettes, pop, and a lot of other stuff. Billy had his stuff put away in a box with straw on top of it. The watchman looked at the straw, but Billy told him it was for a rabbit. Billy would sell "cartoons" (of cigarettes) for a half a dollar apiece.

Billy would plan things for our gang. He would get us a place to sleep when we were bumming away from home. He would get us keys to the bread boxes, so that we could get food when we were hungry. We would get the bread after the bakers left it early in the morning before the stores opened. I still have my duplicate key to a Livingston bread box. If we'd get caught robbing bread, they'd let us off if we were hungry. Sometimes the kids would not "give me to eat," and when I had money, I'd tell them to get away. Billy would find us a place to sleep in some house or basement. He would go around everywhere to see if there was a place to sleep or rob; he was a regular investigator.[2]

Like the jester of old, the "funny boy" is tolerated in spite of behavior that might otherwise be insulting. His irresponsibility is generally excused because of its humorous possibilities. This type of behavior is sometimes the result of an attempt to compensate for some trait—such as a high-pitched voice—which gives undesirable status in the gang.

A very undesirable status in the gang is that of a "sissy," a rating which may arise through effeminate traits, unwillingness to fight, or too much interest in books or other cultivated pursuits. It usually carries with it a girl's nickname. Ordinarily boys will go to any length to avoid such a rôle.

Another personality type which often emerges in the gang is the "show-off." He is the egotist, the braggart, the boaster, the bluffer, the "loud-mouth" of the group; and the other members usually discount him accordingly. He may resort to "loudness" to gain attention not otherwise forthcoming, or, in his naïve conception of his rôle in the gang, he may simply be overestimating himself. His resulting status is certainly unforeseen by him and even unsuspected in certain cases.

Every gang usually has its "goat." He is a boy who is considered uncommonly "dumb"; he may be subnormal, as measured by psychological tests; and he can usually be depended upon to get caught if anybody does. Boys of this type are sometimes known as "goofy guys," if they combine some special peculiarity with their dumbness. Inexperienced boys are often used as "cats-paws" in the exploits of the gang.

The nature, number, and variety of specialized rôles,

[2] Gang boy's own story.

which in their interrelationships constitute the action pattern of the gang, must depend to a large extent upon the nature and complexity of the activities and enterprises undertaken. If the gang maintains a team, individual aptitudes play an important part in assigning places. Special abilities are useful in carrying out certain types of activities. The gang itself may become highly specialized (a functional type), as in the case of the development of some particular line of athletic sport or criminal pursuit. *The more specialized the gang, the more highly differentiated is usually the division of labor among its members.*

Social rôles and status are similarly determined in the so-called orgiastic group, except that individual traits which count in the organization of such personalities with reference to each other are different from those in the gang, or at least are held in different esteem.

The diversity of talent—singing, dancing, joking, and so on—expressing itself in Boston gangs, is also characteristic of such groups in Chicago. These diversions often develop abilities which later find a place on the vaudeville stage. This is illustrated in a young New York gang recruited in and about Hell's Kitchen—the "Ten Tumbling Tonies"—who amused theater crowds on the sidewalks near Forty-fourth Street and Broadway.[3]

PERSONALITY AND NICKNAMES

Personalities are recognized by the names applied to the members of the gang. Individual peculiarities, which have an important effect in determining status, are likely to give color to the boy's whole personality. He is named accordingly, and his name often indicates the esteem in which he is held by the group. For obvious reasons, a big,

[3] Lee Raleigh, "New York's Ten Tumbling Tonies," *New York Times*, November 2, 1924.

strong boy does not ordinarily receive a "humilific" name. In one case the real, though not the nominal, leader of the gang would not permit himself to be nicknamed.

EFFECTS OF FORMAL RECOGNITION AND CONTROL

The natural struggle for recognition in the gang is largely a spontaneous process leading to social selection. The general pattern of the gang (its organization) arises for the most part out of the necessities imposed by concerted action in attack, defense, raiding, and other collective enterprises; but members qualify for the various personality rôles thus created, through the internal process of struggle and selection. In this way, the status acquired by boys in a gang determines its natural organization.

When the gang gets a more formal organization it usually gives fresh recognition to distinctions and status which have already been acquired spontaneously; but it cannot *confer* these distinctions, for they are the result of collective experience. When the more important formal offices do not happen to go to the natural leaders, they still retain their power as dictators in the group, while the officers are more or less convenient figureheads. Sometimes the imposition of a formal organization on the natural structure of the gang results in dissensions and is the first step toward disintegration.

A certain amount of outside control of the gang may be achieved through the conferring of distinctions upon members and upon the group as a whole. Decorations and awards conferred by the dignitaries of a different or more inclusive group have a human-nature appeal. American colleges confer "varsity" letters upon athletes for their service on college teams; and these honors are often valued more highly than diplomas. In a like manner settlements, playgrounds, business organizations, politicians, and other agencies dealing with gangs may confer distinctions in the form of ribbons, medals, and cups. The limitations of this type of control, however, are apparent. The decoration tends to be regarded, in many cases, as of more consequence than the service performed. Properly safeguarded, however, decoration capitalizes a basic human wish and may be used with success as a means of control.

The social agency which would incorporate or use the gang must exercise great care in imposing a formal organization upon the natural action pattern of the group; otherwise, much effort will be misdirected and energy wasted, dissension and strife will arise, and disintegration will probably follow.[4] The boys' worker must work *with* the natural forces and mechanisms in the gang rather than against them; his function is to lead and direct, rather than to impose something foreign from without. Any formal scheme of organization and award of honors or decorations must take full account of the boys' own conceptions of their rôles, which are essentially of themselves as loyal gang members and prospective gang leaders rather than as participants in more formal groups or as citizens of the larger community.[5]

[4] See document 163.

[5] The sort of recognition, for example, which would confer great prestige upon an assimilated Boy Scout, might be of indifferent account or quite repugnant to an untamed gang boy because outside of his social world. The recognition which appeals to him must be of a sort to advance his status in his own social group.

CHAPTER XVI

Leadership in the Gang

The marks of leadership vary from gang to gang. The type of boy who can lead one gang may be a failure or have a distinctly subordinate rôle in another. The personality of the leader is to a large extent a response to the personnel of his group, which may vary from other gangs with regard to age, interests, race, nationality, cultural background, and so on. Physical and athletic prowess, which stand the leader in such good stead in most gangs, for example, would not be valued in the following type of group.

198. The boys in this gang, with a few exceptions, seem to be mentally deficient. They are all Italian, fifteen to eighteen years old, and are rather a shiftless bunch, hence the above name, which is not of their own choosing. None of these boys is at all athletic and we have been unable to get any of them interested in the gym. They hang around street corners and talk and get into all sorts of mix-ups; driving off automobiles, stealing, etc. Some of them work; two go to high school; two or three of them do nothing. Two of them have shown talent for drawing and other art work, and the whole group has been recently interested in a Saturday afternoon dancing class where they do social and folk dancing with girls.[1]

These variations in personnel produce sharp contrasts in types of leaders; the "hard rock," the "dare-devil," the

[1] Unpublished study by boys' worker.

"politician," the desperado, the "wise guy," and the "Puritan" are some of them.

The natural leader of the gang is a very different person ordinarily from the leader of a conventional group chosen in some formal way, and in gangs which elect officers, the natural leader may not be selected for an office. His dominance of the group, however, is none the less real.

199. When a certain gang became a club, under the supervision of a social center, it was suggested that an election be held to determine the officers. Before this, however, a card game had been played downstairs and "Irish" won the game. In the subsequent election held up in the clubroom Irish was elected president by secret ballot—a procedure which merely confirmed the more primitive method employed downstairs. Once elected, he ruled with an iron hand.

The interesting fact about the whole business, however, was that Jack, the boy who had been elected treasurer by formal balloting, was the real leader of the gang. He was clean-cut and had a high grade of intelligence. His high status is shown by the fact that he would not permit a nickname. He controlled the nominal leader absolutely, and in the club activities a simple word from him was enough to determine the course of group action. While he, like all the other boys, had a court record, he was by far the most decent member of the gang and helped to elevate its standards more than any other member.[2]

TRAITS OF THE NATURAL LEADER

The chief trait of the natural leader as revealed by the majority of the cases studied is "gameness." He leads. He goes where others fear to go. He is brave in the face of danger. He goes first—ahead of the gang—and the rest feel secure in his presence. Along with this quality usually goes the ability to think clearly in the excitement of a crisis.

Sometimes the highly esteemed quality of gameness

[2] Unpublished study by a boys' worker.

becomes developed to the point of pathological exaggeration, and the dare-devil type of personality results.

200. The daring and bravado of a tiny lad with a doll's face enabled him to qualify for the leadership of the "Clutchy-Clutch" gang at the age of nine, although the other members were all older, some of them thirteen. "Bobbie," as the diminutive leader was called, was chiefly interested in adventure; indeed, his desire for prestige and excitement had almost become a mania. He would take any dare—"would not stop at anything." He was the leader of two gangs at one time and also a member of a third. He had been in court more than any other boy in Chicago for his age.

The record of the Clutchy-Clutch, which began as the "Sunday Afternoon Boy Burglars," goes back to 1915. Its members, ten in all and mostly Italian, were drawn from that unstable complex of life in the South State Street area, where most of the families live above the stores and there is no place for the children to play except the streets. The life of this region is so exciting—things are happening there twenty-four hours a day—that it is very difficult for the boys to get the proper amount of sleep.[3]

Bobbie's unlimited nerve is shown by many incidents in the history of the gang. On one occasion at a nearby school he tripped and threw down one of the women examiners. He entered a social center in a drunken condition. Backed by his gang he turned in a 4–11 fire alarm and had most of the Chicago Fire Department headed in his direction. He stole a spirited horse with a buggy and drove down State Street. The chief target of the depredations of the gang was the Polk Street railroad station, from which the boys stole frequently. Their main interest in this activity was not the property they acquired, but the thrill experienced in performing the feat. After stealing money, the whole gang would attend a show and Bobbie would steal candy and peanuts for the bunch.

Under Bobbie's leadership in the early days of the gang, the boys would rush into a saloon, snatch the beer from under a customer's nose, and drink it before anyone could interfere. They burglarized stations, restaurants, and saloons simply to show their nerve; incidentally, they drank so much that some of them had to be taken to the county hospital where stomach pumps were used.

It was not uncommon for Bobbie at the age of ten to shoot craps all day. Many of the boys of his own age were afraid to play

³ See document 60.

with him because he was so venturesome. When examined by the
state psychologist, it was found that he was not sufficiently retarded to be classed as feeble-minded. The disorganization of
family and neighborhood life in this district—the situation complex—goes far toward explaining the freedom and amusements he
enjoyed. The gang did the rest.[4]

The natural leader is usually, though not always, able
to back up his daring with physical prowess. He is very
often the best fighter, and many times he champions the
gang in the face of opposition. As in the days of chivalry,
we find two gangs agreeing to let supremacy depend upon
the fighting ability of their individual champions. This
may be a primary combat or a more orderly fistic encounter with the gloves. Sometimes if the leader is
licked, the whole gang turns in and there is a free-for-all
fight pending the defeat of one side or the other or the ar-
rival of the flivver squad from police headquarters.

201. Eddie was the leader of our gang and the best leader any
gang ever had. He wasn't always the leader, because before he
came Danny was leader for seven or eight months. When Eddie
first moved around there, Danny offered him a fight. Then Eddie
beat him up badder than hell. Eddie became our leader and Danny
did not want to hang with us guys no more because he was afraid
of Eddie.

Eddie was a better leader than Danny, although Danny was
supposed to be better. Danny took lessons in a gym down town,
but Eddie was a better fighter 'n everything. Danny was smaller
than Eddie, but never went out looking for so much fights.

Eddie was the bad guy in the family. His mother did not know
what was the matter with him. His father was dead and his mother
had to work every day and that is how he got to roaming around.
He had two older brothers and they were good kids; one of them
makes $35 a week. But Eddie never had nobody to take care of
him and he never went to school hardly. When he quit school his
mother got him a job where she worked, but he quit because he did
not like the work.

Eddie was our captain and I was Eddie's best pal [proudly].

[4] Interviews and court records.

The gang had two lieutenants, Red and Bud, but Eddie was the leader. They used to do all the planning with Eddie. They had the most brains except Eddie. If they would ever say they had more brains than him, there would be an argument.

We would get the whole gang together to wreck a place; and when we wrecked a place in our neighborhood, we *wrecked* it. We busted a lot of windows in a big hardware store and then we went in and stole a lot of baseball things. We were going to leave the blame on them other guys by writing a note with their names on it. We'd wreck other places, too, by breaking windows. We would bust the windows of the kid supposed to be the leader of another gang. Nobody never knew where Eddie lived, so they could not sneak around and break his windows. If they had, Eddie would have come out with a gun and a club. We broke into a grocery and Eddie nearly pried the big doors out trying to get in. We only got about two dollars, but Eddie made himself at home; he "ett" all he could.

Eddie was such a great fighter that he'd always go round looking for fights and picking fights. Lots of times he'd come out on the bottom, but that never made no difference to him. We had so many fights, I forget half of them. We fought some Jewish guys and licked them. Then we came back after a while and fought over again, but we lost because somebody had told them and they were ready for us. They had got half of another gang of bigger boys. They took half of one of our guys' eyes.[5]

The gang boy has great admiration for the professional pugilist. The developed gang usually has two or three boys with definite aspirations to get into the prize ring. One of the city's hardened criminal groups, the WWW's, has as one of its leaders a professional fight referee; about one-fourth of its membership are trained pugilists; and two or three of them, well-known prizefighters. The successful boxer is many times the product of gang training. As a result of this tradition many gang boys take boxing lessons from professionals.

Another quality that seems requisite to the natural leader is quickness and firmness of decision. He is a man

[5] Gang boy's own story.

of action. He brings things to pass. He makes a rapid judgment and is resolute in backing it up. If later developments prove him mistaken, he uses skill as best he can to explain why the error was made. He is convincing. He "sells himself to the gang." These are the characteristics which enable him to rule; for they give him the confidence of the group.

Other things being equal, the imaginative boy has an excellent chance to become the leader of the gang. He has the power to make things interesting for them. He "thinks up things for us to do."

202. George was usually the leader of the group, although five of us together constituted the dominant element in the gang. George, however, was an outstanding personality; even his enemies liked him. He was naturally an "A-number-1" man. He was ingenious, full of ideas, and possessed of much imagination. He was thoroughly responsible and very ambitious. Although he he was not an athlete, he was very clever, and that counted more than athletic prowess in our gang. We had a pretty well-rounded group after it had developed. We aimed at general abilities and the best in several different lines.[6]

The possession of "brains" or imagination is sometimes sufficient to confer the leadership of a gang upon a boy who is entirely unfitted for it from a physical standpoint. A hunchback was a very successful leader of a gang of healthy boys. An undersized boy may retain his power in the same way.

Occasionally a boy possesses the qualities of natural leadership to such an extent that he becomes a leader of several gangs.

203. Danny was seventeen or eighteen years old, but he wasn't a big kid. He was short and dark and looked more like French than Irish.

Danny's father and mother, who are dead, had been rich. Danny did not like his brother. His brother lives in a hotel and is

[6] Interview with a former member.

a boxer; but Danny, he robs stores every night and the cops are always firing and saying, that if we see Danny they will give a reward for him.

Danny used to have a lot of gangs. He knows a lot more too. One gang he had was a hard one and became so tough that all the other gangs were a-scared of him. He wasn't a-scared of nuttin. He handled a gun well. He pasted anybody in the teeth. He would jump on a copper too. He is dying now from being shot by a copper. He got in with the big guys and would go robbing with the big gangs, holding people up. He'd rob guns and everything. He would take Fords. The flying squad got him and took him to St. Charles, but he ran away from there. He also ran away from Pontiac, and they are looking for him now.

He would make the little kids steal for him. When he wanted things, he would send the little kids, and if they don't go, he would hit them. If a bigger kid would not do his bidding, then he'd tell the whole gang, and they'd jump on him.[7]

Lacking the traits of a natural leader, a boy often manages to exert control in the gang through the possession of some special qualification. He may be the oldest resident and "know the ropes"; he may possess a knowledge of some special technique useful to the gang; he may control some material advantage such as an automobile or athletic equipment; or the mere show of superiority through "sportiness" may be sufficient to assure leadership, at least for a time.

THE LEADER GROWS OUT OF THE GANG

While it may sometimes be true that a gang forms about a leader, the reverse is generally true: the gang forms and the leader emerges as the result of interaction. It is true also, however, that the way for his emergence may have been prepared by the existence of previous relations of palship or intimacy.

The process whereby the leader attains his superior position in the gang is unreflective so far as the members

[7] Gang boy's own story.

are concerned. They are quite naïve about the whole matter; they do not stop to puzzle out why they follow one certain boy rather than another. Many times they are quite unaware of the natural leader's pre-eminence among them. When asked why a certain boy holds his place of leadership, they are often hard put to it to find a reason. They show their admiration for him and they know they want to follow him, but the reasons have never been verbalized.

In certain cases this ignorance as to who is the leader is only pretended. The boys say there is no leader or that they are all leaders for fear that an acknowledged leader ("ring-leader") may have to bear the brunt of the punishment in case they are caught in some delinquency promoted by the gang.

In some cases leadership is actually diffused among a number of strong "personalities," who share the honors and responsibilities. Leadership once concentrated may become diffused owing to the gradual development of abilities among the rank and file. A group of outstanding boys, whose individual abilities are supplementary, may combine to form a dominating inner circle. Or there may be a sort of rotation of leadership as activities requiring different abilities are undertaken. As the gang develops, however, and acquires tradition, one boy with more influence than the rest is likely to emerge as a natural leader.

HOW THE LEADER CONTROLS

The natural leader in a gang exercises what appears to be almost absolute sway. He can direct the members of his group in almost any way he sees fit.

204. The leader of this gang of Italian boys is older than the others, perhaps seventeen or eighteen. He can do almost anything with the group, for they will take correction and treatment

from him that they would not take from anyone else. This is particularly noticeable in school where he can always line up his gang and get good response from them, when they might otherwise fail. The leader is a good-looking chap, with a very pleasing personality and a brilliant mind.[8]

Ordinarily the members of a gang will not attempt any new enterprise without the leader's approval.

It has been suggested that the leader sometimes controls the gang by means of summation, i.e., by progressively urging its members from one deed to another, until finally an extreme of some sort is reached. Those who hang back are confronted with the argument that they have already done worse things. In this way the gang gradually commits more and more serious offenses.

Bulldozing is a method of control employed by a certain type of leader—the bully, who holds his sway chiefly through the fear which he instils. The boy who can retain his position for any length of time, however, must be something more than a mere bully. *With all his show of power, the leader must in a very real sense accommodate himself to the wishes of the rest of the gang.*[9]

The gang leader holds his prestige in the group because he presents the boys with patterns of behavior which are agreeable to them. They would like to imitate him, but often, through shortcomings of their own, they are unable to do so; they must be content with admiring him and following as best they can.

No matter how great the leader, however, his tenure of power is never certain. Some change in the personnel of his gang or in the situation complex may bring his rule to a speedy end. He makes mistakes; the gang loses con-

[8] Manuscript prepared by an observer. See document 162.

[9] The reciprocal dependence of leader and subjects is well recognized. It has been stated by Georg Simmel, a German sociologist; see Nicholas J. Spykman, *The Social Theory of Georg Simmel*, Book II, chap. i, "Submission," pp. 95–111.

fidence in him, and he is "down and out." If he becomes conceited and bossy, he is sure to find himself summarily deposed, although he may for a time retain his power through sheer physical force. A new boy may appear, moreover, to contest the old leader's power through fighting him or in some other test of skill. The democracy of the gang, primitive though it may be, is a very sensitive mechanism, and, as a result, changes in leadership are frequent and "lost leaders," many.

DEMOCRACY IN THE GANG

The fact that the leader of the gang, even at the height of his power, is not an absolute monarch, but plays his part through his response to the wishes of his followers, is illustrated in the crude sort of democracy which is almost universal in such groups.

207. The Seventeenth Streeters had from eighteen to twenty-two members between twelve and fifteen years old. They were mostly Lithuanian, although there were three or four Polish boys in the gang. There weren't any Jewish, because they do not come around our street; they stay on their own streets.

The way I got started with the gang was one warm day when they were going swimming down to the lake; I went with them. I was supposed to clean the house that day and so I was a-scared to go home when evening came; I was afraid I'd get hit. I was up all that night walking around trying to find a place to sleep.

After that I hung away from home for a long, long time, playing with the gang and picking up a living anyway I could. One day some of the boys came up to me and said they seen that empty house and it would be a good place to have a club. So we went up and fixed it up. Nobody knew it. We got tables and chairs out of some yards and put them in the best room in the old house to make a clubroom. One boy had a talking-machine which he brought there. We also had checkers and a lotto box. We used to go up there to play cards, but we'd shoot craps in the street or alley.

We had dues of 15 cents a week and that way we raised money to buy baseball stuff for our ball team. We'd put up $2 or $3 against some other team. We'd get an umpire first from one street then from another; they'd try to play fair.

We only had two officers in our club, a cashier, who looked after the money, and a president. The officers were the ones we thought were the best. We choosed them by having those who wanted to be, stand up, and then the boys would stand up behind them and the one that had the longest row would be the president.

There were ten or eleven members at first. Some were brothers and there were three boys fom Halsted Street. If we wanted a new member, we would ask the president if he wanted him and if he did, he'd take him. We'd ask the new member if he'd pay and if he said yes, we'd let him in.

We had rules for our clubroom too. To get in you had to knock three times. We also had a rule that every time you swore, you'd have to pay 2 cents. We collected a lot that way to buy baseball stuff. We didn't allow smoking because we was afraid of setting the place on fire. If they smoked we'd charge them a nickel or throw them out. If they spit on the floor, we'd make them clean the place out.

We won three games of baseball and at the end of the month we had a party in our club. The president, he made it up. We just had the members and had ice-cream, cakes, and soda, and we ate and ate and played cards. Then we played a lot on the roof. We used to have lots of gang wars. The one that went first, we'd follow; there weren't any captains or generals like that. We'd follow the one we thought was wisest. We'd do as he'd say. We'd choose the wisest guy for the leader of the war, and he was pretty nearly always the strongest.[10]

The leader of the gang is what he is because in one way or another he is what the boys want. The function of leadership is an inevitable growth out of the conflicts and other activities of the gang. The natural leader is the boy who comes nearest fitting the requirements of this function: he "fills the bill."

THE INFLUENCE OF LEADERS

A real leader manages his gang with ease. So great is his influence over his fellows that, if he is "bad," he may lead them to prison.

[10] Gang boy's own story.

208. A group of seven or eight boys who lived in the neighborhood of a small park, used to congregate every afternoon after school in the playground and interfere with the games and activities of the younger children. The policeman on the beat, being an indulgent, fatherly sort of person, always shooed them away with a good-natured warning. One afternoon they noticed a new policeman at the playground. Immediately the leader of the gang suggested that they "kid the cop," and he threw a snowball at the minion of the law. When the policeman, red and angry, reached the gate, there was no sign of the boys to be seen, but they had discovered a new pastime and were not slow to renew their sport.

For several successive afternoons they hung around the children's playground, and then, when nothing happened the leader of the gang suggested that they slide down the shoots and swing in the swings. The policeman asked them to get out, and they laughed. He pulled his club out of its holder and menaced them. "Let's get the cop," shouted the leader, and before the policeman knew what was happening to him, six of the seven members were beating him up.

When the officer brought the case into the Boys' Court, the boys were . . . . sent to St. Charles, where, it appeared later, they grew more intimate than they had been before, with each other, and with the sort of crimes that are committed by boys sent to such a place. When they came out, they seemed to have agreed among themselves that the first thing they would do would be to punish the policeman who had taken away their liberty. There were various suggestions, but the leader finally said that the only way they could be sure to put him out of the way was to kill him. Most of the boys, so they told the court afterward, shrank from that, but the leader finally prevailed with them, saying that he would head the attack and that the others should follow him. . . . . The policeman was found dead with his head crushed by a heavy club that lay near him, and there were bruises over his face and body from other weapons. The boys confessed that they had all had a hand in the affair, though they admitted that none of them wanted to do it. When asked why they did, then, the reply was practically the same in all cases, "T. told us to, and we've got to do what he tells us." "Did he ever threaten you?" the court asked each boy separately. "No, he never had to. We always did what he said." . . . . This boy was truly a born leader, though he led his followers to prison.[11]

---

[11] Unpublished manuscript by D. L——.

In sharp contrast is a gang become "righteous" through the influence of a strong leader with a rather puritanical tradition behind him.

210. Our gang stuck together for several years. It was composed of five boys—Arthur M., the two C. brothers, Warren and Hugh, J. C. M., and myself, Phil R.—all living within four blocks of each other on the extreme outskirts of the city of X——, Illinois. There were three Protestants, one Catholic, and one Jew in the group, but that made no difference in our ardent devotion to each other.

One characteristic which set this gang off from others in the community was its insistence on certain ideals of conduct from its members. Very early we were enthusiastic about the idea of doing what was right. It was an established rule that anyone caught using profanity should receive a kick from every other fellow in the gang. One of the fellows said he had read in a eugenics book that every boy should build up his body while young; for it would have to last him a lifetime. Accordingly we went in for everything that would improve our health. We went camping often; we did not smoke. The gang went out for all the high-school sports and different members made the tumbling, the basket-ball and the football teams. Later, Art was chosen as All Northern Illinois halfback.

The other fellows in our neighborhood laughed at us for not smoking and doing other things which they did. We became known as the "righteous" gang but later when our group achieved athletic fame in high school and also beat up a few of them, they had more respect for us. We also formed a wrestling team so that we could challenge another gang who thought they were invincible. Finally the other fellows in the neighborhood decided to quit kidding us on our stand on the smoking question and to fall into line by quitting smoking themselves.

The largest fellow in the gang was Art, who was six feet tall and weighed 185 pounds. He possessed a wonderful personality and also the qualities of leadership which enabled him to assume control of the gang. He was outspoken, courageous, and frank. On one of our hiking trips in the country a huge dog made for us with ominous intentions and we all scurried for the trees. When we looked down we saw the dog sullenly walking away and Art standing a few feet away with a club held over his head in a menacing position. It was such demonstrations of fearlessness that made us respect him. He was the one who organized us into an independent Boy Scout troop, brought about the prohibition of swearing and smoking, and also inspired us to go in for athletics. In high school Art used to chide the other fellows for drinking and smoking. He once remonstrated with a certain fellow on the football team for breaking training, but did not report it to the coach. He went out for all forms of athletics in high school, making the basket-ball, football, and track teams. In the latter two he starred. Last year he played on the college team.

Art's father was a man of enlightenment, having had a somewhat liberal education in Germany and wishing to see his own children with all the educational advantages possible. The children were brought up in the Puritan style—going to the Catholic church every Sunday and working while attending school so as to learn the value of money.

Warren C—— was good in athletics, but he was very impatient and did not like to study. Not having the patience to stick to it, he left high school and joined the air service. His brother, Hugh, was radically different from Warren. He applied himself constantly to his studies and stuck to things. In high school Hugh went out for all sports, making the football and basket-ball teams. He was active in our neighborhood athletic activities such as boxing, tumbling, etc. He got on the honor roll in the matter of grades for the second consecutive year. Having finished high school, he is now attending college.

J. C. was the only member of the gang not interested in athletics. He was very handy on hikes and hunting trips, however, for he loved the out-of-doors.

The influence of the Boy Scout type of organization upon the gang was considerable, although the group was never organized as a formal Scout troop. Art was elected captain of our independent troop composed only of the five of our group. This was merely a change from our previously tacit to an external recognition of him as our leader.

Majority rule controlled our gang in important decisions, but aside from these the leadership of Art determined and directed the activities of the group. On our hiking, camping, or any other kind of activity Art led the rest in stumping and assumed the chief responsibilities. He knew where and how to put up a tent, how to make a fire, cook, and what food to take along. On hunting trips in the winter he could differentiate between the tracks of different animals.[12]

The nature of the influence which the leader may exert is indicated in the case of this "righteous gang." The character of the gang is to some extent determined by the habits, attitudes, and interests which its members have previously acquired—the nature of the tradition which they bring with them when they enter the group. This is particularly true with reference to the leader. A gang will often become whatever the leader makes it and that will be determined by the forces which have already played upon him and molded his character.

This document shows, among other things, that the energies, which under certain conditions lead to mischief, can be directed into other channels. It also indicates that it is group action—directed toward ends that are intelligible to the boy members themselves—through which order is established and habits are formed that are wholesome, or at least, harmless.

[12] Manuscript by a former member.

PART IV

The Gang Problem

Introduction

The problems arising in connection with the presence of gangs in a community are many. The undirected gang or gang club demoralizes its members. It aids in making chronic truants and juvenile delinquents and in developing them into finished criminals. It augments racial friction in some areas. It complicates the problems of capital and labor in certain fields. It organizes bootlegging and rum-running into profitable business. It contributes to perverted politics and governmental corruption. It promotes the corrupt alliance between crime and politics. In making more acute these various types of social maladjustment it lays a heavy burden upon the community.

The gang problem with all its various phases is not peculiar to Chicago. It is present in every American city where the disordered conditions of the intramural frontier have developed. Studies made in New York City, Boston, Cleveland, Los Angeles, St. Louis, Minneapolis, El Paso, Hammond, Denver, and other cities have revealed the same phenomena on a larger or smaller scale. The problem is better in hand in some of these communities than in others, but the findings of the Chicago investigation indicate a type situation. Even in rural areas the gang tends to appear when community life breaks down and opportunities are present for boys to congregate.

The more serious aspects of the gang problem are created by the older groups. Yet the continuity of life from the younger gangs to the older is so unbroken, the passage from one stage to the next is so gradual, that the serious crimes of young adult gangs can hardly be understood apart from their origins in adolescent groups. Most of the practices of the criminal gang are begun in fact or in principle among the boys. There is no break to mark the place where the adolescent gang leaves off and the adult gang begins. This is an important fact in explaining the criminal community and the development of the other phases of the gang problem, most of which have their genesis in younger gangs.

CHAPTER XVII

Demoralization in the Gang

There are many demoralizing influences in the undirected gang. The period of adolescence, which is particularly given to ganging, is one of plasticity and habit forming. For this reason the nature of the conditioning to which the gang boy is subjected is exceedingly important from the standpoint of his later adjustments. It is these early acquirements which often make him a difficult problem for the community in later years.

Demoralization begins with the boy's entrance into the gang or earlier. The extent of the worldly knowledge displayed by little "punks" of seven or eight amazes the investigator. The process continues progressively as the gang boy grows older. He often undergoes a rather dramatic evolution, passing through a series of stages, each growing out of the preceding. Beginning as a truant, he becomes in turn a minor delinquent, a hoodlum, a reckless young sport or a daredevil, an occasional criminal, and finally, if nothing intervenes, he develops into a seasoned gangster or a professional criminal. Training in the gang is periodically interrupted by visits to various correctional institutions. He comes to regard these as little more than side excursions; and he may even point to them with some degree of pride. Although they are de-

signed to "reform" him, in most cases they simply speed
up the process of demoralization.[1]

THE GANG INVITES TRUANCY

The process of demoralization often begins in "playing hookey," which in itself seems innocent enough. A
lot of the fun in sneaking away from school is in going
"wid de gang"; boys seldom "bum" from school alone.
The gang invites truancy and truancy encourages the
gang.

"Truancy is one of the first steps in the formation
of the gang," asserts an experienced officer of the Chicago
Department of Compulsory Education. "Nearly every
habitual truant over twelve becomes the nucleus for a
gang and delinquency follows. The gang, on the other
hand, is the basis for truancy. The demoralizing influence of truant gangs in school districts is rapid. . . . .
Gang boys are truants and lead others to become so."[2]

The consensus of opinion among the sixty-three Chicago truant officers who prepared special reports on the
gang problem in their districts was that the gang augments truancy. They had under observation at the time
the study was made a total of 238 boys' gangs and 94 un-
attached and unsupervised clubs of the gang type.

"Playing hookey," which is quite natural to any boy,
is defined by society as truancy. When it recurs frequent-

[1] Compare H. E. Barnes, *The Repression of Crime*, p. 375. The
term "demoralization" may be used to denote a falling away from
the customs (mores) or a disintegration of morale. Here it is used,
however, to include the development of attitudes and habits which are
out of adjustment with the dominant social codes. Truancy, incorrigi-
bility, hoodlumism, delinquency, criminality may be considered as successive stages in this process of demoralization. A criminal gang may have
its own mores, which govern the relations of its members to each other,
and it may have a high degree of morale, developed in fighting other gangs
or defying the law. Yet, in either case, its members may be considered as
demoralized from the point of view of the larger community.

[2] From reports of officers in the Department of Compulsory Education.

ly the gang boy receives special treatment at the hands of officials who seek to enforce their definition of the situation. If a truant, placed in an incorrigible room at school, does not standardize his conduct, he enjoys the first side trip of his career in being "put away" in the Chicago Parental School, maintained for the institutional care of chronic truants. He may be held first for a few days in the Juvenile Detention Home, which the gang boys call the "Juvenile County Jail." This experience gives him great prestige with the other boys when he gets back into the gang and tells his story. Too often it is the first milestone in a course of personal disorganization, which often leads either to successful criminality or to prison.

An intensive study of twenty-eight confirmed truants disclosed the fact that twenty-two of them were members of delinquent gangs and five, of mischievous or crap-shooting groups, while only one was free from gang influences.[3]

Although playing hookey seems innocuous to the casual observer, under city conditions of the gangland type it contains the germs of later delinquencies. Boys in truant gangs soon learn to sleep away from home and eventually they may absent themselves for weeks or months at a time. They pick up rags, bottles, and barrels to sell and it is but a short step to stealing milk and groceries from back porches and then bicycles for hikes.[4] Most of the boys in the truant rooms and Parental School are restless little urchins who have been initiated into this life and find it difficult to stick to anything of a more settled nature.[5]

[3] The interviews with boys at the Parental School were conducted by I. D. Stehr.

[4] See chap. viii. See also Healy and Bronner, *Judge Baker Foundation Case Studies*, Series I, Case 11, p. 7a.

[5] Document 20 shows the ten-year development of a hardened criminal gang from a group of truants.

Not all gang boys have been truants, however, and many boys attending school regularly are drawn into gang associations.

THE GANG FACILITATES DELINQUENCY

Whether the schoolboy is a truant or not, the unsupervised gang is pretty likely to lead him in the direction of delinquency. If the gang boy attends school regularly he encounters the demoralizing influence of the gang in his periods of leisure. Most boys in gangland, however, quit school as soon as the law allows them, either to loaf or find a job. The working boy's spare time is quite likely to be filled with the same sort of activities as the schoolboy's. Frequent periods of loafing and unemployment among boys in gangland are particularly favorable to the formation of gangs and the development of the sort of delinquencies which they promote.

212. The X—— Y—— Street Club is reputed to be one of the most destructive and demoralizing gangs in the neighborhood. It has no regular clubroom but meets out of doors in the fall, mainly in the rear of the —— School and in nearby alleys and streets. Crap shooting, gambling, smutty story-telling, and planning robberies were said to be its chief activities. There are some twenty boys from twelve years up in the group. According to a probation officer of the Juvenile Court, the leader is an escaped inmate of St. Charles. The principal of the school nearby told me that the leader fell in love with one of the teachers and induced her to elope with him. The two went to Michigan and later the boy was tried there and for a time was imprisoned in the state penitentiary. He is now back in Chicago.

At the time of the study a member of this gang, only twelve years old, was in the Juvenile Detention Home on charge of participating in a thousand-dollar robbery. He said that the other members were trying to put the responsibility on him. It is said that the leader's custom is to commit crimes and then make the smaller boys bear the brunt of the punishment.[6]

[6] Report of a private investigation made by a social agency.

Neighborhood gangs may exercise a demoralizing effect upon a whole school.

213. Twenty-four eighth-grade boys from twelve to sixteen years old were interviewed at this school. Sixteen of them had no wholesome recreation. Five boys went to a social center and three to a settlement. The boys patronized the movies on an average of nearly twice each week.

Twelve boys belonged to gangs. According to the principal, there is extreme need of constructive action in this section: the streets and even school yard are infested with gangs, the activities of which are destructive of property and character. The influence of these gangs over younger boys is most demoralizing. One tough gang operates near the school and is a menace to discipline and normal life even within the school. A public-school center conducted five nights a week would prove of incalculable value to the neighborhood.[7]

The unwholesome influence upon schoolboys of groups of boys who are not working has often been remarked by school officials.

Many gang boys who have not had dealings with social authority as truants, have their first adventure with the law in the Cook County Juvenile Court, which determines whether they shall be paroled to their parents, put on probation under the direction of the court, or put away in some institution for minor offenders. A visit to the court constitutes the beginning of a "record" and as in the case of an experience in the Juvenile Detention Home or the Parental School, it is viewed in retrospect with great pride by the boy, for it gets him status in the gang.[8] This general principle of prestige in the gang through experience with the law has been observed in a large number of cases.

The importance of the group factor in juvenile delin-

[7] Report of a private investigation made by a social agency.

[8] A court record may also operate to keep a boy in the gang by creating a peculiar common experience. In one case it was observed also that a boy's police record prevented his getting a job, thus forcing him back into the gang for friends who would stake him.

quency in Chicago is suggested by a study of 177 boys brought into the Chicago Juvenile Court in one month (August, 1920). In 57 per cent of these cases, the boys were arraigned in groups, while the records indicate that groups were active in many of the other cases, in which only one boy was caught. A similar study of 169 boys for a winter month (January, 1921) suggests the presence of the group factor in 54 per cent of the cases.[9] While these facts are hardly conclusive in themselves, they become significant in the light of statements made by those in close touch with the work of the court.

In the majority of cases of delinquent boys, the defendants are either leaders or members of bad gangs.[10]

In more than one-half the cases that have come under my observation, the gang spirit has been in evidence.[11]

Our observation leads us to believe that the gang is one of the largest factors in delinquency and juvenile crime in Chicago.[12]

My attention has been called to a quotation from your recent address stating that the "gang spirit" contributes largely to crime. I wish to commend your statement in this connection as my experience of twenty-two years in dealing with offenders leads me to agree with you.[13]

Unsupervised boys' clubs in this gang area are an actual or potential source of disorder and delinquency. This is particularly true of the groups of smaller boys, the members of some of which already possess criminal records.[14]

If not paroled to their parents or kept on probation,

[9] *Preliminary Inquiry into Boy's Work in Chicago*, Middle West Division, Boys' Club Federation, February, 1921, p. 11.

[10] Statement by Judge Victor P. Arnold, Juvenile Court of Cook County, Chicago, Illinois.

[11] Statement by Joseph L. Moss, Chief Probation Officer, Cook County Juvenile Court, Chicago, Illinois.

[12] Statement by Miss Jessie Binford and Mrs. L. W. McMaster, Juvenile Protective Association, Chicago, Illinois.

[13] From a letter to the writer from F. Emory Lyon, Superintendent of the Central Howard Association, maintained for men and boys from correctional institutions.

[14] From the report of a private investigation made by a social agency.

gang boys in the first stages of delinquency may be sent
for a term to the Chicago Cook County School for Boys,
an educational institution for lesser offenders. That the
majority of boys received here have been subjected to the
disorganizing influences of the unsupervised gang or gang
club is indicated by an intensive study of 100 of them
(made in connection with this investigation)[15] taken at
random. Of these, 95 per cent were members of delinquent
gangs, and more than 80 per cent freely admitted the influence of the gang in getting them into trouble. A similar
study in 1918 of 100 boys committed by the Juvenile
Court to a correctional institution showed 75 per cent to
have been members of gangs.[16] A re-examination of these
schedules revealed that in practically every case the delinquency of the boy was linked with gang activities.

Although the group factor in delinquency has been
generally ignored by criminologists, some recent students
of the subject have emphasized its importance. E. H.
Sutherland points out that delinquencies are committed
in the majority of cases by groups of offenders rather than
by individuals. While only 38 per cent of the children
brought into the Children's Court of New York City
were arraigned singly, "the actual association is much
greater than these figures indicate for the reason that
many members of the group committing an offense do not
get caught or get caught later and are arraigned separately." Furthermore, the gang encourages delinquency outside its own ranks by setting a standard of conduct for a
whole neighborhood. Franklin Chase Hoyt also corrob-
orates these conclusions. Generalizing from his experience
with boys' gangs in New York City, he points out that

[15] Through the courtesy of O. J. Milliken, then principal of the Chicago Cook County School for Boys, the author was permitted to become
acquainted with the boys and to record their own stories of their experiences in gangs.

[16] Albert E. Webster, *Junk Dealing and Juvenile Delinquency*, pp.
17, 18.

the adventures and street fights of the younger gangs begin innocently enough, but later tend to develop into predatory activities, ultimately developing "typical gangsters, the gunmen, and the criminals of whom we hear so much, and who hesitate at nothing, not even at murder itself, in the carrying out of their objects."[17]

An interesting case of the way in which the gang may become a source of moral contagion on the cultural frontier of a smaller city has been indicated by a study of El Paso, Texas.

214. In the Mexican section of El Paso is a group of three or four hundred Mexican boys composed of from twenty to twenty-five gangs, each with its separate leader. These gangs have been growing steadily for eight or nine years and now embrace a rather seasoned and experienced leadership in all sorts of crime. Eighty per cent of their members are probably under fifteen years of age; most of the older boys are under eighteen. Stealing, destroying property, and all kinds of malicious mischief are their chief activities. In fact, these groups are almost literally training schools of crime and they seem to be related to each other in a sort of loose federation. For the most part, the boys do not go to school or do not work unless it be for an occasional day. Fifty of them have been sent to the State Industrial school, eight are in jail, twenty-five or thirty are being specially investigated, and about two hundred are under surveillance. These boys may be observed in their characteristic groupings every evening on street corners and in vacant lots and alleys. The park, which is their favorite meeting place, with its double rows of tall hedges, its trees and shrubbery, affords them a good place to hide and to conceal their delinquencies.[18]

It is apparent that the gangs in this case have grown up in a culturally interstitial area within which the usual institutions which control the boy have broken down.

DOES THE GANG CAUSE CRIME?

The present study does not advance the thesis that the gang is a "cause" of crime. It would be more accu-

[17] *Quicksands of Youth*, p. 113.

[18] From Roy E. Dickerson, "Report of a Survey of Mexican Boy Life," a statement to the author, September 26, 1924.

rate to say that the gang is an important contributing factor, facilitating the commission of crime and greatly extending its spread and range. The organization of the gang and the protection which it affords, especially in combination with a ring or a syndicate, make it a superior instrument for the execution of criminal enterprises. Its demoralizing influence on its members arises through the dissemination of criminal technique, and the propagation, through mutual excitation, of interests and attitudes which make crime easier (less inhibited) and more attractive.

The abolition of the gang, even if it could be accomplished, would not remove the unwholesome influences with which the boy in gangland is surrounded. Many boys there would become demoralized even without the gang. But the gang greatly facilitates demoralization by giving added prestige to already existing patterns of unwholesome conduct and by assimilating its members to modes of thinking, feeling, and acting which would not be so emphasized without group influence. One bad gang in a neighborhood, furthermore, "starts all the others going in the same direction," and the younger gangs follow the older. Clifford R. Shaw has traced delinquencies directly from one group to another, by means of a sort of interlocking membership, back for a period of fifteen years. In this way the tradition of gang delinquencies comes to be passed along as kind of social heritage in a neighborhood. E. H. Sutherland has pointed out that the Valley gang in Chicago "has had an active life of over thirty years. In the earlier period the district was controlled politically and socially by this gang. . . . . "[19]

The most important educative influences in shaping the tastes, character, and personality of the boy are like-

[19] *Criminology*, p. 154. "Paddy the Bear," leader of the Valley gang in its early period, has been succeeded by men who have continued its activities and have made large fortunes in beer-running.

ly to be those he encounters informally, because leisure-time behavior comes nearest being voluntary and represents more really the boy's own selection of activities. *Even if opportunities for wholesome recreation were present in abundance, it would be difficult for it to compete with the vigorous freedom of exciting gang life.* It may hardly be doubted that intimate association in gang activities is far more vital in molding the boy than any sort of conventional schooling.

Curiously enough, a boy sometimes becomes aware that the gang is providing him with an education. In one case it was maintained that gang schooling in automotive mechanics was better than technical high-school training.

215. G—— is a seventeen-year-old, a handsome, bright-eyed member of the Glorianna gang. A casual conversation is sufficient to indicate that he is full of energy and ideas of his own. In a two-hour discussion with the investigator he maintained that he could get a better training in automotive mechanics in his gang than in any high school in Chicago. Several of the members are expert mechanics and they have a "great big book" which they consult in cases of doubt. This gang is alleged to have from twelve to fourteen stolen cars on hand all the time. Some of these are torn down and the parts sold, others are dismantled, and still others are rebuilt; the gang maintains an outlet store for the disposal of such material; hence, this type of knowledge is directly related to their activities and stands them in good stead in a practical way.[20]

In spite of all of the forces in the unsupervised gang which influence the boy in the direction of delinquency, some writers believe that the gang has been overemphasized as a factor in producing crime.

It is quite clear that not all gangs are criminal gangs. The gang has probably been overemphasized as a factor in crime, in view of the large number of gangs that exist without criminal records. . . . .[21]

[20] Gang boy's own story.

[21] Sutherland, *Criminology*, p. 157. In this conclusion Sutherland is probably following William Healy, who says,

Our impression is that the gang—defined to include the rudimentary type which Healy calls the "delinquent crowd," and to exclude the more formal group regularly constituted and supervised by some social agency—is a very important factor in Chicago crime. An assumption that any large number of gangs exist without delinquent activities is hardly justified in the light of available findings on this point.

The great majority of the gangs studied in the present investigation had engaged in delinquent or demoralizing activities.[22]

J. Adams Puffer, from a detailed study of 66 gangs of younger adolescents, found that 49 of them, or 74 per cent, engaged in predatory activities, such as stealing, injuring property, etc.[23] His comment on the general influence of the gang is also significant. He found that boys from the better class of homes usually formed brief-lived groups of their own, while boys whose home training was deficient tended to join gangs already formed, which were

apt to be tough with fixed and dangerous traditions. . . . . Thus . . . . among delinquents of my acquaintance hardly more than a quarter were original members of their gangs, or could tell how their gangs started. The bad gang, therefore, tends to be

---

"A considerable literature on gang life has been developed, but according to our studies of delinquents, the rôle of the gang has been overdone. Of course there are plentiful examples of harmful influences, but there are many others, as in this case, where gang life has had very little bearing on delinquency. There are gangs that are 'predatory,' and there are many gangs that are quite innocuous, and there are gangs that by no means draw into them all the boys in the vicinity."—William Healy and Augusta F. Bronner, *Judge Baker Foundation Case Studies*, Series I, Case 1, p. 9a.

[22] Compare Emory S. Bogardus, *The City Boy and His Problems: A Survey of Boy Life in Los Angeles*, chap. vi, "The Boy and the Gang," pp. 93–100. "Stealing is perhaps the gang's most common major activity" (p. 98).

[23] J. Adams Puffer, *The Boy and His Gang*, p. 40.

a persistent and dangerous institution, taking in new members as the older ones graduate.[24]

WHAT THE BOY LEARNS IN THE GANG

What the boy learns in the unsupervised gang or gang club usually takes three general trends: personal habits, which in boyhood are conventionally regarded as demoralizing; familiarity with the technique of crime; and a philosophy of life or an organization of attitudes which facilitate further delinquency of a more serious type. This is the gang boy's threefold social heritage.[25]

Vulgarity, obscenity, and profanity of all kinds, usually acquired very early from the general milieu of gangland, are fostered and elaborated in the gang. This is equally true of crap shooting and gambling in most of its forms. The use of tobacco and snuff is a group habit, even when the group is made up of little boys. The use of intoxicants is a pretty general practice in gangs of older adolescents. Even though association with girls is tabooed by younger gangs, premature acquaintance with sex is almost universal in such groups and like other gang interests is greatly stimulated in interaction. Toughness, first developed as a pose, soon becomes a reality. Vices practiced by individual members usually spread to the whole group and the boy who can hold out against such powerful social pressure is indeed a rare exception.

It is not meant to imply that the gang is in any sense inherently bad. It simply lacks wholesome direction. *It is a spontaneous attempt on the part of boys to create a society of their own where none adequate to their needs exists.* Naturally they absorb what is vicious in their environment to the extent that such patterns appeal to

[24] *Ibid.*, pp. 28–29.

[25] The subjective aspect of the demoralization of the boy delinquent is beautifully delineated in Clifford R. Shaw's presentation of the autobiography of a young offender published under the title of *A Problem Boy.*

them, for there are no very potent forces in their social world to define these acts as undesirable.

LEARNING TECHNIQUE OF CRIME

The boy in the gang learns the technique of crime by observing it in older groups. The doings of the older gang are discussed with greatest interest by the younger groups. Not infrequently the older gang uses younger boys. Chicago beer-running gangs employ boys to drive their trucks; the youngsters look innocent and "get by."

The gang boy acquires a more effective knowledge of the technique of crime, however, by participating in and observing the exploits of his own group. The gang's predatory activities include vandalism and all sorts of thievery. Junking leads to petty stealing. "Going robbing" is a common diversion in the gang and this often develops into the more serious types of burglary and robbery with a gun. A gang often specializes in one particular type of delinquency, but the activities of most groups run the whole gamut of offenses, including practically every crime in the catalogue.

Exact information as to the technique of crime is imparted in the gang.

217. Some of the questionable activities learned in the gang were the different methods of unlocking doors without the use of a key. One method requires only a piece of string and the portion of an umbrella rib. Other methods are more complicated. If I desired to get into my room or cupboard in the settlement and did not have my key, any member of the gang would gladly open it for me within a few minutes. It was much safer not to lock a door if you did not want it opened. If it were locked, their curiosity would prompt them to open it and then there would come the temptation to "loot" because the "law" had locked it up.[26]

How to procure junk, open merchandise cars, rob bread boxes, snatch purses, fleece a storekeeper, empty

[26] Unpublished manuscript by boys' worker in gangland.

slot machines, pick a pocket, go shoplifting, "roll" a drunken man, get skeleton keys, steal an automobile, sell stolen goods to "fences," purchase guns, engineer a holdup, operate stills, burglarize a store, trick the police, and so on—this is the type of technical knowledge for which the gang acts as a clearing-house.

Most of the younger gangs do not give their whole time to crime, as some groups do; they may be described as semi-delinquent or delinquent on occasion. The educative effect in the long run, however, is the same.

ATTITUDES DEVELOPED IN THE GANG

It is abundantly evident that there is no lack of patterns in the gang boy's social world for the whole gamut of predatory activities which are possible in a city environment. Nor is there any apparent opprobrium attached to those approved by the gang, which has its own code for its own members. One is reminded of the so-called "criminal tribes" of India, whose customs include a great variety of activities which are regarded as predatory by the larger social organization with which they come into contact, but which they themselves regard as sanctioned by their gods. The gang, however, not having their cultural detachment, usually accepts the code of society but is in rebellion against it. In fact, the diabolical character of *disobeying* the social codes appeals to gang boys. While they accept the moral authority of the community, still it is external to them and they get a "kick" out of their attitude of disrespect for established rules.

Experience in a gang of the predatory type usually develops in the boy an attitude of indifference to law and order—one of the basic traits of the finished gangster. The personal and property rights of outsiders, who are regarded as proper prey, are constantly disregarded. A growing attitude of superiority to the rest of the world is greatly augmented by the feeling of group power and security. Recklessness is generated and in some cases unbelievable daring and impertinence. Too often this attitude is so well taken—through police connivance and political protection—that a terrorized community raises no voice to challenge it. Nor is official collusion always necessary to its maintenance; for the members of a gang, having some reason for enmity, may "mob," beat, or take "pot" shots at officers of the law.

The gang boy very early acquires the independence which is characteristic of the finished gangster—learns to sleep away from home and live on his own resources for weeks at a time. He frequents the parks, the canals and river fronts, the forest preserves; he helps the farmers of adjacent lands in their busy seasons; he "hangs out" in the newspaper alleys. He soon learns to feel dependence on nobody and even if he loses his original gang, it is easy enough to fall in with another. He is ready to cut his moorings when occasion demands.

218. A boy of fifteen ran away from home with a gang of three other boys. He had been a member of a boys' club and his father's employer had paid for a camp membership for him. The gang, however, had greater attractions. He was not heard of until three months later when his gang was arrested in a room in a cheap hotel on Harrison street. Here the police found $10,000 worth of goods, the proceeds of from forty to fifty burglaries. The "racket" was to call up a house and make sure no one was at home and then put a little boy through a window to open the door.[27]

Finally, the boy usually acquires in the gang an attitude of fatalism, a willingness to take a chance—a philosophy of life which fits him well for a career of crime. "What's de odds? Take a chance!" He learns to take

[27] Interview with a social worker.

Charles Dickens, who tells a similar tale of Oliver Twist, must have known gang life in East London.

getting caught stoically. "You get caught sooner or later anyway; so why not take a chance?" Most gang boys are quite familiar with the punitive machinery of society. Boys standing at the window of the Chicago Cook County School, watching the westbound suburban trains of the Illinois Central, are heard to remark, "Dere go de St. Charles coffee-grinders" and "Dat's where we go next." The boys soon become used to the idea of being sent away; and they foresee the next step. One boy looked forward eagerly to the later stages of the journey: "I want to see de inside of Pontiac and Joliet too before I'm t'ru'." This sentiment, developed to the logical extreme, may manifest itself in the "desperado attitude." A boy of sixteen, whose brother was hanged, and who himself was the leader of a particularly vicious gang, made the remark with all show of sincerity, "I want to kill a cop before I have to swing."[28]

219. "I'd just as soon swing as go back to the stir," said one gangster who had participated in a murder during a holdup. "I'm tired of prisons. Maybe they'll give me the rope for this and get it all over with. Harry swung for his job. He told me in the county jail that he didn't care. He said the odds were three to one anyway, and he was willing to pay. He meant that he had taken three lives and the state was only getting one in return. I'm ready to swing too."[29]

What better education for a disorderly life can be

[28] That this boy is making progress toward his goal, despite frequent attempts of society to "reform" him, is indicated by the following news item of gang activities in which he participated three or four years after he was heard to make the above remark:

"Five youths, charged with fifty-four robberies with guns, were held to the grand jury yesterday. . . . . Their bonds were fixed at $50,000 each."

[29] From newspaper accounts. This fatalism frequently expresses itself among boys in the statement: "I've gone too far with this sort of thing to turn back now!"

found than that which the gang provides: inculcation of demoralizing personal habits, schooling in the technique of crime, the imparting of attitudes of irresponsibility, independence, and indifference to law, and the setting up of the philosophy of taking a chance and of fatalism?

THE "HOODLUM" AS A SOCIAL PATTERN

If the younger undirected gangs and clubs of the gang type, which serve as training schools for delinquency, do not succeed in turning out the finished criminal, they often develop a type of personality which may well foreshadow the gangster and the gunman. A boy of this type may best be described as a hoodlum, the sort of "hero" who is extolled in most unsupervised gangs of younger adolescents.

The hoodlum is a definite social type. He takes particular delight in interfering with the orderly pursuits of business and pleasure which he sees about him and indeed, often enough, which may have been planned for his own benefit. He breaks up a party, eggs a speaker, molests school children, taunts women and girls on the streets, or engages in petty thievery of personal belongings. He is a vandal: it seems to give him pleasure to despoil and destroy property wherever opportunity arises. He does not hold a job. He is often on the streets or in the poolrooms. He is a loafer and idles away countless hours in smoking, gambling, and rough horseplay. His bravado is always ready to foment a brawl, but he is seldom willing to engage in a fair fight unless backed by his pals. He is coarse and vulgar in his talk. He is, in brief, a thoroughly disorganized (or, if you like, unorganized) person, and if the trend of his present evolution is carried far enough, he is pretty likely to develop into a criminal.

220. Fatty is about nine years old. He stole 25 cents from a policeman who was waiting to buy lunch. He holds up the little boys when they go with money to buy ice. He took six pool balls from the playroom of the settlement. His brothers "went over the water" (to the bad boys' school). He stole $6 worth of tickets through a hole in the picture show window. He smoked so much that he fainted in line at school. He found a gun which a robber threw away in his alley and used it on the little boys. He took the scissors from his teacher at school. He broke a $200 window in a drug store. He took $2 from a man with a push cart. He plays hookey from school. He stones the girls. Early he had come under the influence of a gang, whose members later acquired court records.[30]

A red-sashed, golden-curled little Lord Fauntleroy is too idyllic to be set up as a pattern for the boyhood of today; he never was a real boy. It is quite another thing, however, to seek to direct the activities of the boy into channels which will enable him ultimately to organize his own life for wholesome personal development and some measure of adjustment to the complex conditions of modern society.

LATER TRAINING FOR CRIME

Unsupervised gangs of older boys and young men continue this process of demoralization in the direction of more serious criminality. Their end product is the slugger, the gunman, and the all-round gangster.

As gangs get older they may attempt to accommodate themselves to society and so become conventionalized as athletic clubs. External earmarks of respectability, however, do not guarantee its reality. Demoralizing habits, disorganizing attitudes, and questionable activities are often carried over into the club organization to be continued and augmented there under the guise of legitimate functions.

[30] Interview with a settlement worker.

221. The Goldenrod Athletic Club, whose career lasted from 1905 to 1920, numbered with its hangers-on about 100 Irish-Americans from twenty to thirty years of age. A clubroom was maintained near Archer and Western avenues. Besides football and baseball, the chief activities were dances and gambling. The club was affiliated with the local Democratic political machine.

Eventually gambling became the leading interest of the group, which developed into what later proved to be a training school for professional gamblers. The members would make it a habit to get on incoming trains near their hang-out and to ride them both ways in order to get next to "suckers," whom they enticed into card or dice games. They would let the greenhorns win for a time and then fleece them. A dozen of the group were engaged in this sort of activity.

Four members, tiring of the neighborhood, began looking for something more lively and finally became leading professional gamblers at the Kewanee race track in the South. One of the leading crapshooters of California, now aged thirty-eight, was also a graduate of this gang. Another member entered the legal profession and can be depended upon to defend any of them when they get into trouble; he was the "brains" of the group from its beginning.

In this way the influence of the group was multiplied. After they were old enough to get set in their habits and get away, they were hopeless from the standpoint of reform, but always agile enough to keep out of trouble. It was in the gang that they were initiated into a life of crime, and it is probable that they started new centers of demoralization elsewhere when the group broke up.[31]

"Scratch a club man and you will find a gangster" is an adage which applies in many of these cases. The club frequently gives the hoodlum an unwonted standing and influence in the community. In the club too are often found the young sport of the reckless type, the dare-devil, and the occasional criminal and gangster in the making.

While conventionalization into a club may be a step in the direction of the gang's disintegration, it may on the other hand serve to contaminate a wider group. The gang club tends to draw in additional members in great

[31] Interview with a politician in the district.

numbers; its social functions may be patronized by hundreds and even thousands of young people who might not otherwise normally be subject to such influences. Thus in the form of an organized club the vicious gang often extends its noxious influences to wider and wider circles of boys and young men.

The case of Walter Krauser, twice a murderer, sentenced to hang, and then adjudged insane, may be cited as one illustration of the demoralizing influence of the gang club.

222. His work-worn mother laid a tearful curse on "that cruel, hounding gang" today for bringing Walter Krauser to the shadow of the gallows.

"He was a good boy!" she cried. "He tried so hard! But they wouldn't let him alone. He is only nineteen. He couldn't hold out against them. They kept coming for him—morning, noon, and night. They called him 'yellow' when he wouldn't go out with them. They haunted my good boy!"

The boy's eighth-grade teacher and even the vengeful police of the Stock Yards station verified the heartbroken mother's picture of her son as the victim of a cruel system—a system which fosters the gang spirit, protects the gangster in petty crimes, ties the hands of the police until finally something happens which is too much for the political "fixers."

"Walter Krauser was a bright, well-behaved lad in 1918, when he was graduated from the eighth grade of the Fallon school.

"I remember him as an unusually nice boy, ... " his eighth-grade teacher said today. "He had a good mind and good habits. I never thought he'd come to this."

But when his school life was over Walter found himself facing a hard rough life. All the "real guys" were gangsters. Gang membership was the sign of caste. When Walter got his chance to join the most powerful, most desirable of all the gangs, he joined.

Presently the police began to hear of him. He was picked up for fighting on the streets, for starting a rough-house in a saloon—for functioning as a gangster should. These arrests meant nothing. One of the advantages of gang membership is immunity from petty police interference. Walter would be turned loose when taken to court. If the judge had not been given that "office," why, some one had let the complaining witness know it wouldn't be wise to talk in court.

Krauser was arrested a dozen times this year, according to the Stock Yards police. Not once was he sent to jail. Toward fall the charges against him became more serious. On September 3, he was arrested for robbing a saloon. . . . . The woman bartender positively identified him. The case seemed cinched. But when Krauser came up for trial, something happened to the state's case. The bartender no longer wanted to identify Krauser. She was not sure. The case was dropped.

On November 27, Krauser was arrested for stealing an automobile. It was another air-tight case, but when the gangster was taken into the Boys' Court for trial, the complaining witness refused to go on the stand and again Krauser went free.

For this protection the Stock Yards police blame an influential politician of the district. Krauser had a protégé's privileges, they say. Those privileges led him to go too far. This time—held on a charge of murder—he is to have no backing, it appears. The "gang" organization has disowned him, though a membership card, showing dues paid in full to date, was found in his coat. Krauser must face the law alone. And the law has his confession.[32]

There has been no way of testing a sufficient number of gang boys to determine the presence of defective heredity in gangs in proportion to that existent in the general population. The general impression from the present investigation, however, is that the majority of boys in the ordinary gang or gang club are of normal mentality both as to intelligence and emotions. The gang boys interviewed in the great majority of cases gave the impression of normal, and ofter superior, intelligence and a normal development of emotional responses and sentiments. There are undoubtedly many retarded and defective boys in the 1,313 gangs observed in the presence study; although the exact percentage is unknown, it is probably no higher than the percentage of the same type in the

[32] *Chicago Daily News.* Krauser's sentence to hang was later commuted to life-imprisonment on the ground of insanity, after he had killed an accomplice in the county jail.

general population. That the gang provides a doubly bad environment for this kind of boy is obvious.

TRAINING IN THE CRIMINAL GANG

The older gang may definitely drift into serious crime without assuming any semblance of more formal organization.[33] A side trip to the Pontiac reformatory or a term in the county jail or Bridewell often vary the monotony of gang activities at this stage. Then, if offenses are repeated or more desperate, there come the last stages in the gang boy's journey: the Joliet state penitentiary, a federal prison, or the gallows.[34]

A remark made by Nicholas Viana, a nineteen-year-old member of the Sam Cardinelli gang,[35] shortly before his execution affords a significant commentary on the influence of the criminal gang and its poolroom hang-out on young boys.

"I entered Cardinelli's poolroom in short trousers," he said. "In a week I was a criminal."

Viana and three other members of the gang were hanged for the murder of a saloonkeeper during a holdup. Cardinelli, the leader, was not present when the crime was committed, but he had furnished the four boys with revolvers and had sent them to rob the saloon.

Canaryville, a district near the Chicago stock yards, was at one time notorious as a breeding-place of vicious gangs,—a moral lesion in the life of the city. Some of Chicago's most desperate criminals are said to have been produced by the "Canaryville school of gunmen."

[33] See document 20.

[34] It is undoubtedly true that many of the demoralizing influences which play upon the gang boy emanate from his associations in penal institutions. These influences are carried back into the gang.

[35] See document 230.

226. The white hoodlum element of this district was characterized by the state's attorney of Cook County when he remarked that more bank robbers, pay-roll bandits, automobile bandits, highwaymen, and strong-arm crooks come from this particular district than from any other that has come to his notice during his seven years as chief prosecuting official.[36]

For years Eugene Geary, protégé of the late "Moss" Enright, and a leader of the gunman school, developed in "Canaryville," the toughest section of the stockyards district, has been known to the police as one of the most dangerous men in Chicago—a man killer, quick on the trigger of the pistol he always carried, and who gloried in the unsavory reputation he had earned through his exploits as a labor slugger, gangster, and all-around "bad man."[37]

It was this section which produced "Moss" Enright, "Sonny" Dunn, Eugene Geary, the Gentleman brothers and many others of Chicago's worst type of criminals. It is in this district that "athletic clubs" and other organizations of young toughs and gangsters flourish, and where disreputable poolrooms, hoodlum infested saloons and other criminal hang-outs are plentiful.[38]

Gerald Chapman, a nationally known criminal who was hanged April 6, 1926, was an end-product of the type of demoralization which the gang initiates. At the age of about fifteen or sixteen he was "graduated from the corner-loafing stage and became a member of a band of roughs known as the 'Park Avenue Gang'"—"a group ranking for the desperate quality of its membership with the Gopher and the ancient car barn gangs."

If the gang may be regarded as one of the products of the economic, cultural, and moral frontier in a great city, the gang boy, too, may be so regarded. He is often a delinquent, but this delinquency cannot be considered in most cases other than a result of the situation complex in which he finds himself and from which he cannot escape.

[36] Chicago Commission on Race Relations, *The Negro in Chicago*, p. 8.

[37] Chicago Crime Commission, *Bulletin*, No. 14, Oct. 6, 1920, p. 3.

[38] Chicago Commission on Race Relations, *op. cit.*, p. 342. Quoted from the *Annual Report of the Crime Commission*, 1920.

"There are no bad boys" is a slogan that has been adopted by the Boys' Brotherhood Republic; the idea behind it is undoubtedly sound—that "bad" boys as defined by society, are largely created by the disorganizing forces consequent upon the confused conditions where American life is in process of ferment and readjustment.

CHAPTER XVIII

The Gang and Organized Crime

To think of the bulk of Chicago's crime as the result of the activities of hardened criminals or adult gangs would be erroneous. There is no hard and fast dividing line between predatory gangs of boys and criminal groups of younger and older adults. They merge into each other by imperceptible gradations, and the latter have their real explanation, for the most part, in the former. Many delinquent gangs contain both adolescents and adults. The adult criminal gang, which is, as a rule, largely composed of men in their early twenties, carries on traditions thoroughly established in the adolescent group. It represents a development and perpetuation of the younger gang or at least of the habits and attitudes of individuals trained in younger groups. It is clear, therefore, that crime, in so far as it is facilitated by the gang, can only be understood by following it to its roots and beginnings in the boys' gang.

While there has been no great increase in delinquency among children under sixteen years of age and while the number of delinquents under this age is very small in comparison with the total number of children, yet there has probably been a decrease in the average age of criminals above sixteen.

One striking fact about present-day crime is the youthfulness of offenders. Statistics on the ages of delinquents are unsatisfactory because they do not usually represent the first offense or even the first conviction of the boy. Statistics with regard to arrests, convictions, and commitments, however, do show that the majority of delinquencies occur between the ages of twenty-one and twenty-four years. Most of the commitments for larceny, burglary, forgery, fraud, rape, and trespassing are of persons nineteen years old. The majority of commitments for robbery, homicide, disorderly conduct, assault, carrying concealed weapons, fraud, adultery, profanity, gambling, prostitution, fornication, malicious mischief, and violating city ordinances come between the twenty-first and twenty-fourth year. It is evident that in most of these cases the career of delinquency was begun long before commitment to a penal institution.

CRIMINAL CAREERS BEGIN IN ADOLESCENCE

The extent to which criminal careers begin in adolescence is partly indicated by the youth of present-day delinquents and by the number of adolescent gangs engaging in predatory activities. William Healy, one of the most careful students of the individual delinquent, says that "the greatest interest for all students of criminology centers about the fact that most frequently the career of the confirmed criminal begins during adolescence." The chief cause, he continues, lies in the "formative conditions of this epoch." During this period the most important needs are for social adjustment.[1]

In Chicago the gang is probably the most important single factor—in that section of the boy population from which the majority of delinquents come—in determining how these needs for adolescent social adjustment shall be met. That approximately one-tenth of Chicago's

---

[1] *The Individual Delinquent*, p. 713.

350,000 boys between the ages of ten and twenty are subject to the demoralizing influence of gangs suggests the importance of devising a practical program to redirect their energies into more wholesome channels. While current suggestions for the mitigation of crime include everything from high bail bonds to doing away with prohibition, very few of them sense the necessity of dealing with the problem at its source.

Statistics on juvenile delinquency in Chicago indicate how early demoralization begins and show the types of misconduct which are most common among boys under sixteen.

While the gangs of younger boys prefer the less risky types of delinquency, the older adolescents are likely to undertake the more serious crimes. The most important types of felonies committed by these boys are those connected with property, viz., robbery, burglary, larceny, and the receiving of stolen goods. Rape and the operation of confidence games are next in importance. Among the misdemeanors, larceny is by far the most important; the others are crimes with automobiles, assault and battery, assault with deadly weapons, carrying concealed weapons, gambling, prohibition violations, and receiving stolen goods. Most of the quasi-criminal cases fall under the heading of disorderly conduct; the others include keeping disorderly houses, gambling, and violating city and park ordinances.

It has already been pointed out that the majority of the boys who pass through the juvenile and boys' courts are probably members of gangs which influence them toward delinquency. While the statistics presented above show the types of crimes committed by adolescents, the number of crimes that may be committed by an adolescent gang before it is caught, can only be indicated by a study of concrete cases. Five boys between fourteen and sixteen years of age, for example, admitted to the police twenty-five burglaries in two months. A gang of four boys nineteen and twenty years of age had engaged in twenty-four different robberies in one night, using a car taken from their first victim for this purpose. A gang of six boys, seventeen to twenty years of age, lived in a rooming-house and maintained themselves by burglary; when caught they admitted six such crimes in six days.

Before discussing the part played by the older gang in criminal activities, it will be necessary to present a brief outline of the general organization of crime in Chicago, within which the gang functions.

THE ORGANIZATION OF CRIME

The seriousness of modern crime grows largely out of the fact that it has ceased to be sporadic and occasional and has become organized and continuous. The numerous individuals and groups who are interested in the promulgation of illegal activities have become so related to each other as to make the commission of crime safer, more effective, and more profitable. Serious crime in Chicago has been placed, for the most part, on a basis of business efficiency.

There is in Chicago as in other large cities an "underworld," an area of life and activity characterized by the absence of the ordinary conventions and largely given over to predatory activities and the exploitation of the baser human appetites and passions. This is the criminal community. Besides the human riff-raff, the hangers-on, the questionable characters, the semi-criminal classes, it includes an estimated population of 10,000 professional criminals, that is, those "engaged habitually in major crimes only."[2]

---

[2] *Bulletin of the Chicago Crime Commission*, June 1, 1920. See Robert E. Park, *et al.*, *The City*, pp. 41–42, for a discussion of the relation of the process of urban segregation to the development of the professional criminal.

In certain respects the criminal community assumes the characteristics of what has been described as a moral region.

Every neighborhood, under the influences which tend to distribute and segregate city populations, may assume the character of a "moral region." Such, for example, are the vice districts, which are found in most cities. A moral region is not necessarily a place of abode. It may be a mere rendezvous, a place of resort.[3]

Such a moral region is constituted by gangland with all its tentacles and satellites. The hang-outs of the gangs in these areas are street corners, saloons, pool-rooms, cabarets, roadhouses, clubrooms, and so on. Each place of resort is subject to influences from others of a similar type; one example of these interlocking influences is afforded by the "grapevine system," whereby information travels very rapidly through the length and breadth of the underworld.

One of the outstanding characteristics of the criminal community is what might be called its fluidity. While there is considerable definite organization, largely of the feudal type, there is no hard and fast structure of a permanent character. The ease of new alliances and alignments is surprising. Certain persons of certain groups may combine for some criminal exploit or business, but shortly they may be bitter enemies and killing each other. One gang may stick closely together for a long period under favorable conditions; yet if cause for real dissension arises, it may readily split into two or more bitter factions, each of which may eventually become a separate gang. Members may desert to the enemy on occasion. Leaders come and go easily; sometimes with more or less violence, but without much disturbance to the usual activities of the gangs. There is always a new crop coming on—of younger fellows from whom emerge men to fill the

[3] Park, et al., op. cit., p. 43.

shoes of the old barons" when they are slain or "put away." The passing of an O'Bannian simply transfers the crown to a new head or creates an opportunity for a new gang.

Although organized crime must not be visualized as a vast edifice of hard and fast structures, there is a surprising amount of organization of a kind in the criminal community. There is a certain division of labor manifesting itself in specialized persons and specialized groups performing different but related functions. There are, furthermore, alliances and federations of persons and groups, although no relationship can be as fixed and lasting as in the organization of legitimate business.

The specialized individuals in the criminal community are sometimes free lances, sometimes incorporated into a definite group. At the top are the professional criminals, who might be called, to use a business term, criminal enterprisers (or entrepreneurs). They provide the organizing energy and business brains of crime; they are the so-called "silk-hat" gangsters who engineer the larger illegal enterprises.[4] They must keep in close touch with certain specialized persons or groups, who perform certain indispensable functions for them. Fences or syndicates of fences must be employed to dispose of stolen goods or securities; doctors and sometimes even hospitals must be relied upon to furnish medical assistance to criminals without giving information to the police; fixers and political manipulators must be depended upon to use their influence with the law; professional or obligated bondsmen must be found to provide bail; shrewd criminal law-

[4] Sometimes these gangster entrepreneurs have a different genesis from that of the ordinary gang boy. In some cases at least, they seem to be men of questionable character or easy ethics who come from presumably reputable or well-to-do families, but who have been drawn into the activities of organized crime, particularly the illicit liquor business, because of the possibilities of large profits.

yers must be engaged to handle criminal interests in the courts;[5] and corrupt officials and other "inside men" must be sought out to help engineer illegal exploits— all these together constitute, to borrow another commercial phrase, the "functional middlemen" of the underworld.

Besides these more specialized factors, the criminal enterpriser uses many other elements in the criminal community. There are habitual criminals who can be depended upon for definite assistance or parts in special jobs. Then there are numerous bums, toughs, ex-convicts, and floaters who frequent underworld areas and who are willing to make casual alliances for the commission of crime. Besides these there is a semi-criminal class of hangers-on and abettors who are more or less continuously employed at legitimate work, but who engage in questionable practices for side money.

THE FORMATION OF THE CRIMINAL GANG

Some criminal gangs are direct perpetuations of adolescent groups which have drifted into crime. In many cases, however, the seasoned criminal group represents a coalescence of various elements in the criminal community, which has been described above. As gang boys grow up, a selective process takes place: many of them become reincorporated into family and community life, but there remains a certain criminal residue upon whom gang training has, for one reason or another, taken fast hold.

Some of these boys may be mental or temperamental

[5] "I read the statute and I found that in 1919 the criminal lawyers of this city secured in the legislature, when nobody was looking, legislation by which they could admit defendant to bail after conviction. That makes the action of the court ineffective."—Judge Harry Olson, *Bulletin of the Chicago Crime Commission*, December 10, 1924. It was pointed out recently, however, that a large number of professional criminals in New York City had, as a group, engaged an eminent member of the New York bar to act as their permanent counsel.

variants, but many of them are the victims of peculiar combinations of circumstances which make social adjustment difficult. Among the most important of the factors which contribute to make them gravitate toward crime are the possession of court records and the experiences and associations undergone in so-called "reform" and penal institutions.[6] It is not surprising, therefore, that so many of the members of our criminal gangs are ex-reform-school boys and ex-convicts. Once having become habituated to a life of crime they continue to attach themselves to criminal groups as the opportunity may offer. Thus, from one point of view, organized crime, manifesting itself in gangs and in the larger structures within which gangs function, may be regarded as the result of a process of sifting and selection whose final product is a criminal residue.[7]

This residue may be thought of as constituting a large part of the criminal community (the underworld). The gang forms in this social stratum for much the same reasons that it forms among the free-floating boy population of Chicago's junior gangland; it enables its members to achieve a more adequate satisfaction of their wishes than they could have as individuals. It provides fellowship, status, excitement, and security in much the same way that the adolescent gang does for the gang boy. Unlike the juniors, however, the chief motive which usually prompts the member of the criminal gang to enter such a group is economic. He enters its fellowship with a much

[6] After a survey of the history of American penal institutions, H. E. Barnes (in *The Repression of Crime*) concludes that "present penal institutions obviously fail to achieve this result of reforming the criminal. Instead of reforming criminals, they are in reality institutions for the training of more efficient and determined criminals" (p. 375). The present study confirms this opinion.

[7] See the statement by Robert E. Park on the diversity of congenial milieus in the city. Park, *et al.*, *The City*, pp. 41–42.

more definite conception as to what he is to derive from it—namely, profit, and that profit from crime.

There has been a general tendency among criminal gangs to evolve into purely commercialized groups—a trend also related to the efficiency of governmental control. It is possible to classify these groups into three types, which have followed each other in a sort of rough historical sequence. First, there is the frontier type such as that of Jesse James and the notorious Ashley-Mobley gang of the Florida Everglades. This sort of group develops just beyond the control of the law in the interstitial reaches of the frontier or the wilderness. The second type, which is represented by the Rats gang of St. Louis and by many contemporary Chicago groups, is that which depends for its life and protection, to some extent at least, upon political influence or official connivance.

Finally, there is the type of criminal gang which, while it may have official connections, depends primarily upon its business-like organization and the efficiency of its methods of executing criminal activities. Such was the "Cowboy" Tessler gang of New York City which has been termed "the most highly organized and commercialized group of bandits in history." This gang, most of whose members were apprehended in October, 1925, used silencers on its guns, employed a jeweler to remount its stolen gems, maintained two garages where stolen cars could be renumbered and disguised, established a warehouse and a business office where miscellaneous loot was sold, and maintained a sinking-fund to provide bail and legal fees. This type of group is manifestly more or less independent of governmental interference because of the superiority of its methods.

The guerrilla gang of fifteen or twenty years ago, the prototype of the present criminal group in Chicago, presents a decided contrast to the commercialized gang of today. It was usually composed of fighters of the rough and tumble sort, much of whose activity was directed toward maintaining their local prestige and territorial jurisdiction.

228. Along one street on the West Side there are three names that stand out in the history of the earlier gangs: the Healeys, Shaneys, and Canaleys. There were between one hundred and one hundred fifty of them there from eighteen to twenty-eight years old, with headquarters in a certain saloon on a nearby corner. They had a baseball team and ran dances to raise money. They had fights with another notorious gang which had influential political connections. They carried on a war between 1906 and 1910, using sticks, stones, blackjacks, and saps as weapons. If a fellow of one bunch was trimmed by a member of another, he would have his revenge; he would come and get his gang and a street fight would result. When the movies came into the neighborhood, these fellows would use slingshots to shoot the ushers. They were mostly loafers and some were criminals, hanging around the saloons and doing very little work. They had a stand-in with the politicians and four or five of them were always on the public pay-rolls. The use of firearms in their altercations was rare.[8]

While most criminal gangs in Chicago are still dependent upon a large measure of political influence for the continuance of their operations, there has been a considerable substitution of economic motives and business technique for the old adventure interests and swashbuckling methods. *The romantic element which still inheres in the life of the younger gangs and gang-like clubs, described in previous chapters, seems to a large extent to have faded out for the adult groups.* Such gangs as the Hudson Dusters, the Gophers, and the Car Barners of New York City, the old Bottoms gang of St. Louis, and many of the old Irish gangs of Chicago; have succumbed, for the most part, to the Industrial Revolution.[9]

Since the profit motive is probably the dominant note

[8] Interview with a politician who grew up in the district.

[9] See Herbert Asbury, "The Passing of the Gangster," *American Mercury*, March, 1925.

in the life of the new type of gangster, the affiliation of the professional criminal may be changed fairly readily. If his own gang is broken up, he joins another without great difficulty, particularly if he has some trait of character or possesses some type of knowledge which may be useful in gang enterprises. This may also explain why fear is more potent than loyalty in the prevention of squealing in the criminal gang of today.

THE RÔLE OF THE GANG IN ORGANIZED CRIME

The gang, then, while it is not the only element in organized crime, plays an important part in the mobilization of the criminal and the organization of the criminal community. Its influence in training criminals and facilitating crime has been partly described in the preceding chapter. It is probable that most of Chicago's supposed 10,000 professional criminals have received gang training, and it is evident that crime in Chicago roots in the gang as its basic organized unit, no matter how it may have become elaborated into rings and syndicates.

Chief of Police Morgan A. Collins in instructing his men with reference to a crime drive asked them to break up the gangs, remarking that "most major crimes and bomb plots are hatched at such gatherings."[10] It is these more highly developed and closely integrated gangs of older boys and young men, often guided by older men of long experience in organizing criminal enterprises, that give organized crime its vitality.

The successful commission of most crimes, even on a small scale, requires accomplices and co-operation. Both are to be found in the criminal community. A "job" can be "pulled," therefore, without a permanent gang.[11] Yet

[10] *Chicago Herald and Examiner*, June 20, 1924.

[11] A good example of this is afforded in the criminal community established in the town of Madison across the river from St. Louis when an active police commissioner drove out the criminal population.

this is dangerous and the "lone wolf" is not common, for when he gets caught he must fight the law alone or with such meager resources as his relatives can provide. The temporary group, also, lacking the powerful backing which a well-knit gang usually commands, is more likely to be caught and convicted.

The absolute number of criminals in the city may decrease, but improved gang organization enables a smaller number of them to create a far more serious problem than would otherwise exist.

While it appears to be a fact that crime has been increasing in a greater proportion than the population, it appears to be equally true that criminals have not.

The business of crime is being more expertly conducted. Modern crime, like modern business, has been centralized, organized and commercialized. Ours is a business nation. Our criminals apply business methods.[12]

In a city of a million or more inhabitants, one or two master gangs, such as the Rats of St. Louis, the Tessler or Whittemore gangs of New York City, or the Valley gang of Chicago, especially if linked with politics, would be sufficient to give the impression of a crime wave. To the Rats gang, for example, have been attributed more than twenty murders and twenty-three major robberies. The Tessler gang is credited with being able to commit seven holdups within an hour in the Bronx.

THE COST TO THE COMMUNITY

While there is no way of estimating accurately the cost of such gang crimes it is undoubtedly enormous. The ascertained loot of one St. Louis gang in its major burglaries and robberies during a five-year period was approximately $4,700,000.[13] That dozens of other master

[12] H. B. Chamberlin, *Bulletin of the Chicago Crime Commission*, November 20, 1919, p. 4.

[13] See document 96.

P. & A. Photo

A CRIMINAL GANG

This is a portion of the "Candy Kid" Whittemore gang, which operated on an interstate basis. This group has been held responsible for many murders and for robberies involving more than $1,000,000. Its leader, Richard Reese Whittemore (fifth man from the left), was hanged August 13, 1926, for the murder of a prison guard. Gangs of this type are at work in most large American cities. (See chap. xviii.)

gangs throughout the country take a similar toll, is evidenced by the frequent reports of large hauls secured in highly organized robberies.

Repeated bank raids bringing bandit gangs millions of dollars, the failure of ordinary police protection, and the consequent high insurance rates have led to the adoption of special methods of safeguarding moneys in banks and in transit. At the suggestion of their state associations, banks of many states have armed their employees and trained them in marksmanship; vigilantes have been organized; and military mobilization has been provided for in emergencies.

Illinois experienced 73 raids in 1924 with losses of $327,000.[14] The Illinois Bankers' Association, which has spent large sums for experimental and protective work, has reported a decrease both in bank robberies and burglaries since 1924. The Chicago Cook County Bankers' Association has developed a system of patrolling each of its twelve districts by means of two men riding a motor cycle and a side car, each armed with a revolver, a sawed-off shotgun, and a rifle. The 1924 average of a bank raid in Chicago every seven weeks, together with the frequency of murders which were incidental to such raids, led to a standing offer by the state bankers' association of a reward of "$2,500 to any person who lawfully kills a bank bandit in the act of robbing or attempting to rob any member bank."

Similar raids on the United States mails have brought millions of dollars to criminal gangs. For many years it was customary to deliver valuable mails from open wagons of the type used for distributing groceries. These were eventually replaced by locked vans driven by armed chauffeurs. The marines were then pressed into service

[14] Data on bank raids in Chicago and Illinois were furnished through the courtesy of the bankers' associations of Cook County and of the state.

for a time to guard mails in transit.[15] Finally, in 1924, the government had built 3,000 bullet-proof railroad cars constructed of battleship steel and equipped with riot-guns, firing shields, calcium flares, and bullet-proof windows. Armored mail trucks were adopted for city service.

Along with this development in the technique of protecting the mails, have come highly specialized methods for the protection of pay-rolls. "All important holdups today are pulled by organized gangs," declares the head of a large company organized for guarding pay-rolls.[16] These companies now transport millions of dollars each day in trucks specially constructed to resist the attacks of bandit gangs. All these methods of protecting banks, mails, and pay-rolls are expensive and their cost must also be added to the more direct losses from robberies suffered by the community.

Besides the money cost of gang crime, the gang takes a heavy toll in human life. Black Hand gangs play a large part in extortion and murder, especially in the Italian-American community. The number of murders resulting from gang activities in Chicago is large: many innocent persons are killed incidental to robberies; in 1920 more than 36 per cent of persons murdered in Chicago lost their lives in resisting holdups and burglaries.[17] A number of policemen die each year in fighting gangsters; while the gangsters kill each other at the rate of about one a week in their internecine strife. It has been estimated that, between November, 1924, when Dion O'Bannion was murdered in his florist's shop, and October 11, 1926, when Earl ("Hymie") Weiss was assassinated, more than one hundred and fifteen men had fallen in

[15] They were employed again in October, 1926.

[16] Forest Crissey, "Beating the Bandits," *Saturday Evening Post*, February 20, 1926.

[17] Sutherland, *op. cit.*, p. 65.

Chicago gang wars. According to a newspaper estimate Weiss was the fifty-seventh gangster to be killed between January 1, 1926, and October 11 of the same year.[18]

A famous American surgeon, addressing a London audience, once made the remark that gang wars in America were not to be taken seriously because the gangsters were only killing each other off. That this is not always the case was indicated by the murder of William H. McSwiggin, known as the "hanging prosecutor" and one of the "aces" of the state's attorney's office. Two companions of McSwiggin's, alleged to be underworld characters—one a gangster, the other a politician—were assassinated upon the same occasion. Innocent by-standers are often hit by gang bullets and gangsters sometimes mistake identity and kill the wrong man.

At times Chicago has seemed helpless before the depredations of her criminal gangs.

The community finds itself thrown back upon medieval conditions where the robber chieftains and their respective bands of armed retainers work their wills and cow the timorous populace. The law is impotent and is disregarded. The one influence effectively curbing the activities of each robber chief is the imperious automatic or the categorical demand of the sawed-off shotgun in the hands of opposition law-breakers. These unpleasant realities inspire some degree of caution as the man above the law proceeds on his triumphant way.[19]

Yet other communities have not been free from the problem. In St. Louis the names of the Rats, the Jelly-Rolls, and the Cuckoos are well known; and in the same city the White House gang, the McCandles, the Pirate Crew of Duncan Island, and the Bottoms gang gave trouble during the war. San Francisco has had its Black Stocking, Howard Street, and Thirty-strong gangs. The

[18] *Chicago Daily News*, October 12, 1926.

[19] Editorial, "Crime Triumphant," *Chicago Daily News*, November 15, 1924.

history of the gangs of New York City is probably the longest and most picturesque.[20] Then, there were the Hole-in-the-Wall gang of Salt Lake City, the Robbers' Roost gang of Portland, and so on; almost every American city has harbored groups which have become notorious for their criminal activities.

THREE TYPES OF CRIMINAL GANGS

Three types of criminal gangs may be distinguished with reference to their resources, power, and potential damage to the community. The first of these is illustrated in those temporary groups which are constantly forming and re-forming in the criminal community. The second is the ordinary garden variety of criminal gang, such as the Cardinellis, which does not have great resources but which hangs together and commits many crimes. The third type, such as the Valley gang, is the more permanent and powerful group which has great resources in money, political influence, and intelligence.

The number of the less powerful type is large. Their usual "racket" is "stickups" and the ordinary types of robberies and burglaries. Yet their depredations have been so bold and so numerous in recent years that even bootleggers and the gamblers are afraid of them. The Sam Cardinelli gang, which was successful for a considerable time, appears to have been of this type. Although the leader and two of its members were hanged and a fourth was sent to prison for life, the surviving members of the group are still said to be working together as a Black Hand gang.

230. The Sam Cardinelli gang was known as one of the most vicious groups of criminals in Chicago. It was held responsible for many murders and from fifty to one hundred robberies about which evidence was obtained. The nature of its activities may be indicated by a brief summary of some of its more important crimes.

[20] See Asbury, *op. cit.*

Five members of the gang, including Nicholas Viana, the "choir-boy," entered a saloon and in the course of a holdup killed the proprietor and one customer. The gang escaped in an automobile driven by Santo Orlando and found later at his home. Ten days later Orlando was found in the drainage canal with several bullets in his body. The police believe that the gang, fearing the arrest of Orlando and that he might confess, murdered him in cold blood.

Several months later four members of the gang were accosted by two police officers at Twenty-first and Indiana Avenue. While being searched Viana shot one of the policemen in the groin and the other was also wounded. The gang escaped.

On one occasion, Errico, one of the members, planned the holdup of a South Side poolroom. He entered the place and at his signal Nicholas Viana, Frank Campione, and Tony Sansone entered with revolvers and robbed fifteen customers, Errico among the rest. During the holdup one of the customers put his hand in his pocket and was immediately shot through the heart by Campione. He died instantaneously. After the trio had fled, Errico remained only long enough to avert suspicion.

Individual shares of the loot in some of these cases were ridiculously small considering the chances taken. The reputed mastermind of the gang was Sam Cardinelli, aged thirty-nine. He did not take an active part in the more important crimes, but is said to have planned them. Most of the other members were young, Viana being eighteen, while several of the others were only nineteen.

Cardinelli, Viana, and Campione were hanged while Errico's sentence was commuted to life-imprisonment because he turned state's evidence.[21]

Even this type of gang is not without legal resources and power, as is indicated by the fact that at the time the above account begins Cardinelli was already out on bail and had a criminal case on appeal to the supreme court.

MASTER GANGS

The more successful and permanent type of adult group, also largely made up of young men, may be called the master gang. There are operating in Chicago ten to twenty of these groups whose names alone are sufficient

[21] Records of the Chicago Crime Commission.

to strike terror into the hearts of the peaceful residents of the districts where they hold sway. Most of them grew out of small beginnings in one of the three chief divisions of gangland. The Valley gang may be cited as typical of this class.

231. The Valley gang on Fifteenth Street, Chicago, has had an active life of over thirty years. In the earlier period the district was controlled politically and socially by this gang. But the population of the district began to change, the members of the gang no longer had parents on the police force, and they came into conflict with the police, as the result of which two policemen were killed. The leader, "Red" Bolton, is now serving a life sentence in the state prison. The result is that the gang has weakened and almost disintegrated.[22]

The Valley gang, however, did not disintegrate, but prospered under the leadership of "Paddy the Bear," who was the feared and fearless dictator of the district. In June, 1920, he was assassinated supposedly by another member of the gang, one of the younger hangers-on, who bore him a grudge. At his death the control of the gang passed to its present leaders, whose names have frequently adorned the front pages of Chicago papers in recent years.

Members of the gang have boasted that they have worn silk shirts and have ridden in Rolls-Royce automobiles since the war. Their great opportunity for wealth came with prohibition and their entrance into the rum-running business. Eventually they controlled a string of breweries both in and out of Chicago, and their leaders are said to have made millions in these enterprises. One of them occupies an exclusive North Shore estate purchased for $150,000. Their money has stood them in good stead, for they have been able to employ the most expensive lawyers to defend them and when serving sentences in certain penal institutions they have been permitted to come and go almost as freely as though they were living at a hotel. At present they dress in the height of fashion, ride in large automobiles with sleek chauffeurs, and live on the fat of the land.[23]

The major interest of the master gangs is probably the illegal manufacture and sale of spirituous liquors, but

[22] Sutherland, *op. cit.*, p. 154.

[23] Interviews and news accounts.

many of them are not averse to other types of crime such as the various types of robbery: bank, pay-roll, bank-messenger, jewel, fur, and mail. Many of them are also identified with the promotion of other illicit activities such as vice and gambling.

SPECIALIZED TYPES OF CRIMINAL GANGS

In so far as the criminal gang requires special organization for the achievement of its ends it may be regarded as a structural, as well as a functional, type. This is illustrated in the specialized gangs, which devote a major portion of their efforts to some one line of criminal activity (a "racket") for which they have developed a special technique, due to some special knowledge or experience previously acquired. Some of them successfully undertake or control a number of different lines at once; while others go from one type of crime to another, working out one field and then turning to something less hazardous or more profitable.

So far has this division of labor been carried that a specialized gang of beer-runners does not even have to do its own bombing or killing, but may employ a still more specialized group for that purpose.[24]

Successful gangs of burglars, such as the so-called "Electric Light Ring," usually operate in groups. Some thieving gangs specialize on certain kinds of stores or individuals, such as chain stores and chauffeurs. Gangs of expert freight-car thieves have necessitated the employment by the railroads of large forces of private police to protect their property. Jewel and fur stealing have proved lucrative to some groups. The so-called "high

[24] See editorial, *Chicago Tribune*, November 28, 1925.
There were approximately 119 bombings reported in Chicago in 1925. Most of these seem to have been instigated in an effort to intimidate, although some were undoubtedly for revenge or to get rid of troublesome persons.

society" gang is not entirely a creation of the movies, but actually preys upon the wealthy.

The following case of a pickpocket group may be presented as an example of the organized activity of a specialized gang.

232. There is a gang of about fifteen pickpockets ranging in age from nineteen to thirty which hangs out near the park. During the non-rush hours they pitch horseshoes and play a little unorganized playground ball. They are real crooks and not interested in athletics, although they do spend some time in the park.

"I don't see how in hell a fellow can get his mind on this game," one of them was heard to remark when playing "indoor."

They "work" when others are coming home from business. In addition to working up and down State Street when the factory employees are going to and from work, they prowl around at night.

This gang works in groups of three or four. They station themselves along the street at one- or two-block intervals. Several will first board a car and produce a blockade. Others get on and shove. Another gets on later and does the actual work. Their method is to attract attention by pressure on one part of the body, while they manage to get at a pocket with the least contact sensation possible. They divide their spoils in the park. They do not have a political drag. All of them drink; some are dope addicts; and some of them bite their fingernails to the quick.

If the vagrancy laws were enforced they would be picked up. They have been in and out of jail, but jail has not reformed them.[25]

The value of a good automobile, its usefulness to the criminal, and the ease with which it may usually be stolen by an expert have combined to make this sort of theft attractive to the gang. The stealing of automobiles has come to be quite an extensive industry with many branches and ramifications. A boy who was formerly a member of a San Antonio gang was offered three jobs when he came to Chicago, and one of these was filing numbers from stolen automobiles for a concern which specialized in that sort of business. There are many gangs whose chief interest is this sort of crime.[26]

[25] Interview with a park director.   [26] See document 64.

Other types of specialized gangs deal in blackmailing (e.g., the Red Peppers), kidnapping, confidence games (e.g., the Woodard and the Yellow Kid gangs and the Norfleet defrauders), check and security forging, counterfeiting, dope-peddling, pandering, smuggling, arson, hijacking, and jackrolling. Each of these tends to develop its own type of personnel and its own particular technique.

THE RING AND THE SYNDICATE

Limitations of space do not permit a complete discussion of the ring and the criminal syndicate; it must suffice for this study to point out their pertinent relations to the gang.

A ring[27] may be regarded as a permanent conspiracy usually made up of "inside men" associated secretly for some illegitimate purpose profitable to themselves. They are called "inside" men because they are persons ostensibly engaged in innocent vocations but usually obtaining inside information to be used in the commission of crime or in some other way employing their positions for the furtherance of illegal activities. An example of the ring without ordinary gang connections was that uncovered in the government printing office. This exposure led to the dismissal of 268 employees who had been bound together under oath. Members of the ring had engaged in bootlegging and race-track gambling, using government wires for the transmission of tips; one of the foremen even operated a still in his private office. There are also rings of other types involving inside men in distinct vocations. One of the most elaborate of these was the notorious Tweed ring of New York City, which included both a state and a city political machine and which succeeded before its downfall in stealing some $30,000,000 outright

[27] A ring is sometimes erroneously referred to as a gang. An example is the Ohio gang, a graft ring engaged in oil frauds during the Harding administration.

of the city's money and increasing the municipal debt to $50,000,000.[28]

A gang often performs a very important function in the ring, of which it is many times an integral part. If action is required, a gang is usually depended upon to accomplish it; the gang, therefore, may be regarded as the motor part—the muscle, so to speak—of the ring when such a combination exists. This is clearly indicated in the case of the elaborately organized rum ring which "milked" the Jack Daniel distillery warehouse of 831 barrels containing 30,000 gallons of whiskey; the job was actually "pulled"—the whiskey was actually removed by members of the Rats gang of St. Louis. In this case the gang was not a permanent part of the ring but was simply associated with it for a special purpose. In other cases a ring may employ gangsters, as individuals or as a group, either as gunmen or for strong-arm work.

It often happens that a gang forms its own ring by the addition of inside men to get information on particular jobs. A post-office inspector and a politician may be needed for a mail robbery, as in the Rondout case. Minor employees or government agents may be added as needed; or associates of the gang may be worked into positions of trust with a view to later usefulness in criminal enterprises. Inside men, such as fences, may be enlisted to help dispose of the loot, and criminal lawyers and politicians may have a place in order to provide protection from prosecution. Successful gangs and gang leaders have been instrumental in organizing some of the most prosperous and extensive rings.

[28] Rings may be classified on the basis of the particular illicit purpose which they serve. Some of the types exposed in recent years are those organized for looting public institutions such as prisons; making graft from public improvements such as paving; issuing fake passports; collecting exorbitant fees in bankruptcy cases; illegal manufacture, withdrawal, distribution, and sale of intoxicants; promoting illegal commerce in habit-forming drugs; and the smuggling both of goods and of immigrants.

The criminal syndicate differs from both the ring and the gang. While the ring is a single group of individuals associated together in business or governmental institutions, a syndicate represents a multiplication of units under a more or less centralized control either inside or outside legitimate institutions. These units may be vice resorts, gambling houses, breweries, and so on, or a variety of types of gangs or rings; diverse units may be syndicated in various combinations or those carrying the same type of illegal activity may form a single organization such as a vice or gambling syndicate. This multiplication of units is brought about by the necessity of covering a larger territory or carrying on an increased amount of business, which may be local, regional, or national in scope. The syndicate must be run on business principles to be successful. It usually has political linkages which afford protection.

Illicit liquor, gambling, and vice have provided the greatest opportunities for the syndicate type of criminal organization in Chicago. This is relatively more profitable and less dangerous than robbery. Judge Daniel P. Trude of the Morals Court of Chicago presents a document prepared by one on the inside of the "system of organized, protected gambling, beer-running, con game, picking pockets, and vice which had grown up in Chicago in 1922–23." This document describes a protected vice syndicate and shows how it was able to perfect a powerful organization.[29]

The existence of liquor syndicates has made it difficult at times for the city of Chicago to enforce the prohibition laws.

233. There existed . . . . great syndicated associations that had taken on the proportion of complete business organizations

[29] *Sixteenth, Seventeenth, and Eighteenth Annual Reports of the Municipal Court of Chicago*, pp. 88–89.

and which through their influence and power had acquired a definite control over our law enforcement agencies. These organizations had bought up several of the old breweries whose former proprietors had ceased business upon the adoption of the eighteenth amendment.

Beer manufactured for $4.00 or $5.00 a barrel was sold to retailers at $55 to $65 a barrel and part of this wide margin between the cost of production and the retail price was distributed to persons, many of them in public office and directly charged with the enforcement of the law. The inevitable effect was to paralyze law enforcement in Chicago, so far, at least, as this traffic was concerned.[30]

The office equipment and records of a huge vice and liquor syndicate, which were seized in a raid on its South Michigan Avenue headquarters, revealed its control over a string of vice resorts and its extensive wholesale and retail dealings in illicit liquor, as well as its probable connection with interstate freight thefts. This type of syndicate, as well as those controlling gambling, has operated extensively in the suburbs and among the roadhouses which fringe Chicago. Several of the master gangs of the city have been instrumental in organizing and later maintaining these large syndicates.

The superiority of the syndicate in the promotion of crime lies in its ability to furnish bonds quickly and in cash if necessary; to hire the best lawyers who are adept at securing continuances and ferreting out technical complications to defeat the law; to buy political and often official protection; and to employ powerful gangs for purposes of intimidation and strong-arm work.

GANG CRIME AND THE PROBLEMS OF CAPITAL AND LABOR

One interesting ramification of gang crime, which

[30] From an address by Mayor Dever to the Citizen's Committee of One Thousand for Law Enforcement quoted in the *Chicago Tribune*, January 7, 1925.

cannot be neglected in any complete survey of the subject, is its relation to the problems of capital and labor. Wherever and whenever strong-arm work or "rough stuff" is required either by the employer or the employee or by their respective organizations, the gang, particularly of the criminal type, is a ready instrument. Strike-breaking, intimidation, blackmail, acid or rock throwing, bombing, dynamiting, slugging, and similar methods, gang-executed, have been used not only between capital and labor, but also between rival unions and between rival organizations of business enterprisers. That criminal, political, and labor activities may all enter into the program of a single gang is indicated in the following document.

234. The L—— Street gang, numbering between fifty and sixty Irish and German Americans, flourished chiefly in the decade between 1900 and 1910. The district in which they lived was a hotbed of gang fights even prior to 1900. Friction within the gang led to the murder of one of its members by another, who was sent to Joliet for fourteen years. After serving eight and one-half years, he was let out and put on the pay-roll of the sanitary district. Later he married and settled down.

The gang was composed for the most part of hoodlums, fighters, and thieves, few of whom did any work. Some of them were sand-baggers, while others were interested in gambling; there was no interest in athletics. After 1910 the group tended to disintegrate, moving out of the district before an influx of Lithuanians and Poles.

The connection of this gang with politics was direct. It was this and a few other groups like it which gave a start to one of Chicago's leading politicians, a man who was at one time connected with the state's attorney's office, later on the Board of Review, and who once unsuccessfully aspired to become a candidate for mayor.

This gang also constituted the right hand of a building-trades grafting boss, who extorted money from contractors through his ability to control labor conditions. Through the use of this gang he could not only stop work on a building and prevent other workers from taking it up, but he could also bring about violence to work already erected. He used the gang to intimidate contractors and in this way to extort money from them.[31]

There has been a tendency among labor unions of a certain type to enter into alliance with gangsters and criminal gangs. Labor and business organizations which have resorted to violence have usually relied upon gangs for bombing and similar activities designed to bring outsiders or competitors into line.[32] Groups of this type usually have a regular scale of prices for various kinds of work. As revealed in a strike in 1918, this schedule was as follows: $100 for a complete job of bombing, $75 for a fair effort, $25 for throwing a stench bomb successfully, and $10 for breaking a plate-glass window.

The control of a few labor unions by gangsters and gunmen and the employment of these ruffians for strong-arm work by some unions have played a part in prejudicing public opinion against unions in general. Two brothers, leaders of the notorious WWW'S, have been heads respectively of the Master ——s' Association and the Master ——s' Association, two distinct and unrelated organizations. They were employed obviously on account of their ability to marshal a hundred or more gangsters for strong-arm work. This phase of the relation between the gang and labor was pointed out by Justice Kickham Scanlan of the Chicago Criminal Court in his famous charge to the grand jury called to investigate "miscarriages of justice" in labor trials in March, 1922.

SCOPE OF GANG ACTIVITIES

Gang activities in Chicago are carried on throughout the areas of gangland and the criminal community. Vice and crime, as promoted by the gang or other agencies, tend to hide behind the curtain of anonymity that is to

[31] Interview with a politician and former member of a gang club.
[32] See document 20.

a large extent drawn over the slums and the deteriorating neighborhoods in the semicircular poverty belt about the Loop. When crimes are committed in other parts of the city, the gang flees from constituted authority to its hang-outs in these regions.

There are certain advantages, however, in having a sanctuary outside the city limits where the authority of the law is less able to cope with well-organized crime. For this reason, there has always been a tendency for vice and crime areas to hover close to the city limits, but just outside the reach of the city police department. Most of the old vice districts got their original locations in this way.

There are also certain satellite towns and villages which are an integral part of the city geographically, but whose politically independent governing bodies are in some cases none too responsible with reference to the enforcement of the law. In certain of these villages, some with a population of 50,000 or more, it is possible for the gangs to wield great political influence to terrorize elections, to organize gambling and vice, and to maintain hang-outs in saloons and elsewhere as places of criminal rendezvous.[33]

[33] On September 20, 1926, a machine-gun attack was made upon a hotel owned by an alleged gang leader in one of these suburbs adjoining Chicago on the west where gangs are alleged to have thrived after being driven out of Chicago proper. The building and several other places of business were riddled with bullets; the assailants escaped with an escort of a number of automobiles. This was the third time that machine guns had been used by gangsters in this area. One attack had been made the previous spring upon a beauty shop while an alleged gangster was inside; and Assistant State's Attorney McSwiggin and two companions were killed by machine-gun fire in front of a saloon in the same region. Gangs have often terrorized local elections in this suburb.

On October 1, 1926, seventy-nine residents of the same suburb were indicted by a federal grand jury for conspiracy to violate the Volstead Act. The list of those indicted included the town mayor, his secretary and town assessment commissioner, the town chief-of-police, several alleged

The roadhouse fringe that borders the edge of the city has been described above as representing a portion of the cultural frontier between the urban and the rural districts. This area too constitutes an important branch of the underworld; escaping the official controls of the city proper, it provides a favorite haunt for vicious gangs and a place where illicit enterprises may be carried on or planned with comparative impunity. Many of these roadhouses, more inaccessible to official scrutiny than city hang-outs, are owned and most of them are patronized by gangsters. These satellites of vice and crime encircle the city like a ring, yet the gangs are not welcomed by the law-abiding residents of the areas in which they have established themselves.

Cabarets, no matter where they may be located, and dance halls of a disreputable type, are always likely to be hang-outs of vicious groups. A number of notorious cabarets in the Loop district have long been known as places of rendezvous for master gangs. Many of these so-called "crime-nests" act as feeders for the underworld. In them the prosperous gangster takes his pleasure, meets his friends, and often plans his crimes. Some of them are entirely controlled by gangs, but in many other cases the management is in collusion with such groups.

The location of its rendezvous, however, makes little difference to the criminal gang of today so long as it can escape supervision. This is easy under modern conditions. Hard roads and high-powered automobiles have resulted in an amazing mobilization of the criminal. It has been estimated that 90 per cent of Chicago's robberies are preceded by the theft of motor cars, most of which are

---

notorious gang leaders and their henchmen, saloon-keepers, still-operators, minor politicians and fixers, and others. One of the saloon-keepers indicted was the same man in front of whose place of business McSwiggin met his death.

abandoned after they have been used in the commission of crime.[34] Lonely farmers, country banks, peaceful motorists, and even moving trains are no longer safe from criminal attack. For this reason the gang ceases to be merely a local problem in cities whose disorganized life breeds such groups.

No longer are the depredations of the gang confined to its immediate neighborhood, but they are state-wide and interstate in their scope.

235. Beginning about 1895 as a group of fifteen Irish, German, and Polish fellows stealing hogs from the railroad cars, the Brighton gang later developed into a band of copper thieves operating all the way from the mines in Michigan to the U.S. mint in Washington. They enjoyed a certain immunity and success in their work, and this led to an increase in numbers and a division into two sections. As time went on they ceased to specialize entirely in copper-stealing, and went in for general merchandise as well. They have been known to take about $100,000 worth of metal in a year, and an equal amount of other commodities. In one haul they got 25,000 twenty-five-cent cigars—very high-grade tobacco.

At considerable expense these fellows and the receivers of the stolen property were indicted. The cases were continued time after time, until the defendants knew that the witnesses for the prosecution were no longer available; then they secured the dismissal of all the charges. A case was next taken up against them in Indiana. When the case came to trial the judge "non-suited" the complainants (declared that they had no case). This was supposed to have been the result of a legal technicality—an error in the indictment, but it is alleged that pull and bribery played a part.

Two members of this gang were killed by railroad watchmen when caught in the act of robbery. Several of them are in Leavenworth, having been convicted when the railroads were under federal control. A few are now in Joliet and still others are awaiting trial. Their hang-out is in a saloon operated by one of their own mem-

[34] See the *Bulletin of the Chicago Crime Commission,* "Motor Cars and Crime," April 2, 1923. Commissioner of Police Richard E. Enright of New York City points out the close relationship between taxicabs and crime in that city. See William McAdoo and Richard E. Enright, "Taxi Evils," *New York Times,* February 22, 1925.

bers. Several of them, most of whom have prison records, have set up as saloon-keepers—a comment on our system of licensing.[35]

This document shows how a gang becomes more mobile and acquires a greater spread as it grows older and more experienced.

SPECTACULAR CRIMES AND "CRIME WAVES"

Gang raids which involve large losses, and murders perpetrated in the execution of gang wars possess a spectacular quality which have given the impression that the United States in general and Chicago in particular are being deluged in a great crime wave. The truth, however, is that the so-called "crime wave" is a state of mind. Crime is an ever-present reality. It is the attention and the interest of the public which moves in waves. While certain spectacular crimes, such as gang murders, have become more frequent due to internecine warfare among beer gangs, there has been no general increase and there is no reason to believe that Chicago is the "crime center of the United States" or the "murder capital of the world." These impressions are created very largely by the spread of news about spectacular crimes through improved means of communication and modern journalistic technique.

Popular misimpressions about crime waves and the extent of crime, however, do not lessen the gravity or the widespread disorder and injuries consequent upon the crime which does exist. At its best the problem is serious enough and demands the attention and the best efforts of any scientific procedure which can be called into service to aid in solving it.

The most important point, perhaps, to be noted here is the general lack of an adequate program to deal with crime. One reason for this is that many who are attempt-

[35] Interviews with railroad detectives.

ing to alleviate the situation are either groping blindly for a solution or are giving their attention to methods of treating the criminal and protecting the community against him, rather than attacking the underlying maladjustments which contribute to the creation of the criminal.

We know very little in a comprehensive, systematic way about the underlying causes and conditions of crime and effective methods of controlling them. In spite of this lack, however, crime commissions and similar bodies have been so interested in the detection, trial, and punishment of the criminal that they have given little more than passing notice to the possibilities of prevention by attacking the problem at its roots. This study, it is hoped, will throw some light upon the genesis of crime in a great city and the necessity of dealing with the problem at its sources.

No more cogent evidence for the need of further scientific study of the causes of crime and the effects of punishment need be cited than the great body of highly contradictory opinions, statistics, and cures advanced by individuals and agencies purporting to deal with the problem. The mere summarization and utilization of tested knowledge already available for practical application would constitute an important contribution to the solution of the problem.

CHAPTER XIX

The Gang in Politics

The political boss finds gangs, whether composed of boys or of men above voting age, very useful in promoting the interests of his machine. He usually begins with the neighborhood boys' gang with whom he ingratiates himself by means of money for camping, uniforms, rental or furnishings for clubrooms, and other gratuities.

236. A former mayor of Chicago is alleged to have presented at Christmas time a pair of skates to each member of a gang of a dozen dirty little ragamuffins from twelve to fourteen years of age. He asked each of the boys to write him a personal letter, thanking him for the skates, and they used a typewriter in a nearby settlement for this purpose.[1]

Whether the politician uses school children's picnics at a popular amusement park or some other type of patronage, the effect is to "get him in good" with potential voters, to gain the support of the boys' parents and friends, and to attract the favorable comment of the neighborhood.

The political boss knows exactly how to appeal to the gang because he himself has usually received valuable training for politics in a street gang from which he has ultimately been graduated and with which he may still

[1] Interviews.

retain connections in an advisory capacity.[2] The gangs
and clubs of younger boys are considered feeders for the
older groups, and as a matter of fact, the juniors and the
midgets often fall heir to the charters, the equipment,
and, most important of all, the tradition of the seniors,
whom they imitate.

Under such conditions it is inevitable that boys in
gangland regions shall have an intimate knowledge of
political chicanery and corruption, not possessed by boys
in other districts. They often acquire attitudes of disrespect for law and tend to come to regard the whole
governmental structure as largely providing opportunities for the personal emolument of successful politicians.
Typical attitudes are indicated in the following documents.

238. Eddie is fourteen years old and in the eighth grade at
school. It is his ambition to be a lawyer and to specialize in crime
cases, because "those are the kind where you get the most money."
When asked what he would do if he were chosen to defend a man
whom he knew was guilty of murder, he said,
"First, I'd go to see who the judge is; to be a lawyer, you have
to have a whole lot of political pull. To be a lawyer, you have to be
a little bit of a liar, too."
Legal training is the smallest part of the preparation for entering the legal profession, in his opinion. Rather—and he got his
knowledge from direct contact with the criminals and crooks who
infest this part of gangland—one must know what strings to pull
and must have allies on the legal force of the public attorney's staff.
"To be a lawyer, you have to have plenty of political pull
behind you," he continued. "I'd work day and night, t'ink it over,
go to my friends and tell 'em. They might go to the judge's house
and tell 'im about it and continue the trial and give me a chance to
t'ink it out." Then, he pointed out the importance of getting an
attorney who had the right political connections. For this reason,
he would have to go into politics.

[2] It has been said that a "blue book" of city administrators would
show that at least two-thirds of them have come from these training
grounds of self-assertion.

When asked whether he would practice law for the betterment of humanity or in order to become rich, he replied emphatically, "For money!" Then he added apologetically, "At least, I wanna make my livin'."

Eddie finally decided to brave any protest which I might make and give me his real attitude on dirty politics. He is after the cash, let ethics go! He said that dirty politics requires lots of brains and that he does not believe in it, but will go in for it anyway. He knows several people who practice dirty politics, one of whom is a bailiff in a neighborhood court. He also knows "Jewelry Jim," a police character and a local political boss who runs a restaurant. According to the boy, he goes to the judge and the police to help his friends.[3] "Jim" would not make a good alderman "because he's too crooked and he can't speak good English, and if he became alderman, he would help only his friends."[4]

239. When a noted criminal is caught, the fact is the principal topic of conversation among my boys. They and others lay wagers as to how long it will be before the criminal is free again, how long it will be before his "pull" gets him away from the law. The youngsters soon learn who are the politicians who can be depended upon to get offenders out of trouble, who are the dive-keepers who are protected. The increasing contempt for law is due to the corrupt alliance between crime and politics, protected vice, pull in the administration of justice, unemployment, and a general "soreness" against the world produced by these conditions.[5]

THE POLITICIAN AND THE GANG CLUB

The political boss probably achieves most ready control of the gang by encouraging it to become a club, often

[3] This politician, who has also been implicated in election frauds, is said by a former police official to have great influence in local courts. "No matter what a fellow may be charged with, if he comes in, the magistrate will listen to reason. He is hated by the better element in this Italian community." A school official is authority for the statement that he "has made his million" furnishing bond for the members of these young gangs, some of whom he has provided with clubrooms. He is also said to be associated with the Black Hand, so that if the boys do not make good their promises, their mothers and sisters are in danger. He has given banquets attended by prominent politicians and office-holders.

[4] Interview with a gang boy by Ted Iserman.

[5] Statement by a leading worker with gang boys.

giving it his own name for advertising purposes, such as "McFlaherty's Boosters," "O'Mulligan's Colts," etc. If he can get his name attached to a successful athletic club, he is able to attract considerable support from the "whole athletic fraternity." It is surprising how many men have been "made" politically as patrons of the sports. So potent are the possibilities for political control in this type of organization, that it is said that an alliance of South Side clubs, formed to control the politics of Chicago, was blocked by a powerful city official. A park attaché was at one time employed by politicians to organize street gangs into clubs. Charters for such groups could be obtained free of charge through the ward boss.

The tendency of the gangs to become athletic clubs has been greatly stimulated by the politicians of the city. It has become a tradition among gangs throughout Chicago that the first source of possible financial aid is the local alderman or other politician. There can be little doubt that most of the 302 so-called athletic clubs listed in this study have first developed as gangs, many of them still retaining their gang characteristics. The ward "heeler" often corrals a gang like a beeman does his swarm in the hive he has prepared for it. The boss pays the rent and is generous in his donations for all gang enterprises. He is the "patron saint" of the gang and often leads the grand march or makes a speech at gang dances and picnics. In return his protégés work for him in innumerable ways and every gang boy in the hive is expected to gather honey on election day. It is doubtful if this sort of athletic club could long survive if it had to depend solely upon the financial backing of its own members.

A citizen of one of the West Side communities where athletic clubs are numerous divides them all into two classes.

240. There are two types of athletic clubs—the political type which is subsidized and to which you belong because you get something out of it that you do not pay for directly, and the self-supporting type. The latter usually fails because its members cannot make a go of it financially. There were twenty such clubs in this neighborhood during the past three years, and practically all of them went under. They spring up, flourish for a time, and then die out. Most of these clubs, both the self-supporting and the political type, are first gangs which hang together in the poolrooms or on the street.[6]

Many instances of political connections between unsupervised boys' and athletic clubs have been observed in typical areas in gangland.

241. The club at ——— Street with a membership of eighty is evidently simply a political instrument of ———, a local politician, whose restaurant is upstairs. The president of the club states that it is active only in campaign seasons and that the rent of the clubrooms is donated by the politician.

The ——— Arrows, with over forty members, pay a small rent for their rooms. A member indicated that this was made possible by a subsidy from a politician, whose name was not disclosed.

The ———'s occupy a whole building at nominal rent. Members say that a local politician and his political lieutenant regularly hold meetings there.

There is little doubt that many of these independent so-called athletic clubs are utilized politically and that small clubs of younger boys (like ———'s next door to the larger club) are considered as feeders for the more adult groups. In this connection may be indicated the need for careful scrutiny of all clubs as to their actual and potential political relations.[7]

The way in which the politician uses the gang club as a tool in building up his own personal or local political machine is indicated in the following document. It is significant that the process is self-perpetuating, for out of every such group come men trained in the methods of

[6] Interview with the president of an athletic club.
[7] Report of a private investigation made by a social agency.

the boss and themselves headed for political offices and similar "boss-ship." Out of this group, for example, came a successful politician who now acts as patron for a baseball team from another gang, which has a following of about 150 men.

242. One of the most politically powerful athletic clubs in Chicago originated as the "kid followers" of an older club with a long political history. These boys were taken over by a politician just beginning his career and given his name. He had been associated formerly with the older club and with a Democratic political society. He became their president and his first step was to rent them a clubroom and buy them uniforms and equipment (this was about 1908). This was the beginning of a well-built organization, out of which were to come athletes, aldermen, police captains, county treasurers, sheriffs, and so on, some of whom have made good records in public service.

With the aid of this club, its president was enabled to become a member of the Board of Commissioners, the chief governing body of Cook County, and here he allied himself with a spoils-seeking majority and was known for his crude and violent conduct.

The members of this club have been so well protected, as a rule, in the execution of their delinquencies that they have become a rather lawless group and have succeeded pretty well in terrorizing their immediate community.

In one case three of them were suspected of a murder—and this instance indicates to some extent why a general exposé of these conditions is so difficult. A saloon-keeper was keeping them in hiding, when the public demand for action became so insistent that the police inspector in the district brought pressure to bear upon the club to turn up the suspects. It was then disclosed that the inspector's son, who was treasurer of the club, was short in his accounts. Whereupon action was immediately dropped and the suspected individuals were safe until sought out by the down-town bureau.

In spite of these facts, however, many of those who discussed the club felt that it could still be made respectable under proper guidance.[8]

---

[8] Interviews.

Photo by Author

Photo by Author

ATHLETIC CLUBS

At the left is the headquarters of an athletic club popularly known as "Ragen's Colts," an influential group in the South Halsted Street district, an area which is sometimes called the "aristocracy of gangland."

At the right are the clubrooms of a less prosperous group. The typical legend, "For Members Only," is on the door and displayed in the window. The group of younger boys at one side is typical of the boy followers or admirers of the older club. Every street gang in Chicago aspires to be an athletic club with rooms of its own. (See documents 150–51.)

In such cases as this we get the most vivid picture of the roots of political power in certain areas of Chicago. But here again, we find that Chicago is not unique, for political power has similar roots in other large cities in America in which we find the same type of cultural disorganization.

THE GANG PROMOTES THE ALLIANCE BETWEEN CRIME AND POLITICS

The unsupervised gang or gang club facilitiates the demoralization of its members and promotes crime and disorder, but there is still another way in which it augments the problems of a great city. It impairs the efficiency and integrity of local government by facilitating an extensive alliance between crime and politics. That such a corrupt alliance has existed and still exists in Chicago is indicated by statements of judges, the president of the Chicago Crime Commission, and the United States district attorney. Yet that Chicago is not unlike other American cities where like industrial and social conditions prevail is attested by the existence, at one time or another, of similar alliances in Boston, New York, Philadelphia, St. Louis, and other cities.

To be morally certain of this alliance, however, is one thing, and to be in possession of such facts as can be used for legal evidence is quite another. The legal links in the various chains of cirumstantial evidence have been largely lacking. The large number of people involved, the danger of mutual incrimination, the fear of violence, indirect business relations with illicit groups, and a certain repugnance against telling on one's friends have all played a part in preventing any general expose which would lead to convictions.

The study of gangs conveys a very vivid impression that the whole structure of municipal politics is at base a complex of personal relationships and mutual personal obligations which make service in the interest of an impersonal public and an abstract justice very difficult. The influence of personal relations in dissolving a moral order has been indicated by Robert E. Park.

> Personal relations and personal friendships are the great moral solvents. Under their influence all distinctions of class, of caste, and even of race, are dissolved into the general flux which we sometimes call democracy.
>
> It was a minor statesman who said: "What is the Constitution between friends?" As the embodiment of a moral doctrine, this question, with its implications, is subject to grave qualifications, but as a statement of psychological fact it has to be reckoned with. What, between friends, are any of our conventions, moral codes, and political doctrines and institutions? It is personal friendships that corrupt politics. Not only politics, but all our formal and conventional relations are undermined by those elemental loyalties that have their roots in personal attachments. There is no way of preserving existing social barriers, except by preserving the existing animosities that buttress them.[9]

The gang, both young and old, plays an important rôle in this complex of personal relationships which serves to join crime and politics in Chicago in such an intimate unity. In order to indicate clearly how politics encourages and promotes the gang and how the gang facilitates the inter-connections between crime and politics, it will be necessary to describe briefly the organization and workings of the types of political machine which have operated in Chicago.

THE GANG AND THE POLITICAL MACHINE

The influence of the boy or adult gang in city politics has arisen largely through its ability to trade some advantage in the way of votes, influence, money, or what not, with the politician in return for subsidies, immunities,

[9] "Behind Our Masks," *Survey*, May 1, 1926, p. 139.

and so on. In this way gang influence has been enlisted in the support of the political machine, whose potential development is one of the weaknesses of democracy in cities. The usual type of American city government was designed for "a small community based on primary relations," where the town meeting could function efficiently.[10] The average citizen in the modern American city, however, cannot vote intelligently to elect officials because their functions are so varied, there are so many of them, and most of them are so inaccessible to him personally. He must, therefore, rely upon "some more or less interested organization or some more or less interested advisor to tell him how to vote."[11]

"To meet this emergency, created primarily by conditions imposed by city life, two types of organization have come into existence for controlling those artificial crises that we call elections."[12] One is the civic association and the other is the boss and his political machine. The latter is a technical device invented in the interests of party control for the purpose of capturing elections. While the former is based on secondary relations and depends largely upon publicity, the latter is based on primary relations, which depend upon intimate acquaintanceship and friendly service by the boss.

The political machine is, in fact, an attempt to maintain, inside the formal administrative organization of the city, the control of a primary group. The organizations thus built up, of which Tammany Hall is the classic illustration, appear to be thoroughly feudal in their character. The relations between the boss and his ward captain seem to be precisely that, of personal loyalty on one side and personal protection on the other, which the feudal relation implies. The virtues which such an organization calls out are the old tribal ones of fidelity, loyalty, and devotion to the interests of the chief and the clan. The people with the organization, their

[10] Robert E. Park in Park, *et al*, *The City*, pp. 34–36.

[11] *Ibid.*   [12] *Ibid.*

friends and supporters, constitute a "we" group, while the rest of the city is merely the outer world, which is not quite alive and not quite human in the sense in which the members of the "we" group are.[13]

While gang influences seem to touch all phases of Chicago politics, the gang probably plays its chief part in its relation to ward and factional political machines. The factional machine, which may be city-wide or even of greater scope, is built up in the interests of one or more politicians and their hangers-on, who form political alliances wherever their own purposes are advanced. It is the ward machine, however, which serves as the basic unit of informal political organization and which in turn is integrated with similar units in larger machines. While the ward organization is usually subdivided into many smaller units, it is the ward boss who serves as the focus of political power and integrates the efforts of precinct politicians.

Public indifference[14] in political matters, among other factors, has aided the development of that unique personality, the ward boss, the czar of local politics.[15] The classic example of this functionary in Chicago is "Hinky Dink," who with his associate, "Bath House John," has held undisputed sway in the old First Ward since his first election as alderman in 1897, and this, in spite of the recurrent characterization as "utterly unfit," applied to him biennially by the Municipal Voters' League. He is a type representing the perennial class of undefeatable alderman, the so-called "gray wolves" of the Chicago City Council.

[13] *Ibid.*, pp. 35–36.

[14] See Charles E. Merriam and Harold F. Gosnell, *Non-Voting: Causes and Methods of Control.*

[15] For an admirable brief description of the boss and his part in politics, see William B. Munro, *Personality in Politics.*

One of the most important elements in the control of the ward boss in gangland areas is the immigrant population. His hold upon the people in the immigrant colonies, particularly those of first settlement, is due not so much to his capacity for "corrupt manipulation or police oppression," in the first instance, as it is to his ability to render friendly services, such as getting the immigrant a job with some big corporation with which he has influence.

Whatever other local or state office he may hold, the ward boss is usually the ward committeeman of his political party and since his indorsement is required for all office-seekers and appointees, his position is commonly regarded as more important than that of alderman. The immediate henchmen of the ward boss are the captains of the precincts. They are usually political job-holders, who under the direction of the ward committeeman, form an organization (with a president and a secretary) which is the real ward machine. Subordinate to each precinct captain are three clerks and three judges of election, all party adherents. In Chicago they constitute a small army and an important element in machine control of elections.

The local and factional machines acquire power through their ability to spend money, to dispense patronage, and to secure political and other favors for their constituency. At election time from $15 to $150 is ordinarily spent in each precinct to hire men and women workers who have friends who will vote their way. They are usually paid $5.00 each, although a good precinct worker gets as much as $25.[16] This money flows into the party coffers from a variety of sources. Some of the lower grades of city employees have at times found it necessary

---

[16] The committee of the U.S. Senate, investigating "slush" funds in the Illinois primaries of April, 1926, discovered that two of the Chicago Republican factional machines had expended approximately $130,000 and $170,000 respectively in these primaries.

to contribute a certain percentage of their wages. There are many outright donations from candidates and others whom the machine is in a position to favor in some way. In addition there are receipts from the sale of tickets (sometimes forced) to party picnics, balls, and other functions—besides hidden income in some cases from the more direct forms of graft.

The machine in one ward may co-operate with others in trading votes, interchanging influence, and so on. It not infrequently happens that there is a bi-partisan alliance in a factional machine in which the local machines of both parties co-operate. In commenting on the notorious primary election of April 13, 1926, in which gangs played such an important part, a high official stated that "in every precinct where votes were stolen for certain Republican candidates, there were also votes stolen for certain Democratic candidates. It was a perfect bi-partisan alliance."

The ward machine is sometimes enabled indirectly to influence certain city courts in favor of gang members because some judges who are more or less dependent on machine support for re-election cannot remain entirely insensitive to its demands, particularly with regard to prohibition enforcement. The machine also exerts pressure upon the working class through employers whom it has favored and who are in a position to suggest how their employees should vote. It gets votes by obtaining jobs for the poor, doing political favors for the rich, and being able to perform a twofold service for the ordinary voter, viz., get him excused from jury service or "fix" his personal property taxes.

POLITICAL ALLIANCES WITH GANGSTERS AND CRIMINAL GANGS

Not only does the political boss utilize the boys' gang and the gang club, but he enters into more or less definite alliances with the gangsters and the criminal gang. The kind of group which is often enlisted to support him is indicated in the following document. It will be noted that this type of gang originates with younger boys who have probably been favored by the politician and who have gradually become criminals, in which rôles they are probably even more useful to him.

244. This gang centers about the H. brothers, whose father, in the meat business in a South Side gang area, permitted the boys to have a clubroom in the bar in the rear of his shop. There were sixty or seventy boys and young men, mostly German and Irish Americans, between the ages of eighteen and thirty years. They were not interested in athletics, but in gambling and holdups for which they usually went unpunished. This gang did strong-arm work for a politician who at one time was a candidate for sheriff of Cook County.

Most of them have now drifted out of the district, spreading their influences in many directions. One of them, who had once been a waiter for Colossimo, became manager of a cabaret and sporting house in the South Side badlands. Some of them went to Florida and became active politically there. It is said that they forced a roadhouse-keeper there to divide his profits half-in-half for protection and later murdered him. One of them became a "bookie" at the races, while others went in for beer-running. One went to West Madison Street to run a house of prostitution, while another became allied with a recent political-criminal "outfit" on the South Side. While the members of this gang have scattered far and wide, the old virus is still in them.[17]

Some of these gangsters are so powerful in their districts that they can swing an entire ward if they are disposed to exert themselves. In Chicago and Cook County where party and factional power often tends to be pretty evenly divided, the ability to swing a few doubtful wards heavily into line for one candidate or one faction often means winning an election. For such support the politicians are willing to pay, and sometimes they sacrifice the

[17] Interview with a politician and former member of a gang club.

public interest by thwarting justice to give their gangster-vassals immunity.

Political alliances with members of gangs have become so common in recent years that there has been a disposition to regard gangsters as "inlaws" rather than as outlaws. It has become customary in Chicago to refer to these gangsters as "immune criminals." This merely means that these men have escaped punishment, sometimes in one way and sometimes in another, but often through political influence brought to bear at some weak point in the long series of legal steps between detection and punishment. O'Banion was alleged to have been a case of this type.

246. When Dion O'Banion was shot and killed, Chief Collins congratulated Chicago on the death of "an arch-criminal, who was responsible for at least twenty-five murders." Yet in his thirty-two years of life O'Banion had spent only twelve months in jail. Before he had risen to be anything more than a daring young robber, he served two brief sentences in the house of correction. That was all. The twenty-five murders for which Chief Collins says he was responsible were committed after that.[18]

The immunity which the politician confers is not without its effect upon gang boys, who are prospective gangsters.

This feeling of a right to immunity came out clearly in the uncontrolled activities of politically sponsored gangs and gang clubs in the race riots of 1919.

248. They seemed to think that they had a sort of protection which entitled them to go out and assault anybody. When the race riots occurred it gave them something to satiate the desire to inflict their evil propensities on others.[19]

[18] See Charles Gregston, "Crime in Chicago Now on Business Basis," *Chicago Daily News*, November 15, 1924.

[19] Testimony of a municipal judge, quoted in Chicago Commission on Race Relations, *op. cit.*, p. 13.

There was considerable talk of the non-interference by the police with the lawless activities of these groups during the riots on account of the political influence of some of their leaders. In one case members of a club broke into a police station and stole the weapons and other evidence to be used against some of their associates.

Another type of "pull" enjoyed by a youthful gang is indicated in the following case.

249. A gang of from eighteen to twenty fellows of from eighteen to twenty-one years of age came to a playground one Saturday afternoon and insulted the instructor. They refused to get out when told to do so by the director and finally had to be taken in charge by the police-patrol wagon. When taken before a magistrate at a nearby police station, they were confronted by the playground director and the instructors who were witnesses to their misconduct. The magistrate, however, in the absence of marks of physical violence, refused to find them guilty of disorderly conduct and even to fine them $1.00 each and suspend the fine, as the director requested, in the interest of the neighborhood and the principle involved. This was clearly a case of political pull. Three or four people also approached the director in a similar case and requested that there be no prosecution.[20]

Police protection, often extended at the command of the political boss, has always played an important part in the immunities enjoyed by gangs and their members. The following case illustrates how a certain type of police protection works with the leader and members of a boys' gang.

250. It was only a week or so ago that we called at the police station near our social center to get the captain's report upon the leader of the gang in which we had been interested. It happened that only three weeks before the boy had been caught, with his gang, in the very act of stealing in one of the prominent Loop stores. The whole gang was arrested and taken to this station. It was announced that the leader was in for good and that the policeman had said that he would be sent to Pontiac, St. Charles already having assumed in his career the rôle of a "vacation school."

[20] Interview with playground director.

The next day, however, the boy leader had been released and was never recalled for a hearing. The rest of the gang were released soon afterward. A few days later the same boy was arrested for stealing a bicycle, and was again promptly released. When asked about this, the detective said simply,

"O, you mean that little ——— youngster? Oh, he's a good kid; we just let him go. . . . . He comes from a nice family, all good people, and it would be too bad for him. . . . ." None of the police officers could furnish any details, nor had they any record of the arrests on their books for these two days.

The boys say quite frankly that there is no need to fear a "cop" in this street so long as a fellow has spare cash. The members of the gang have more than once been out trying to raise money to bail out one of their friends who has been caught, and it is common knowledge that if the boys caught shooting craps run quickly and leave the "stakes" for these particular policemen, nothing more happens.[21]

No generalization must be drawn, however, to the effect that the Chicago Police Department countenances or encourages such irregularities. When they do occur, they are usually confined to some local territory or to a small element on the force, which higher police officials are attempting constantly to oust. A certain number of men of this type do, however, tend to persist in the department in spite of the efforts of their superiors to expel them, and it is this group which often abets gang activities.

251. Police protection has been an essential element in the existence of organized crime. Collusion between grafting police officials and various criminal groups has been shown and during the administration of the present state's attorney [1919], criminal police officers have been convicted and sent to the penitentiary.[22]

252. All gambling houses and regular houses of prostitution invariably pay for police protection. Gangs of pickpockets and

[21] Manuscript by a resident of the district and a close observer of the gang.

[22] H. B. Chamberlin, *Bulletin of the Chicago Crime Commission*, November 20, 1919, p. 4.

regular safe-blowers also pay for police protection if they keep going for any length of time.[23]

The recognition of the possibility of police alliance with gangs is indicated by frequent "shake-ups" of police officers in gang districts. In some cases the transfers have been so complete that the only vestige of the former staff to be found in a police station was the office cat. After the disclosures with reference to the extensive operations of the Genna gang, for example, all police sergeants on duty at the station located in this area were transferred to other districts.

Another way in which the machine politician maintains his hold upon the gang and the gang club is through his ability, by means of the spoils system, to put their members on official pay-rolls. Even where civil service is in effect, the politician and the gang assists members by special coaching and instruction, and in certain cases methods of evading civil service regulations, such as temporary appointments, have been employed.

253. At one time the man in charge of one of Chicago's playground systems had been president of one of the politically powerful gang clubs for many years. The only physical culture he had received was in gang sports and as captain of the gang's football team. Many gang members were given playground and park positions; some of them were crippled, worn-out, or broken-down servants of the political machine with no qualifications whatsoever for the positions they were to fill.

Another case is cited of a gang leader, who began as a newsboy at sixteen and had a bunch of boys helping him in "rolling" drunken men. As he grew older he became a procurer and now has a following of about one hundred men from nineteen to twenty-eight years of age. These young fellows hang out in cigar stores and poolrooms, gambling, betting, and procuring. Through his ability to swing their votes, the leader has held several minor appointive offices in the City Hall, but has not been required to do any actual work. He dresses exceedingly well and has often been seen around down-town hotels where he procures girls for traveling salesmen.

[23] Interview with a former vice inspector.

The difficulties involved in operating the school playgrounds in the face of pressures to employ political favorites became so great in the spring of 1925, that an assistant superintendent of schools threatened to close the whole system. He made the following statement:

"We cannot allow broken-down cripples to be placed in charge of neighborhood centers where there is frequent trouble with gangs of potential criminals. My office swarms all the time with individuals trying to round up jobs for some one to whom they owe political favors. The situation is becoming intolerable—particularly when they try to foist on us by threats and other means candidates, unfitted physically, mentally, or any other way, for work as playground attendants."[24]

The prospect of obtaining a "soft job" or a lucrative one through the influence of a politician is particularly effective in controlling the members of younger gangs or those whose members are on the verge of becoming voters.

Politicians, public officials, and their subordinates have also catered to gangsters in the liberties permitted them with regard to penal institutions. This seems to have taken place both with reference to undue freedom permitted within jails and prisons as well as to premature pardons and paroles. It appears that a jail, bridewell, or reformatory in many cases turns out to be little more than a political institution used to provide jobs for loyal machine-supporters and to manipulate the patronage of underworld gangs by extending favors to inmates, shortening or extending sentences, and similar expedients.

WHAT THE GANG GIVES THE POLITICIAN

To repay the politician for putting gang members on official pay-rolls, and providing subsidies, protection, and immunities from official interference, the gang often splits with him the proceeds of its illegitimate activities; controls for him the votes of its members, hangers-on, and friends, and performs for him various types of "work"

[24] Interviews and published accounts.

at the polls, such as slugging, intimidation, kidnaping, vandalism (tearing down signs, etc.), ballot-fixing, repeating, stealing ballot boxes, miscounting, falsifying returns, etc.

A partial insight into how the methods of the gang supplement those of the political machine may be indicated by a review of gang activities in the primary election of April 13, 1926.

254. Some of the methods employed by the gang in connection with the political machine are indicated in the petitions for recounts filed by some of the defeated candidates in the April primaries. It was alleged that certain politicians had used the powers of their office "to intimidate voters, terrorize election officials, enlist gunmen and gamblers to prevent a fair election and employ repeaters at the polls." It was further asserted that "saloon-keepers were required to transport floaters and repeaters from precinct to precinct and that groups of unqualified voters were registered and voted under fictitious names and paid for voting according to instructions."

"Groups of turbulent and lawless persons openly displayed and fired revolvers in the polling places, circulated throughout the precincts in certain wards, kidnapped judges and clerks and created such conditions of fear and terror as to cause large numbers of prospective voters to refrain from voting."

"During the official canvass, gunmen and gangsters intimidated employees of the election board, circulating around the tables where the count was being made."

A special grand jury under the direction of a special state's attorney found that gangsters had been most active in certain suburbs outside of the city of Chicago proper. After the coming in of the Dever administration, which made conditions in Chicago more difficult for the criminal gangs, many of them attempted to establish spheres of influence in these suburbs, where in some cases they acquired almost complete political control.

"The recount showed that hundreds of thousands of votes had been stolen with the aid of criminals of the worst type." The jury indicted the leader of one of the most notorious master-criminal gangs together with the president of the village board and chief of police of one of the suburbs and several gangsters. Some of these men were accused of conspiracy to instigate perjury on the part of election officials. It was also charged that 114 armed floaters were brought in and voted. One of the gangsters had led in a veritable reign of terror on the same day that he was supposedly being sought as a suspect in a gang murder case. Some of the other charges were voting under an assumed name, drawing a gun with intent to assault, illegal voting, assault with intent to kill, and kidnapping.[25]

That gang methods in politics are not new in Chicago, however, is indicated by a description of how the political boss of a few decades ago made use of such groups.

255. The X gang, which hung out in the South Side division of gangland, was organized as the G—— Colts by an influential politician and part owner of the G—— brewery about 1904. The group had about a hundred members between twenty and thirty-eight years of age, who met in the clubroom provided by their patron. Their activities consisted largely of handball, boxing, baseball, crap shooting, gambling, and fighting with two other gangs in the vicinity. Gang battles were carried on chiefly by means of stones and clubs, but at times there was gun play.

During one administration, the patron of the gang was practically the mayor and chief of police of the district. He was the political boss of the area until his death in 1918. With the aid of the gang, he ruled the police and shifted them to suit himself. The police often held court and assessed fines, although this did not appear to be legal. The boys of the district, who took delight in pelting the policemen with paper bags filled with water as they came from roll call, were always protected by the boss and would be promptly released after they had been brought to the station-house.

This gang ruled the polls by various methods, stealing ballots and ballot boxes, and kidnapping the challengers for the opposing party during election day and holding them prisoner until evening. They had such pull that they could never be brought to justice for their misdeeds.

As time passed the members of the older gang entered into various lines of business, chief of which was lucrative employment by the city and large public utilities, obtained through political influence. One of them became foreman of the water-pipe extension of the City Hall at $10 a day. Others became saloon-keepers. A few were sent to Joliet, but were soon pardoned. So great was the

[25] Published reports.

influence of the boss that a former governor has been seen to put his arms around the boss's neck and kiss him (he was really kissing his influence).

At the death of the old boss, he was succeeded by his son, who, although not so powerful as his father, is still a member of the local Republican central committee. He has a following of about 250 hangers-on, who, although not primarily strong-arm men, can still be depended upon for crooked work at the polls.[26]

While the power of the gangs to corrupt public officials has been due in part to their ability to deliver votes, it has been greatly augmented by the enormous profits which they have derived in recent years from the manufacture and sale of illicit alcoholic beverages—profits which have undoubtedly amounted to millions of dollars. Two leaders of one beer gang are reported to have paid for one year alone an income tax of $250,000. In 1923 this gang is said to have purchased one brewery for $600,000 cash, making a total at that time of six plants under its control. A congressman and several state legislators were said to be sharing the profits of the business which were $28 per barrel on beer that cost $2.00 per barrel to make.

These huge profits have in some cases enabled gang leaders to purchase protection from interference.

256. Two leading gangs of rum-runners on the south side of Chicago for a long time enjoyed political protection. One of them brought in liquor along the ———— Avenue route, formerly controlled politically and to a certain extent administratively by a state senator from the district. One of the leaders of this gang was on the pay-roll of the senator as his private secretary. The other group used the ———— Street route which at that time was controlled by a certain police captain with whom the leader of the gang had a "stand-in."

It was not unusual in those days (before Mayor Dever and Chief Collins drove the gangs into the suburbs) for a police squad to escort these beer caravans right into town. The police would also ride on their wagons, and when once the gangs got something

[26] Interview with a politician of long experience.

on a policeman, they knew how to use the art of blackmail. Police protection was not only necessary in convoying liquor in order to allay suspicion, but it was also desirable to prevent hijacking. One case has been cited in which two groups of policemen engaged in a battle, one group protecting a truck-load of illicit beer, the other attempting to steal it from them.[27]

To Chief of Police Collins is attributed the statement that in 1923 beer-running gangs in Chicago "were spending money at the rate of $1,000,000 a year to 'fix' the law."[28]

There is no doubt but that in many cases politicians and office-holders have been actually in partnership with the rum gangs. Certain branches of the government, in other words, have been in partnership, in some cases at least, with the actual business which other branches have sought to suppress. A prominent city official in Chicago, for example, was owner of a brewery which the government found necessary to close by injunction; and the case had to be carried to the United States District Court of Appeals before a permanent closing order could be obtained against it (in 1924). The government's case was based upon the seizure of real beer at the brewery. A West Side politician was captured in the plant on one of these midnight raids. As a result of investigations into the illicit traffic in "sacramental wines," it was discovered, according to the allegations of government operatives, that a city official, an important prohibition enforcement agent, and other enforcement officials were involved in deals which netted millions of dollars to the conspirators. It was alleged also that a state legislator had collected $50,000 to be used in facilitating the wine sales. The Sibley warehouse robbery (1923), in which 2,248 cases of pre-war Lancaster whiskey having an illicit value of something like $1,000,000 were removed by

[27] Interview with a former vice inspector.
[28] Gregston, *op. cit.*, November 15, 1924.

means of forged and raised permits, was engineered by a powerful criminal gang with the alleged co-operation of several officials.[29]

This gradual undermining of the integrity of public officials in all departments of the government is probably the most serious of the unforeseen effects of prohibition. Yet it is not without a parallel in American history. A similar assault upon the integrity of the government, although probably not so widespread, was made by railroad interests in the latter quarter of the past century. It occurred at the time of the notorious Crédit Mobilier, a railroad company, whose corrupting influence reached even to the vice-presidency.[30]

The whole complex of relations between crime and politics in American cities needs to be thoroughly and impartially studied as a preliminary step in any hopeful program designed to bring about social control. The findings of the present study indicate the necessity of redirecting the activities of the gang so as to leave as little opportunity as possible for political manipulation.

[29] For a further account of alleged relations between criminal gangs and politics, see Oliver H. P. Garrett, "Linking State and City Politicians with Chicago's Gangsters," *St. Louis Post-Dispatch*, May 9, 1926. Reprinted from a series in the *New York World*, May 3 to 9, 1926. See also article by the same author, "Politics and Crime in Chicago," *New Republic*, June 9, 1926, pp. 78–80.

[30] See H. U. Faulkner, *American Economic History*, pp. 458–61.

CHAPTER XX

Attacking the Problem

The general perspective obtained from the survey of gangs in Chicago shows that the gang and its problems constitute merely one of many symptoms of the more or less general disorganization incident to rapid economic development and the ingestion of vast numbers of alien workers. Like the industrial countries of western Europe, America has passed through the throes of a revolution of economic technique; but unlike these countries, we are still, for the most part, in an epoch of feverish mobility and expansion consequent upon the peopling of a new continent and the exploitation of virgin natural resources.

The process of breakneck competition in the development of this new wealth and the consequent tendency toward increasing division of labor and specialization have stimulated the rapid growth of cities and all the internal processes of kaleidoscopic movement and rearrangement which this growth has entailed. The result has been that American industrial cities have not had time to become settled and self-controlled; they are youthful and they are experiencing the struggles and instability of youth. The apparent chaos in certain phases of their life may be regarded as a case of "cultural lag."[1]

[1] See W. F. Ogburn, *Social Change*, pp. 200–213.

Conditions are changing too rapidly to develop corresponding controls of an efficient type. As a result there is a blind groping for order, without much understanding of the nature of the problems involved or their difficulties.

As a great industrial and commercial metropolis, Chicago both typifies and epitomizes these conditions. Life is in constant ferment physically, economically, and culturally. Rapid change and enormous movement have tended to prevent the development of a consistent social code supported by all members of the community and even to break up such codes as have existed among the older white stocks and the diverse cultural groups of the polyglot immigrant population which comprises three-fourths of Chicago's inhabitants. The result is a high degree of disorganization, manifesting itself in vice, crime, political corruption, and other social maladies, which tend to escape to a suburban fringe or to become segregated within the city in the semicircular "poverty belt" around the Loop, an area which provides easier escape from control than other portions of the city. The fact that the gangs of Chicago are to be found for the most part in this "zone of transition,"[2] which is the region of greatest disorder in the city, is in itself significant, for they not only find an environment favorable to their development, but their life and activities are colored by the disorganization they encounter there.

Recognizing, then, the probability of the continuance of this state of social disintegration for some time to come, the more ultimate problem resolves itself into one of reducing the disorganization incident to prosperity and progress to the minimum necessary for progressive reorganization. The immediate need is to study the present difficulties with a view to controlling and directing social change to this end.

[2] For a description of this zone see E. W. Burgess in Park, et al., The City, pp. 55-56.

FACTORS UNDERLYING GANGING

Boys in gangland areas enjoy an unusual freedom from restrictions of the type imposed by the normal controlling agencies in the better residential areas of the city. Their play is usually unhampered and the extensive railroad, canal, and industrial properties furnish them a realm for adventure that is unexcelled in the playgrounds or in the more orderly portions of the city. There is no dearth of excitement in this disorganized environment, and in the gang they find an instrument for the organization of their play and the satisfaction of most of their wishes. The free, wild life they lead under such conditions constitutes one of the chief obstacles to the sort of direction which any boys'-work program attempts. The problem of competing with the care-free activities of the gang is a difficult one and requires a high degree of intelligence and understanding on the part of any leader or agency attempting to meet it.

In describing in a summary way the underlying conditions of disorganization in gang areas, we are simply attempting to explain the factors that make possible the freedom which leads to ganging. We are merely describing the soil which favors the growth of gangs. Such underlying conditions as inadequate family life; poverty; deteriorating neighborhoods; and ineffective religion, education, and recreation must be considered together as a situation complex which forms the matrix of gang development. It seems impossible to control one factor without dealing with the others, so closely are they interwoven, and in most cases they are inseparable from the general problem of immigrant adjustment. Thus, in any individual case of the entrance of a boy into a gang, several of these factors usually interact to create such an opportunity.

While recognizing the importance of studying the interplay of the forces of disorganization in the case of any given gang boy, it is possible, however, to disentangle these underlying conditions from one another and, for purposes of discussion, to treat each separately. The value of this method lies in making clearer the influence of each factor and in suggesting methods of attacking the problem in each case.

Any condition in family life which promotes neglect or repression of its boy members, indirectly promotes the gang by stimulating the boy to find the satisfaction of his wishes outside the plan and organization of family activities. This, like such other underlying factors as ineffective religion, inadequate schooling, and unguided recreation, is a purely negative factor so far as the gang is concerned, merely creating an opportunity for ganging or any other kind of substitute activity. The family deficiencies which may make ganging possible are of a great variety of types—poverty; immigrant maladjustments; disintegration; and ignorant, unsympathetic, immoral, or greedy adults, but their general effect is the same: the family fails to hold the boy's interest, neglects him, or actually forces him into the street. These family conditions interact in the usual case, but it is noteworthy that, either singly or in combination, they are rarely absent from the homes of gang boys.

The failure of present-day religion to penetrate in any real and vital way the experience of the gang boy may be cited as a second negative factor which makes possible the free life of the gang. The lack in this case is the failure to provide controls of the boy's behavior and interesting activities for his leisure time to supplement those of the home, the school, and the playground.

The third negative factor which contributes to an opportunity for the free life of the gang, is the type of schooling which does not interest the boy or provide for a satisfying organization of his lively energies. This occurs in two ways: first, the procedure within school hours does not interest the gang boy, who resorts to truancy; and secondly, the school does not have an adequate program of extra-curricular activities to supplement the work of other agencies in meeting the spare-time problem.

The fourth negative factor which contributes to a situation favorable to ganging is the lack of proper guidance for spare-time activities. The recreation of boys who become "wholesome citizens" is guided by parents, friends, teachers, and recreational leaders, but this guidance is largely absent in gangland areas. The point is not that children do not play in gangland. They do.

259. I am impressed more and more with the fact that the boys of our streets are able, with very little help, to carry out a rather active program of recreation for themselves. I am thinking now of the unorganized street play, pick up ball games, handball, card playing and crap shooting, if you please. A great many of our boys' workers labor under the mistaken impression that unless they provide these boys with activities, they will remain idle. A walk down any of our streets in summer time will show that most of the children are busy. Some of us went out last summer and conducted street games in two certain streets twice a week. On the nights we were there the playing was more intense, and more children took part, but on the other nights most of the children were playing in that and other streets where we never had games.[3]

The common assumption that the problem of boy delinquency will be solved by the, multiplication of playgrounds and social centers in gang areas is entirely erroneous. The physical layout of gangland provides a realm of adventure with which no playground can compete. The lack is not of this sort. The real problem is one of developing in these areas or introducing into them leaders who can organize the play of the boys, direct it into wholesome channels, and give it social significance.

[3] Statement by a leading boys' worker in gangland.

Thus, it becomes apparent that ganging is merely one symptom of more deep-lying community disorganization,[4] which frees the boy from ordinary controls and in this way makes possible the development of the gang. An authority on the early gangs of New York City holds a similar position.

260. I do not think there is any doubt of the correctness of the thesis that the gang is a symptom of community disorganization. I believe that most, if not all of the great gangs of New York—not the modern bootlegger and killer groups, but the old organizations such as the Gophers, the Hudson Dusters, etc.—grew out of such disorganization; and they can be traced directly to conditions in the old Five Points section, which appears to have been the last word in depravity. This district was once the scene of an old dive, which was first a brewery and then a tenement, called "The Old Brewery," which was never anything but a hive of wretchedness and poverty.[5]

These disorganized conditions do not directly produce gangs, but the gang is an interstitial growth, flowering where other institutions are lacking or are failing to function efficiently. It is a symptom of the disorderly life of a frontier.

REDIRECTING THE GANG

The social maladjustments described above are negative factors in the genesis of the gang because they do no more than give the boy an opportunity to roam about and choose his associates and his amusements for himself. It is probable that these underlying conditions can ultimately be reduced to some extent with intelligent, collective planning, but in the meantime there is bound to be ganging and kindred manifestations. While we are struggling with the problems of immigrant adjustment; of poverty; and of inadequate homes, schools, and churches;

---

[4] Long ago Jacob Riis, who knew the life of the disorganized areas of New York City, said, "The gang is a distemper of the slums; a friend come to tell us that something has gone amiss in our social life."

[5] Statement to the author (July 20, 1926) by Herbert Asbury.

there still remains the gang. Its existence must be recognized and some sort of place must be made for it in the life of the community.

This brings us to a second type of procedure for attacking the gang problem, viz., the treatment of gangs already formed and forming. In general, two kinds of agencies have to deal with the gang in a practical way: those interested in boys' work, and those representing the law.

THE GANG AND THE LAW

While considerable progress has been made in the modification of laws and legal procedures to meet the special needs of children, the representatives of the law have not learned, for the most part, how to deal with the boy delinquent and his gang in an effective way. This arises through no lack of good intentions, perhaps, but more largely from a failure to comprehend the problems involved.[6]

As a rule policemen assume that the gang must be suppressed—must be broken up. They fail to understand that boyish energies, like tics, suppressed at one place are sure to break out at some other. And when the breaking-up of the gang has been accomplished, there is usually no attempt to provide substitute activities for the boys. Under ordinary circumstances, then, the "cop" becomes the natural enemy of the gang, a rôle which he usually assumes with equanimity, but one which may involve considerable discomfort and peril to his person. There is, of course, a considerable amount of tolerance of juvenile disorder by policemen in gang areas. This merges in some cases into official connivance at or even protection of gang delinquencies and criminality.

[6] How complete this misunderstanding of the needs of the boy can be is indicated in Clifford R. Shaw, *A Problem Boy*.

THE TREATMENT OF THE DELINQUENT AS A PERSON

Probably the most important conclusion, with reference to the treatment of gangs, to be drawn from the present study is that the inadequacy of our official machinery for handling delinquents, particularly boys, is due largely to a failure to recognize the group factor in delinquency.[7]

In 1915 William Healy wrote an epoch-making volume, *The Individual Delinquent*, showing the importance of studying every offender with reference to all the factors operating to produce delinquency in his own individual case. He abandoned the general and unitary causation theories of his predecessors and pointed out that each case must be treated on its own merits. "Trained in psychiatry and psychology, he emphasized physical examinations and mental tests without ignoring social factors. However, he relied upon the experience of the social worker instead of calling into service the technique of the sociologist."[8]

While in no way minimizing the importance of the principles of study and treatment formulated by Healy, E. W. Burgess has emphasized the necessity of studying the delinquent as a person (that is, as an individual with status).[9]

In the explanation and control of delinquency, it is significant to determine the nature of the participation of the person in the social organization, as in the insecurity or degradation of status, the type of personal behavior pattern, the degree of mobility, the change of the social environment, and the collapse of the social

---

[7] See Robert E. Park in Park, *et al.*, *The City*, p. 111.

[8] Abstract of E. W. Burgess, "The Study of the Delinquent as a Person," *American Journal of Sociology*, May, 1923, p. 657.

[9] It has already been indicated in chaps. xv and xvi that the term "person" has come to mean an individual considered in the rôle which he plays in a social group. Personality in this sense is the estimate which the group places upon him and the position it assigns. The individual's *conception* of his rôle is also an important factor in determining his behavior.

world of the person. In the study of delinquency, the psychiatric, psychological, and sociological methods of investigation are not in conflict with each other, but rather are complementary and interdependent.[10]

Following this line of thinking, the present study reveals something of the social world of the boy delinquent and shows the importance of the gang in the development of his personality and his attitudes toward his delinquencies.

But it is not only necessary to study the delinquent as a person, merely to understand him; it is also essential to *deal with him* as a person in any practical situation demanding the formulation of a program of treatment. He must not be treated as if he existed in a social vacuum, but he must be dealt with as a member of all the various groups to which he belongs—not merely the gang alone, but the family, the neighborhood, the school, the church, the occupational group, and so on. While the importance of the group factor in dealing with delinquency has been pointed out occasionally, the implications of this point of view have not been understood or taken into account in the official treatment of delinquents.

Too often the boy delinquent has been dealt with as if he were a purely biological, predetermined, individual mechanism.[11] To treat him in this way is to neglect what is usually the most essential element in the problem, viz., his own attitudes with reference to various factors in the situation and to possible plans formulated in his behalf. The phantasies and dreams that have grown out of his social experience are important determinants of his be-

[10] Burgess, *op. cit.*, p. 657.

[11] We are not meaning to imply in any sense that physical and mental defects which impair the capacity of the boy should or can be overlooked in formulating a plan for his future adjustment. The "whole child" must be treated, but there has been a tendency in the past to ignore the part played by his social world in his behavior problems.

havior. The personal relations which have been developed within his own social world, as a member of the groups which are most vital to the organization of his wishes, cannot be ignored.[12] His own conception of the rôle he thinks he plays in his social groups must be fully understood in any attempt to prescribe a program for his future adjustment. We need a new penology which shall be penetrating in its insights into the subjective aspect of the boy's life and which shall be much broader in scope than institutional care and the present system of probation and parole.[13]

Among the groups within which the boy delinquent finds expression, the gang is one of the most vital to the development of his personality. It often supplants other groups and comes to occupy a predominant place in his scheme of life. He feels many times that it is his gang which gives him what he wants most and he is more interested in maintaining his status in the gang than in any other group. In such cases his relation to the gang (that is, his social world) becomes the paramount issue with which the official agencies must deal, if they are to achieve any measure of success in handling the boy.

Experience shows that there are really only two alternatives in successfully reforming the boy who has become delinquent through the influence of his gang: he must either be removed completely from the gang and the social world it represents, or his gang must be reformed. Official agencies have usually attempted the former alternative without success and have, for the most part, completely neglected the latter. The point may be made

[12] In Shaw, *op. cit.*, the whole history of the boy is shown to be very largely the result of his social relationships.

[13] The importance of taking full account of the boy's total social situation has been suggested from another source with great cogency, viz., the *Gestalt* psychology.

clearer by describing some of the attempts which have been made to deal with the gang boy as an individual rather than to treat him as a person. The social factors in the following case seem to have been ignored.

262. The characteristic method of official agencies in dealing with the delinquent members of the Clutchy-Clutch was to treat them as individuals entirely apart from their social worlds. Apparently there was no attempt to reckon with the rôles they were playing in the gang or their own conceptions of those rôles.

The boys were repeatedly paroled to their parents under supervision of probation officers. In these cases they were simply returned to the old disorderly environment where they re-entered the gang and behaved much as before. The probation officer, underpaid and burdened with so many cases that he could give little more than perfunctory attention to any one of them, was unable to exercise supervision of a sufficiently intensive and intelligent type to reshape the characters of his charges or prevent their delinquencies. In some cases boys were arrested and brought into court even before he was notified.

No constructive work with the gang as a group was undertaken during this entire period of five or six years. No effort was made, so far as was ascertained, by any social agency, either public or private, to improve the highly disorganized environment within which the gang had developed.

Another type of method, equally unsuccessful, was to send the members of the gang to an institution for the purpose of discipline and "reform." Several of them were sent to the Parental School (for chronic truants) for varying periods. The only apparent effect of serving these terms in most cases was to keep the boys out of neighborhood mischief for the time they were sent away. No lasting improvement could be noted upon their return to the old gang associations. At this time the Parental School was run almost entirely upon the repressive principle. About the only effect of this sort of treatment was to embitter the boys and arouse attitudes of rebellion and intense hatred toward any agency of "reform."

As the members of the gang grew older and continued their delinquencies, they were sent to the Chicago Cook County School for Boys (for first and lesser offenders). Here they received excellent care and good training in school and manual work. Yet, even without the harsh features of many other institutions, this school could effect little lasting alteration in their characters, attitudes, and habits because it created for the boys a necessarily artificial environment where the ordinary temptations of the boy's native milieu and spontaneous group life were lacking.

After release from this institution after a term often of only a few weeks, the boys were returned to assume again their old rôles in the Clutchy-Clutch, usually with added prestige for having had this adventure with the law. Instead of deterring them from the demoralizing activities of the gang, these experiences with the authorities prepared them for more active participation in gang exploits and delinquencies by putting them more or less in the light of heroes in the eyes of the rest of the gang. In fact, full standing in the Clutchy-Clutch could only be secured by a court record; and the longer the record, the higher the standing.

In the case of one of the most difficult boys, the court tried the expedient of getting him out of the neighborhood. The family finally purchased $50 worth of land in the outskirts of the city. A shack was built and the boy was taken out there with the father, who worked on a garden plot during the summer. The lack of any adequate social world for the boy in this new environment, soon led to his returning to be with the gang each week-end, and it was not long until he was back again in the old neighborhood.[14]

If some interested social agency such as a playground, a settlement, or a boys' club had been enlisted by officials to co-operate with official agencies in directing the energies of the Clutchy-Clutch—if it had not ignored the organization and interrelations of life in the local neighborhood—a larger measure of success would have been conceivable.

"TAKE THE BOY OUT OF HIS GANG"

It is an easy matter to advise that "the boy should, of course, be taken out of his gang and other recreational activities substituted," but it is usually very difficult to accomplish this feat without resorting to the method of repression. The usual procedure is to put the boy in an

[14] Records, interviews, observations, and boys' own stories. The leader of this gang has been described in document 200.

institution for a time in the hope that the methods employed there will remodel him sufficiently to prevent his delinquencies when he is returned to the old environment. Many boys make good resolutions when undergoing the more or less rigorous discipline of an institution.

264. If I ever get out of here, I'm through with that stuff. I could rob a lot, but I don't want to. I know what that means for me. I'll soon be seventeen and that means St. Charles for sure. Judge Arnold will say "I'll have to put you in a place where you'll behave." I wish I could go home. I don't care to stay here. I don't get enough sleep; they wake you up early. Nothing is better than home.

When I get out I might hang around with the gang again, but I won't do any robbin'.[15]

An experience in an institution is probably a sufficient deterrent to further delinquency in some cases, but it is very doubtful if these good resolutions are long remembered when the average boy gets back to his gang; group controls and pressures are too strong to be long withstood in such cases.

The outstanding objection to the usual type of institutional treatment, even at its best, is that the boy is learning to adjust himself to a purely artificial situation, which, even with the so-called "cottage" plan, in no sense approximates his environment when he has been released. The "practice of good habits for a definite period" in the coercive atmosphere of an institution gives no assurance whatsoever that these habits will carry over into a totally different situation when the irksome restraints are removed. There is no military drill in the slums. Confinement in steel cages and doing "pull pen" and "the squats" are strangely absent in the free life of gangland. When the unnatural restraints are removed, the more logical tendency is to indulge even more freely in the old adventures, so long denied. Moreover, the boy

---

[15] Gang boy's own story.

returns to his gang with a "record," which usually operates either to classify him as an undesirable in the community or to give him greater prestige with his gang. *The
conclusion seems justified, therefore, that sending a gang
boy away to an institution turns out to be little more than
one method of evading the real problem—that of adjusting
him in his actual social world.*

That this is coming to be recognized by men of vision
is indicated in a statement by O. J. Milliken, who took
charge of the Chicago Parental School following the scan-
dal of 1923.

> 265. Were I to think only of the boys and their welfare, I
> would spend a large part of the money expended on institutions
> in hiring "Boy Men" to cover the city and spend their entire time
> with the gangs. . . . . Unless an institution can do constructive
> work, it does more harm than good. . . . . A limited number of
> corrective institutions are necessary, but they should be for the
> mentally ill, what our hospitals are for the physically ill. . . . .

George W. Kirchwey goes so far as to say that no normal child should *ever* be placed in an institution; such
treatment should be reserved for the "hopeless and helpless, for the mentally defective and psychopathic (if you
ever can find out who and what the psychopathic are),
and the insane."[16]

Another expedient which has been employed in an
attempt to "take the boy out of his gang" is that of getting the family to move from the neighborhood. This procedure is usually unsuccessful; for most families of this
type can only move to some other gangland area where
the boy enters another gang. If they do succeed in moving to what is for them some isolated or obscure portion
of the city, the boy's whole social world collapses, he bitterly complains that "there ain't any kids out there," and

[16] "Institutions for Juvenile Delinquents" in *The Child, the Clinic
and the Court*, p. 336.

it is not long until he is making long trips back to the old neighborhood to be with the gang again.[17]

To keep the boy away from his group while the family remains in the same community is next to impossible on account of the superior attractions of gang activities. The only alternative which remains, therefore, is to deal with the whole gang. This may be done by recognizing the gang and making a place for it in the program of the community, redirecting its activities into wholesome and socially significant channels. Or, it may be done by incorporating the leader and each member of the gang into some larger institution, to which their loyalties can be developed.

TRANSFORMING THE GANG

The usual policy of boys' work agencies has been to redirect the activities of existing gangs into wholesome channels by some sort of supervision. While this method is difficult and not always successful, its usefulness has been conclusively demonstrated by many Chicago agencies. The gang is usually taken over by the agency as a club, given a name, and affiliated with the larger structure. Subsequently, the members of the group are made to understand the rôles they play and given some part in the life of the community. While the following document does not present the exact technique of this process, it illustrates the general principle involved.

266. When the new garage of the F—— Company was opened, a small group of boys made it about as unpleasant for the company as they possibly could. The building had a wide expanse of glass and it was this shining mark that attracted the attention of two score or more active urchins in the neighborhood. They worked out an organized scheme of attack whereby they were enabled to

---

[17] Clifford R. Shaw has made some interesting studies showing how these boys go long distances to return to their old gang associations and tend to come back year after year, no matter where their families move to.

elude watchmen, employees, and specially detailed police. Annoyance and property loss were continual and efforts to stop the trouble were ineffectual.

At length the president of the company had the Scout movement brought to his attention. He ruminated over the matter for some time and finally called upon the Scout Commissioner and enlisted the co-operation of one of the finest Scout Masters in the city.

In a casual way, this Scout Master made friends with the boys and one day suggested in an offhand manner that the Boy Scouts were a jolly bunch of boys and it might be fun to organize a troop. The suggestion made a big hit and the troop was formed.

Soon the "Holy Terrors," as the gang was often called, were so busy with their first aid, their endeavors to fathom the mysteries of signaling, and their study of Scoutcraft that there was no time for throwing stones. More than that, the inclination seemed to have vanished. Now with an old gang leader in command, they are as proud of their new task of defending all the property in the neighborhood as they used to be of their clever schemes for making trouble.

All the officers of the company have become deeply interested in the youngsters. Several times the Scouts have had turned over to them two or three of the company's coaches and have gone off for a day's practicing in the country.[18]

The preceding case is presented as typical in general principle of the redirection of the gang by such agencies as the Young Men's Christian Association, the Boy Scouts of America, the settlements, the parks, the playgrounds, the Boys' Brotherhood Republic, and the Chicago Boys' Clubs. The politicians and saloon-keepers have also learned the trick of taking over these gangs and making clubs out of them, but their motives have usually been rather more for their own aggrandizement than for the good of the boys.

The generally recognized importance of boys' clubs in dealing with the gang has given rise to a demand for more scientific measurement of the effects of boys' club work upon gangs, gang boys, and juvenile delinquency in

[18] *Scouting*, April 1916.

A GANG TRANSFORMED INTO A BOY SCOUT TROOP

The group pictured above was a destructive gang which was transformed by skilful handling into the Boy Scout troop shown in the lower picture. The notion of solving the problems of difficult boys by formulating projects for them is being developed by Clifford R. Shaw and William I. Thomas. The foregoing pictures illustrate how a project may be worked out for a whole group. The alternative method of handling a gang is to break it up and give the boys individual or group projects in a larger frame of reference, such as that provided by the Union League Boys' Club. The important point to be noted is that where the gang is broken up, the social world of the boy disintegrates and a new one must be substituted for it—not of the artificial type found in an institution, but one which will provide for a redirection of his energies in the habitat in which he must live. (See document 266.)

general. As a result, at the behest of the Boys' Clubs of America, Inc., the Boys' Club Study, financed by the Bureau of Social Hygiene (at a cost of $37,500.00), was undertaken, under the direction of the author, by the Department of Sociology of the School of Education of New York University. This investigation attempted to measure the efficiency in delinquency prevention of a large boys' club located in New York City. The results of the study, covering the initial four years of the club's existence from 1927 to 1931 and completed in 1935, apply only to the boys' club unit investigated except where conditions in other clubs and their communities are similar.

This study, which used the descriptive, ecological, statistical, and case-study methods,[19] showed that this particular club was not an·important factor in delinquency prevention during the period considered.[20] The club did not succeed in reaching the large number of the boys it was designed to serve, although from the standpoint of race and nationality, occupational background, family status, school status, intelligence, educational achievement, emotional stability, and the incidence of truancy and delinquency, it did succeed in enrolling a more "underprivileged" class of boys, probably including more potential delinquents than among the nonmembers of the same age groups. A large number of boys in the immediate neighborhood of the club build-

[19] The methods of the Boys' Club Study are described in the September, 1932, issue of the *Journal of Educational Sociology* (VI, 1-64) in a series of six articles by Frederic M. Thrasher, R. L. Whitely, Janet Fowler Nelson, Irving V. Sollins, and Zola Braunstein, members of the staff of the Study.

[20] The findings of the study have been summarized by Frederic M. Thrasher, director of the Boys' Club Study, in an article, "The Boys' Club and Juvenile Delinquency," *American Journal of Sociology*, XLI (1936), 66-80.

ing were never enrolled in the membership, and the history of those who did join showed a high percentage of membership turnover and mortality. The club lacked an adequate system of human accounting both for its members and the boys in the area most in need of its services. There was never any conscious attempt to enlist the potential delinquent as such, and many delinquents among the membership were not known as such to the club. Known delinquents were not accorded the recognized treatment used in the best guidance clinics. Boys'-club delinquency rates were higher than those of the community in general, an expected result because of the types of boys enrolled; yet it was not shown that the club had any effect in decreasing these rates since the great majority of delinquencies among boys'-club members occurred during periods of membership or after such periods. It seems probable that the increasing delinquency rates discovered among club members were the result of increasing age rather than the effect of participation in boys'-club activities. It is obvious, in any event, that the club failed to prevent delinquency among its members and that they continued to become delinquent in the same or higher proportions than the non-members of the club. *A study of the criminogenetic factors in the club community leads to the most significant conclusion of this study, viz., that crime prevention is a function of a concerted community program designed to achieve this purpose rather than of any single preventive agency.* In such a concerted community program the boys' club undoubtedly has an essential function to perform.

During the years following the end of the Boys' Club Study period, the Boys' Club in question adopted many of the recommendations of the Study; and there is evidence that it has corrected the defects in its program brought out by the preceding researches.

GIVE LIFE MEANING FOR THE BOY

The problem of redirecting the gang turns out to be one of giving life meaning for the boy. It is a matter of "definition of the situation," but this has too often come to mean the process of setting up taboos and prohibitions. We need to make the boy understand what he may not do, but it is more important to lead him to see the meaning of what society wants him to do and its relation to some rational scheme of life.

The gang boy's undirected activities are too often only related to the impulses and exigencies of the immediate situation which confronts him. Here he is—surrounded by these particular lead pipes in this particular basement of this particular empty house on this particular holiday. He does not see beyond this immediate situation and the opportunity it presents to get a little junk to sell for spending money. If there is no larger frame of reference for the definition of his behavior, he usually acts upon his immediate impulse without regard to his own future or to the interests of a larger community.

Where the meaning of an activity has been established in a larger configuration, to use a term of the *Gestalt* psychology, behavior is controlled, not by immediate impulses, but by its significance for more ultimate purposes. I get my French lesson even though I am tired and the night is hot and the task is tedious, whereas if I followed the impulse of the moment I would take a swim in the lake or make an excursion with a friend to a soda fountain. I am enabled to control my behavior in this way because I wish to learn French in order to achieve the more ultimate purposes of taking a Ph.D. degree, reading the scientific works prepared by scholarly Frenchmen, and getting along comfortably during the year I am to live in Paris. In this way the particular situation has meaning in terms of more ultimate purposes.

This is not so often the case with gang boys. Most things are done with reference to the immediate pleasure which they give and much energy seems to be spent in purely random activities.[21] Document 28 indicates the surprising instability of interest and the almost complete lack of any ultimate plan or purpose in the life of these boys. In the case described by Clifford R. Shaw[22] the disorganization of the boy may be partly explained by the notable absence of any consistent plan or life-purpose.

The energies represented in these more or less haphazard activities need to be redirected and integrated with the boy's own more ultimate purposes. The first problem, perhaps, is to stimulate his imagination and give him some ambitions. First may come an interest in machinery, then in electricity, and ultimately an ambition to be an electrical engineer. This anticipated goal gives significance to intermediate activities. Attending a technical school now has a different meaning from the vague notion of going to college which was previously entertained.

Yet, the gang is not entirely lacking in ability to organize the interests of the boy. It very often does just this thing for him because it does have some sort of program involving various enterprises to which its members become related. In this way the boy becomes *somebody*, gets a rôle in the group, and participates in its exploits. The point is, however, that these gang activities usually represent useless and often disastrous enterprises which are not ultimately significant, either for the personal development of the boy or the good of the community. The organization of the "Holy Terrors," for the purpose of breaking plate-glass windows and eluding the police, undoubtedly involved an integration of the activities of the members of the gang with reference to a definite plan

[21] See document 27.   [22] *The Jack-Roller.*

and purpose, but, viewed from without, the whole enterprise was not productive of values either for the boys or for society. This is true of any predatory activity engaged in by gangs.

The problem of boys' work is to direct this energy into channels that shall both develop the boy and further the interests of the community.

. . . . When we have sufficiently determined causal relations we shall probably find that there is no individual energy, no unrest, no type of wish which cannot be sublimated and made socially useful. From this standpoint the problem is not the right of society to protect itself from the disorderly and anti-social person, but the right of the disorderly and anti-social person to be made orderly and socially valuable.[23]

The personality of the boy can be developed, for example, by replacing mere wandering with hiking, which has some plan and purpose and a wholesome and educative effect. If boys will fight, let them, but let them fight for a championship with gloves and according to rules. A boxing tournament in which the honor of the club is involved is both personally and socially significant. It tends to develop personal pride in a good physique as well as some conception as to the meaning of loyalty and the importance of co-operation and fair play. The same purpose is accomplished by broader organizations for intergroup competition in the various sports, in debate, and so on. The boy comes to feel that he has a place and a responsibility in a wider scheme of things, which is not without significance for the life of the whole community.[24]

Not only should the organization of the boy's activi-

[23] William I. Thomas, *The Unadjusted Girl*, p. 232.

[24] That the gang is interested in the wider program of the community is indicated by the participation of its older members in the Great War. At the same time the younger gangs were playing at war with play trenches, machine guns, periscopes, etc. One gang, which called itself the "War Club," had forty-two flags decorating the walls of its shack in a prairie.

ties make for his own personal development, but it should promote the betterment of the community. It is curious to note that in this way boys' gangs have been led to protect the very property they sought previously to destroy. In one case a group of boys of a certain college town were known as the "Campus Pests." The problem was solved by making them a "junior university" and assigning them a place in campus life. A destructive gang in Central Park, New York City, was transformed into a Scout troop and given a cabin in the park for a meeting place. Vandalism at once ceased as they took up their new rôles of junior park policemen, protecting life and property.

That the same procedure works with gangsters is indicated by the success of the Marshall Stillman movement in New York City. Criminals have been given a place in a vocational scheme and some of the guerrilla bands have been organized into boxing and service clubs, helping the poor and assisting other gangsters and ex-convicts to become "right guys." It is significant that the advisory board of the movement, which is the most potent element in its success, is composed of former gangsters with long records, among whom the chief are "Red Fagin," who has worked into the movement his former gang of twenty-five members from seventeen to twenty-one years of age; "Tubbo," who was a member of the Wales Avenue gang of the Bronx; and "Dom the Deadliner," who for many years was almost a commuter between Mulberry Bend and the reformatories. A plan was once suggested to interest the gangs of Chicago in the militia. Whatever the scheme which is ultimately adopted, however, it will need to develop a program into which the activities of the gang and its members can be incorporated and through which they can be given significance in a larger plan of life.

CHAPTER XXI

Crime Prevention and the Gang

The growing seriousness of the crime problem in the United States[1] has focused the attention of the educated public from time to time upon the possibility of a more fundamental and more systematic attack upon the under-

[1] Crime and racketeering represent an intolerable condition in the United States today. Some phases of the organization of crime in relation to the gang were discussed in a preceding chapter on "The Gang and Organized Crime." Since the materials in that chapter were prepared, this problem has increased in seriousness not only in Chicago but in other metropolitan areas in the United States. The annual cost of crime has been carefully estimated at approximately $1,207,656,000.00 by the Wickersham Commission (National Commission on Law Enforcement and Observance: *Report on the Cost of Crime, 1931*). A conservative estimate by criminologists places the annual cost at five billions. This is a staggering load for any country when we reflect that the direct cost of education is only about one billion dollars a year.

While no reliable statistics are available as to the increase and extent of crime in this country, it is common knowledge that the problem has become very grave during the past few years. The development and spread of racketeering which has come to prey upon hundreds of different American businesses and industries through extortion, force, violence, blackmail, arson, murder, kidnapping, bombing, and undue influence is an eloquent tribute to the power of the criminal gang and the underworld. Spectacular crimes such as bank robberies, large-scale safety-vault burglaries, wholesale murders (for example, the Chicago St. Valentine's Day "massacre" of 1929 and the Kansas City "massacre"), the killing of innocent adults and children by stray bullets in gangster wars, and the kidnapping of adults and of children of prominent people—all such sensational crimes have directed public attention toward the widespread menace to the safety of life, limb, and property in this country.

lying causes of crime than has yet been attempted, and these later formulations of the problem of crime prevention are closely related to the whole problem of dealing with the gang and with the delinquency it promotes.

The groundwork for this type of attack has now been prepared through the acquisition of important knowledge as to the origins of crime made available through recent scientific studies: first, that *the origins of criminal careers are to be found largely in the social reactions of childhood and adolescence;* and second, that *the concentration of potential delinquents and criminals is to be found largely in typical, interstitial areas which are the characteristic breeding-places of gangs, delinquency, and crime.*[2] These are the so-called "delinquency areas" which have been so well characterized by Clifford R. Shaw.[3] Shaw describes the delinquency area as follows:

> It was found that the areas of high rates of delinquents are adjacent to the central business district and the major industrial developments. Generally speaking, these areas were found to be characterized by physical deterioration, decreasing population, high rates of dependency, high percentage of foreign-born and Negro population, and high rates of adult offenders.
>
> One of the most significant findings in this part of the study is the fact that, while the relative rates of delinquents in these high-rate areas remained more or less constant over a period of 20 years, the nationality composition of the population changed almost completely in this interval. As the older national groups moved out of these areas of first immigrant settlement, the percentage of juvenile delinquents in these groups showed consistent decrease.

[2] Both these generalizations are well illustrated by the findings presented in the present volume.

[3] Clifford R. Shaw and Henry D. McKay, *Social Factors in Juvenile Delinquency,* II, 107–8, Report on the Causes of Crime of the National Commission on Law Observance and Enforcement. See also Shaw, *Delinquency Areas.*

It was indicated also, that the areas of high rates of delinquents are characterized by marked disintegration of the traditional institutions and neighborhood organization. In this type of area, the community fails as an agency of social control.

These two outstanding generalizations, based as they are upon well-authenticated facts, clearly indicate the point of attack for a major crime-prevention program, namely, the behavior problems of childhood and adolescence in the crime-producing areas. How may a practicable program of crime prevention which strikes in a basic way at underlying causes be formulated?

The problem is primarily one of dealing with pre-delinquents or potential delinquents in these areas of deterioration in such a way as to assure the development of wholesome personality and good citizenship. It involves many factors and many techniques, but the fundamental problem is one of synthesis of all methods which are known to be essential, so as to deal consistently and completely with the total situation in a given delinquency area. This involves an inescapable program of social planning which is clearly suggested by any careful sociological study.

Yet criminologists, persons with legal training, educators, and recreational and social workers in general have usually failed to grasp the fundamental principle of crime prevention, viz., the necessity for a definitely organized and thoroughgoing preventive program in the local community from which the bulk of delinquents and criminals are produced. Until recently they have possessed in general neither the technical knowledge nor the inclination to enable them to promote the concentration of local responsibility, the co-operation of local agencies, and the integration of local services which are essential to such a program.

The analysis at the beginning of chapter xx and

throughout the book indicates that the gang is clearly a symptom of community disorganization. The gang, along with other personal and social factors in the interstitial (crime-producing) area, plays an important part in the demoralization of youth and the facilitation of delinquency and crime. The solution of the gang problem, however, is intimately and inextricably bound up with the whole question of crime prevention as applied to *all* factors contributing to delinquency in such an area.

From the analysis of the gang and of juvenile delinquency in relation to crime in this volume, as well as upon the basis of the results of more recent studies, the essential elements of a crime prevention program for a local community appear to be as follows:

I. The general purpose: To achieve a comprehensive, systematic, and integrated social program for the incorporation of *all* children in the delinquency area—especially *all* the maladjusted and those likely to become delinquents—into activities, groups, and organizations providing for their leisure-time interests as well as all other normal needs.

II. Means to the achievement of this purpose:

1. Concentration of responsibility for crime prevention for the local delinquency area in question (a problem of community organization).

2. Research to procure essential facts and keep them up to date as a basis for an initial and a progressively developing crime-prevention program (child accounting).

3. Utilization of services of, and co-operation among, all preventive agencies existing in the given community (a problem of community organization).

4. Application of the preventive program *systematically* to all children in the delinquency area of the local community.

5. Creation of new agencies, if necessary, to supplement existing social organization when and at what points definite needs are discovered which cannot be met by existing facilities (a problem of community organization).

6. Continuing educational program to enlist and maintain public interest and support.

The nature of the program indicated in the foregoing statement of the purpose of crime prevention (1) seems, at first glance, to contain no elements of novelty. And, indeed, its subsidiary techniques are largely the well-known services of the behavior and guidance clinic, the family case-working agency, the recreational organization, the educational institution, etc. Yet such a program represents a radical departure from the methods of social work and community organization as formerly conceived. The elements of novelty, as contemplated here, which hold real promise of effective crime prevention, lie in the direction of *community reorganization* (based upon research) rather than the proposal primarily of new methods of dealing with children either individually or in groups. The new approach is indicated in the six methods of procedure set forth above as means to the achievement of the general purpose of crime prevention.

The cardinal first step in crime prevention is concentration of responsibility for a definite and systematic program in a definite and adequate social instrumentality which will be charged with crime prevention as its sole, or at least as an important incidental, function. It is obvious that traditional social agencies as now constituted are usually not fitted for such a task. Yet it is equally clear that many existing social agencies must play important parts in carrying out such a program. The instrumentality, therefore, which assumes this vital community function must be one which lends itself readily to securing the co-operation of all community institutions and organizations.

It has been suggested that the local council of social agencies serving the delinquency area for which the crime prevention program is being formulated should logically assume this responsibility, since such a council is representative of most of the agencies which must co-operate in putting such a program into practical operation. This may be accomplished through the creation of a committee or section of such a council which would employ a qualified executive with a small but capable staff for performing the essential crime-prevention functions.

In some communities the local council of social agencies may not be in a position to take the initiative in, or to secure financing for, a crime prevention program. In others no effective council may exist. In such cases it is quite reasonable to suppose that any agency which has a fundamental stake in crime prevention, such as a recreational group, the public school, the juvenile court, or the police department, or a committee representing a combination of such agencies may take the initiative in developing a crime-prevention program in which the co-operation of all essential agencies can be enlisted.

The public-school system in any community is in an especially strategic position, in the interest of the adequate performance of its own educational functions, to undertake, without fear or favor, the development of a crime-prevention program which shall enlist the interest and co-operation of all the social agencies of the community. The present trend, however, is in the direction of crime prevention as a function incidental to local community planning undertaken by a comprehensive local council of community agencies.

We have discussed the first element in the six-point program of crime prevention, namely, the concentration of responsibility for the function of crime prevention. The second point is no less important: that the program must be based upon social research rather than the superficial type of survey often employed by social agencies. No adequate program can be formulated or carried on without definite knowledge of facts regarding the children of the area and their problems and the social influences which play upon them. With few exceptions social agencies do not know the communities to which they minister with any degree of thoroughness, and unfortunately they do not ordinarily keep their records in such a way as to enable them to evaluate their own work effectively. They know their own methods; but they are inclined to be "institutionally minded," and they find difficulty in visualizing the community and its problems as a whole and their own proper functions in the larger situation. The social agencies often know certain phases of their community backgrounds very intimately, and separate agencies see one problem or another very vividly. The point is, however, that there is no synthesis of essential knowledge without genuine research, and that there can be no adequate basis for a thoroughgoing crime prevention program without knowledge which is systematic, organized, and complete. This is particularly pertinent in dealing with the problem of delinquency because it is just the child who is missed by the methods of the ordinary leisure-time program, or who drops out of the wholesome group or institution, or who is shunted from one agency to another without any consistent plan for his adjustment or attempt at follow-up, who so often is the pre-delinquent or the candidate for a criminal career.

The third point in the crime-prevention program involves the integration of services of all appropriate agencies with reference to each individual case involving a child, a family, or a gang.

The fourth point involves the application of the preventive program *systematically* to *all* children in the delinquency area of the local community. This is an essential element in any program of effective crime prevention, and it is a relatively simple matter when once the problem is understood and an adequate crime-prevention agency is established. It is assumed that the delinquency area, which breeds crime, has been definitely delimited. This at once reduces the size of the juvenile population which must be dealt with by excluding the non-delinquency areas. Yet, delinquency areas are usually districts of congested population with high ratios of children in the general population. The problem now becomes one of sifting out those cases which we have called "pre-delinquents," that is, children who, by virtue of behavior problems already manifested or conditions in their biological or social backgrounds, are likely to become delinquents. Truants from school and very young delinquents, adolescents who are first-offenders, children with a record of delinquency in their immediate families, children living in blocks with excessively high delinquency rates, non-delinquents associated with delinquent gangs, etc., are cases in point. With the development of research and the availability of numerous records bearing upon the beginnings of criminal careers we shall undoubtedly possess eventually definite indexes which will enable us to predict with some degree of precision what children are most likely to become delinquents. At present we are in possession of sufficient knowledge to enable us to bring a crime-prevention program within the limits of practicability by the process of sifting indicated above and the concentration of effort upon critical cases. When we say that our program must be applied systematically to all children in the delinquency area, we mean that all children must be considered in the sifting process, which will rule out the majority— those who are functioning within an adequate social framework—and leave a considerable residuum of potential criminals whose problems must be dealt with. The emphasis here is upon a systematic approach to the problem, which foregoes the hit-or-miss procedure of the average agency of the so-called character-building type and pursues a method designed to catch all potential delinquents in the area, and especially to forestall the overlooking of any critical cases.

The next procedure in the six-point program for the prevention of crime is the creation of new agencies where existing facilities are demonstrated to be inadequate (by research based on special investigation and experience). It seems plausible that the numerous existing agencies of varied types serving many crime-producing areas at the present time will be found adequate to the task of crime prevention in some communities, once the first four points discussed above have been achieved. Yet in many cases new agencies will need to be created, and here we are confronted with the problem of the community chest and *status quo.*

The final procedure in a crime-prevention program has to do with keeping the public informed and with educating the community to support such a program. A continuous program of public education, not only locally but nationally, is necessary if this type of attack upon the causes of crime is to be permanently successful. The widespread publicity which crime and criminal gangs have received, while it has had some effect in the creation of special agencies for apprehending "public enemies" has done little more than create a general public tolerance of crime and racketeering and a feeling of resignation on the part of the average citizen to the existence of the gangster, the racketeer, and the corrupt politician as a necessary evil in American community life. This widespread public lethargy is an important element in the total problem.

Recently the effective work of the Federal Bureau of Investigation of the United States Department of Justice in apprehending and securing the conviction of notorious criminals and so-called "public enemies" has awakened public interest in this type of crime prevention. It has been much more difficult, however, to enlist public support for the type of attack on crime represented by the co-ordination of community agencies for crime prevention designed to "nip the criminal career in the bud." There is no effective national agency, public or private, charged with the wide dissemination of sound, scientific information on the causes and control of crime.

The possibility of such a basic program of crime prevention becomes more sure as the logic of our knowledge of the problem of the gang and of crime becomes more inescapable. Social planning becomes more and more inevitable as pragmatic tests are applied to our present disorganized social structure. There is no panacea for the solution of the gang problem and its related problem of crime. The market for crime must be considered as well as the supply of criminals, and this is still another problem. Yet, in dealing with the gangster and the criminal we have spent far too much thought and money upon the problem of repressing the finished product of the delinquent career. Economy demands that the emphasis be shifted to the process of prevention, which attacks the roots of crime in those areas of the community which are known to be crime-breeding centers.

Important progress in the prevention of disease and the promotion of public health has come about as the result of various health (disease-prevention) demonstrations financed by contributions from foundations and public-spirited citizens. *Similarly, the time is ripe for adequately financed citizenship (crime-prevention) demonstrations, which shall be carried on experimentally and evaluated scientifically over a period of years in various parts of the country*. In this way the principles of crime prevention can be established and the resulting prophylaxis for crime can be more widely applied by public and private agencies.

Index